THE BORDERS OF SCHENGEN

P.I.E. Peter Lang
Bruxelles · Bern · Berlin · Frankfurt am Main · New York · Oxford · Wien

EUROCLIO is a scientific and editorial project, a network of research institutions and researchers, and an ideas forum. EUROCLIO as an editorial project consists of two aspects: the first concerns studies and documents, the second concerns tools. Both are aimed at making the results of research more accessible, and also at opening up paths through the history of European construction/integration/unification.

The EUROCLIO series meets a dual objective:

- to provide reference tools for research,
- to provide a platform for this research in terms of the publication of results.

The series thus consists of two sub-series that satisfy these requirements: the Studies and Documents series and the References series. These two series are aimed at general libraries and/or university history departments, teachers and researchers, and in certain cases, specific professional circles.

The Studies and Documents series consists of monographs, collections of articles, conference proceedings, and collections of texts with notes for teaching purposes.

The References series consists of bibliographies, guides and other tools. It thus contributes to the creation of a database making up a "Permanent catalogue of sources and bibliographies on European construction".

THE BORDERS OF SCHENGEN

Alice CUNHA, Marta SILVA,
Rui FREDERICO (eds.)

Euroclio
Vol. 93

This volume has been published with the support of the European Commission Representation in Lisbon.

Comissão
Europeia

All chapters have been blind peer-reviewed.

Each author is responsible for the opinions stated on his/hers text

Éditions scientifiques internationales
Brussels, 2015
1 avenue Maurice, B-1050 Brussels, Belgium
pie@peterlang.com ; www.peterlang.com

ISSN 0944-2294
ISBN 978-2-87574-308-4
eISBN 978-3-0352-6576-7
D/2015/5678/60

Printed in Germany

CIP available from the British Library, UK and from the Library of Congress, USA.

"Die Deutsche National Bibliothek" lists this publication in the "Deutsche Nationalbibliografie"; detailed bibliographic data is available on the Internet at <http://dnb.de>.

Table of Contents

Schengen: removing borders while building fences?

Introduction

Alice CUNHA, Marta SILVA and Rui FREDERICO

The summer of 2015 has been marked by daily news reports, many of which have actually made the headlines, about the attempts of illegal immigrants and refugees to reach Europe. Never has this issue been talked about so much nor in such depth. In fact, this huge inflow has captured the attention of not only the media – who to some extent exploit stories of life and suffering – but also public opinion in the European Union's (EU) member states who are far from unanimous about the opening (or closing) of Europe's frontiers as they oscillate between humanitarian concerns and socioeconomic worries. Once again in the history of European integration, Europeans are divided between rhetoric (the desire to receive immigrants) and practice (the costs of this action).

From the time the first Schengen Agreement was signed in 1985, coming into force in 1995, until 2015 a great deal changed, including the EU itself. The idea to create a future Schengen Area which stipulated the gradual suppression of border controls at the common frontiers between these states was not, however, innovative within the European integration process since the Treaty of Rome (1957) had already referred to the concept of the freedom of circulation of people (article 3c).

From 1997 on, Schengen has been part of the institutional framework of the EU. It was included in the Treaty of Amsterdam and in the legal category of European citizenship, later undergoing alterations in the Treaty of Lisbon (2009). It focused on the notion of a "space of freedom, security and justice" with the objective of implementing common policies regarding not only the granting of visas and asylum but also immigration.

Basically, the Schengen area can be summed up as the free circulation of persons within the signatory countries and the abolition of internal borders. This does away with the need for border controls, which thus means that European citizens can circulate freely whenever they so wish without having to identify themselves or pass a border control when they cross the frontier from one country to another.

The idea of the Schengen area is thus essentially simple and efficient. Eliminating controls at the internal borders between member states could contribute to faster journeys with lower costs for the state (in terms of border patrols and border controls), increased exchanges between the different peoples of Europe and even to boosting the economy. At the celebrations commemorating the 30th anniversary of Schengen, the European Commissioner for Migration, Home Affairs and Citizenship, Dimitris Avramopoulos, emphasized the advantages and the importance of the abolition of internal border controls for the everyday lives of Europeans, their society and the economy when he said:

> On a continent where nations once shed blood to defend their territories, today borders only exist on maps. [...] Removing borders, ensuring safety and building trust took many years after two devastating world wars. The creation of the Schengen area is one of the greatest achievements of the EU and it is irreversible.[1]

Even though the advantages and convenience of having movement between the Schengen signatory states made easier for millions of people are known and recognised, in the chapter on free circulation the Agreement contains a list of ambiguities. Illegal immigration, human trafficking and terrorism frequently turn Schengen into a delicate political issue. In this sense, and in parallel with there being open internal borders, the control of external borders has been strengthened, with news reaching us of frequent and mediatized incidents involving boats capsizing and sinking and the humanitarian drama that is unfolding along the shores of the Mediterranean. Following the deaths that have occurred in the Mediterranean in 2015, the European Commission proposed on 13 May a new European Agenda on Migration[2] that seeks to define both immediate and long term answers for the challenges that Europe is facing in this area. It has proposed various concrete measures including, among others, a recommendation that invites member states to resettle 20,000 people coming from third countries within a two-year period and a plan of action against migrant traffickers.

Data from 2014 shows that almost 300,000 people were detected irregularly crossing borders and that over 600,000 asylum applications were submitted, a 45% increase on the previous year. These figures

---

1 Schengen brochure, available at http://ec.europa.eu/dgs/home-affairs/e-library/docs/schengen_brochure/schengen_brochure_dr3111126_en.pdf (last accessed on 03/08/2015).

2 http://ec.europa.eu/dgs/home-affairs/what-we-do/policies/european-agenda-migration/background-information/docs/communication_on_the_european_agenda_on_migration_en.pdf.

highlight the attraction and pull of the EU but at the same time they place under scrutiny and generate public debate on asylum and refugee policies, both of which are feeling the strain owing to the contradictory demands of human rights, internal security and limitations of member states' social security systems.

According to data from the last available Eurobarometer, immigration heads the list of Europeans' biggest concerns (38% of those surveyed[3]), followed by the economic situation and then unemployment. This data shows how immigration is now seen as an external "threat" that, instead of merely rivalling factors of an internal order such as unemployment and economic performance, has now overtaken them. This concern has been instrumentalised by some extreme right parties, European nationalists and populists with a certain degree of success – to judge by election results in some member states – who are using an increasingly intense anti-immigration discourse. But immigration has always been one of the most complicated areas even for those parties of the left considered pro-European and remains so inasmuch as these parties continue to not really know how to resolve the issue; at the same time right-wing parties and conservatives are also being drawn towards a more radical discourse. There is no doubt though that Schengen, which has facilitated the mobility of European citizens, has been one of the EU's major achievements. Moreover, despite the fact that intra-EU mobility has put pressure on national states at the level of social security, for example, it has greatly contributed to boosting the economy in general and to increasing cooperation, multiculturalism and the exchange of experiences between European peoples. Confronted with such data, some questions need to be asked: how can we idealize a European project that does not encompass the security and freedom of its citizens?; How can we protect borders in the global village of which the EU is part – and the Schengen area an even smaller part – while reconciling this *securitist* perspective with the founding idea of Schuman, Monnet or Adenauer?

However, if on one hand the abolition of internal borders within the EU has in fact had a positive and beneficial result, on the other, the question of the EU's external borders, the control of which was not mentioned in the Treaty of Rome, still remains to be resolved. In addition to the illegal immigrants and refugees who arrive every day on the island of Kos in Greece or in Sicily in Italy, a paradigmatic example is what is happening in Calais at the border of France, a Schengen signatory state, and the United Kingdom, a non-signatory state. Immigrants who have legally or illegally managed to enter France only want to use the country where they are at present as a means to get through the Eurotunnel and head for

3 European Commission, *Eurobarometer*, No. 83, Spring 2015, p. 14.

the United Kingdom where they intend to settle and take up residence. We thus have a situation in which, with the non-application of Schengen to the whole territory, situations co-exist within the EU itself in which a national of a third country is able to cross an external border of the Union but then cannot circulate between different member states.

At this moment the continuing debate within the EU centres on the measures that should be adopted to respond to this enormous influx of people from third countries arriving at various EU doors. Member states on their own are incapable of dealing effectively with this situation which in some cases is already presenting signs of a humanitarian crisis to which various non-governmental organizations on the ground are trying to provide the best possible available answer. Several world leaders have also raised their voices, like Ban Ki-moon who urged European countries to "show compassion" and do more to help the migrants[4] and Pope Francis who said that "we cannot allow the Mediterranean to become a vast cemetery".[5]

Free circulation is one of the established rights of European citizens and has allowed over one billion journeys a year to be made within the area. However, despite the benefits, Schengen is an imperfect space whose fragilities point to the shortcomings of European immigration policies, especially with regard to the inefficiencies of the labour markets and the threat to social security models. At the same time the difficulty that member states have to reach agreement on a common immigration policy is highlighted. Borders within the EU have virtually disappeared whilst the external ones are increasingly the target of attention. The debate has developed focusing on proposals such as the reinforcement of information systems, the exchange of these between states and simply closing borders to immigrants from outside the EU and even – in some circumstances and according to more pessimistic analyses – to citizens of other member states. In this respect, we must question whether it is urgent to reinforce information systems? What is the importance of biometric data? Is it important to circulate information regarding the services that control European frontiers? Should we then plan a Europe with full mobility?

---

4 "Ban Ki-moon on migration crisis: EU member states must show compassion", available at http://www.euractiv.com/video/ban-Ki-moon-migration-crisis-eu-member-states-must-show-compassion-314897 (last accessed on 1/08/2015).

5 Pope Francis' speech at the European Parliament on 25 November 2014: Salvador, S., "Papa apela para que o Mediterrâneo não se torne num 'cemitério' de migrantes", *Diário de Notícias*, available at http://www.dn.pt/inicio/globo/interior.aspx?content_id=4259596 (last accessed on 25/11/2014).

In fact, Schengen is based on the idea of the free circulation of European citizens within this space, but this does not apply to citizens from third countries who must pass border controls, thus keeping out millions of people who are seeking a better life and future in the prosperous EU. Two different and opposing notions therefore co-exist: that of a Europe without borders and that of a fortress Europe, so that the Schengen area could even be, in an extreme case, a paradigmatic example of the co-existence of unrestricted mobility for some and the denial of that same freedom for others.

Schengen's complexity arises particularly when the observer places himself on the outside, looking at the Schengen area macroscopically as a common space set within a more extensive and globalized panorama where there are other regions and political "micro-regions" that grant similar facilities to their members. And, paradoxically, when looking inside with his eyes microscopically focused, situations can be identified that call into question the idea of a space of freedom that is especially vaunted by European political decision-makers and therefore the irreversibility that Avramopoulos referred to.

Based on the work of Didier Bigo, Scherrer and Guittet, we can state that the first possible equivocation of this discourse lies in the association of the conception of a securitized space ("ensuring safety"), the supposed idea of freedom ("removing borders") and the certainty that the two result in the construction of a generalized feeling of trust ("building trust"). According to these studies, it can be seen that the technologization of mobility control – which in part tends to be invisible, thanks to biometric body surveillance technology, numerical integration and the deterritorialization of the security apparatus with the construction of databases, thereby giving the impression that people can circulate without surveillance – tends to generate fear and hostility when faced with the other who is mobile and different. Thus, in a world that seeks to be increasingly fast and fluid, categories of individuals are being created: "authorized identities" and the rejected ones who do not satisfy the requirements for integration.[6]

The ambiguity lies primarily in the fact that in an area where there are policies to encourage mobility (for example, academic with the Erasmus programme) the frontier, rather than being diluted, acts as a filter where mobility and security are indissociable, thereby reinforcing mechanisms of domination between regions and creating excluded individuals who might potentially disturb this harmonious space. Control is exercised not only through immobilization or obstaculization when passing through the filter but also by innovating and enhancing identification techniques and

6 Scherrer, A., Guittet, E., Bigo, D. (dir.), *Mobilité(s) sous surveillance. Perspectives croisées EU-Canada*, Athéna Éditions, Outremont (Québec), 2010, pp. 7-24.

technologies in an attempt to foresee risks and anticipate movements.[7] It therefore culminates in the elaboration of a "risk profile"[8] which leads to the stigmatization of undesirable immigrants who are often confused with criminals.

If these identification, control and surveillance practices, despite their progressive technological development, have been a historical constant pervading both democratic and dictatorial regimes[9] inside and outside Europe, the discourse that legitimates their implementation has also been a constant, particularly in three aspects:

- the securitist discourse, in which the need to reinforce border surveillance to prevent penetration by alleged terrorists and criminals (drug, arms and human traffickers) is supported in the name of protecting the locals;
- the humanist discourse, which focuses on the protection of immigrants legitimating the reinforcement of surveillance and the means of intervention – for example, at sea – in order to prevent and rescue victims of capsized boats or to stop human trafficking;
- also associated to this discourse is the construction of the image of the migrant as an unwary victim (from whom, by association, agency or decision-making power is withdrawn), ingenuously enticed by networks of unscrupulous smugglers. With recruiters and smugglers serving as scapegoats for irregular immigration, political leaders continue to claim there is a need to strengthen the instruments used to combat illegality by eliminating any form of help for this type of mobility; they are unaware though (whether deliberately or not) of the complex web of social and informal relations which often lie behind these "structures"[10] and the strategies that intermediaries and migrants (re-)devise to get round new obstacles in order to enter and remain in European territory.[11]

---

7 *Ibid.*

8 Noiriel, G. (ed.), *L'identification. Genèse d'un travail d'État,* Belin, Paris, 2007, p. 24.

9 Noiriel, G., *op. cit*., pp. 22-26.

10 On the informal organization of illegal migrants' networks, see for instance: Carolina, A., *As fronteiras de Nord-pas-de-Calais: um estudo de campo sobre a securitização da imigração na França*, Masters dissertation, ISCTE-Instituto Universitário de Lisboa, 2014; Mazauric, C., *Mobilités d'Afrique en Europe. Récits et figures de l'aventure*, Éditions Karthala, Paris, 2012; Antonopoulos, G., Winterdyk, J., "The Smuggling of Migrants in Greece: An Examination of its Social Organization", *European Journal of Criminology*, 3, 2006, pp. 439-461.

11 "L'histoire de l'identification est-elle également celle des falsifications." Moatti, C., Kaiser, W., "Introduction", in C. Moatti and W. Kaiser (dir.), *Gens de passage en Méditerranée de l'Antiquité à l'époque moderne. Procédures de contrôle et*

The ambiguity of Schengen is also present when we see how the classification that resulted from this agreement, distinguishing between internal and external borders, does not in fact alter the order of things completely. If, to all appearances, one of the symbols of the nation-state's power (the internal border) is eliminated, in practice what has happened and what some studies have shown, contrary to the irreversible nature the path outlined by the agreement might indicate, is that this division does not exist operationally and the borders that Schengen appears to have abolished have not totally disappeared. To see this, all we need to do is think about the temporary closures and compensatory measures provided for by the Schengen Agreement Application Convention, which allows border states to establish bilateral agreements in which they decide how to organize police cooperation and migrant readmission procedures. Such is the case of the Franco-Italian border (practically re-established in 2010) which has reactivated the type of procedures carried out at the old national borders.[12] Reconfiguration of the concept of border (a frontier line), giving rise to "border zones", does not seem to have been a factor in the total dissolution of national "walls" in terms of mobility control. In the case of the *raia* (Portuguese)/*raya* (Spanish) – meaning the border area between Portugal and Spain – for example, police sovereignty is maintained in the police and customs coordination centres on each side and mixed patrols operate that can intervene up to 50 kms on either side of the border line. Mobile controls are led by a national of the country and officers, guards and state employees must wear their regulation national uniform.[13] Observation of the processes Schengen encourages that are rendering frontiers invisible or opaque testifies in fact to a territorial management dependent on numerous factors, demonstrating once again that territorial limits, constantly called into question throughout history, are constructions we tend to view as a natural inheritance.[14]

Gérard Noiriel points to Schengen and the construction of European citizenship achieved through it as being the phenomenon that led to the increased development of police identification practices used to repress illegal immigration as happened in the United States of America after

d'identification, Maisonneuve & Larose, Maison méditerranéenne des sciences de l'homme, Paris, 2007, p. 14.

12 Casella-Colombeau, S., "La frontière définie par les policiers: Sur des fronts des frontières", *Plein droit*, No. 87, 2010, pp. 12-15.

13 Ministério dos Negócios Estrangeiros, art° 12 do Decreto 13/2007, de 13 de Julho, Diário da República, 1ª Série, No. 134, de 13 de Julho de 2007, p. 4432.

14 Moatti, C., "Introduction", in C. Moatti (dir.), *La mobilité des personnes en méditerranée de l'Antiquité à l'époque moderne. Procédures de contrôle et documents d'identification*, École française de Rome, 2004, p. 1.

11 September.[15] In this way, illegality and the concept of immigration as a public problem are constructions for which the states and their representatives on the periphery (who do not always act in accordance with state orders[16]) are, at least in part, the producers.[17] Illegal immigration is, after all, illegalized immigration.[18] In various situations the EU has managed its relations with third countries using the migration question and the need for border controls as the basis for achieving economic and political agreements. This is the case of agreements made with Morocco, while for some Eastern European countries their EU membership is at stake and, as a further example, several African states receive development aid in exchange.[19]

Following a similar line of thought, according to Claire Rodier (a lawyer for the Groupe d'Information et de Soutien des Immigrés and co-founder of the Euro-African network Migreurop), there is also a group of private economic players who use their power to put pressure on states to promote such measures. These groups or multinationals are connected to the markets dealing in surveillance equipment and visa and passport computerisation, or for example the management of detention centres[20], thus contributing to a veritable business built up around migrations and mobility.

All these issues that have given rise to debates that go beyond the party-political and media sphere and have occupied a prominent place in public opinion and academic reflection are what led the editors of this volume to organize an International Conference on *Schengen: people, borders and mobility* in Lisbon on 15 and 16 June 2015. After the Conference some of

15 Noiriel, G., *op. cit.*, p. 24.

16 See for instance Mathilde Darley's case study on the Czech-Austrian border: Darley, M., "Le contrôle migratoire aux frontières Schengen: pratiques et représentations des polices sur la ligne tchéco-autrichienne", *Cultures & Conflits*, No. 71, 2008, pp. 13-29; or Casella-Colombeau, S., *op. cit.*, pp. 12-15.

17 On the production of illegality, see for instance: Ambrosini, M., "Migrants dans l'ombre. Causes, dynamics, politiques de l'immigration irrégulière", *REMI*, Vol. 26, No. 2, 2010, pp. 7-32.

18 Mazauric, C., *op. cit.*, p. 9.

19 On these issues, see namely: Rodier, C., *Xénophobie business. À quoi servent les contrôles migratoires ?*, La Découverte, Paris, 2012; Pian, A., "Le cadre discursif du développement. Des discours et actions politiques concrètes, aux répertoires d'action des associations de refoulés", *Working paper 25*, International Migration Institute, 2010, available at http://www.imi.ox.ac.uk/pdfs/wp/wp-25-10-fr.pdf (last accessed on 24/07/2015).

20 Rodier, C., *Xénophobie business…*, *op. cit.*; Rodier, C., "L'économie de la frontière", Communication in *Colloque international de l'antiAtlas des frontières*, 27/08/2014, available at http://www.antiatlas.net/blog/2014/08/27/colloque-rodier/ (last accessed on 18/05/2015).

the papers presented were selected and this book is the result. Thirty years after the signing of the first Schengen agreement, it has become important to reflect on the processes (and their diversity) involving the circulation of people into and within this space.

In this age of globalization, when the implementation of policies by states and international communities to both encourage and repress the circulation of people can be found, academia has spawned a great deal of activity based on questions and concepts related to migration, borders and mobility. Research in this area, besides that enjoying a more wide-ranging focus[21], is divided among several key issues such as border control[22] and securitization[23],

---

21 For instance: Mau, S., Brabandt, H., Laube, L. & Roos, C., *Liberal States and the Freedom of Movement: Selective Borders, Unequal Mobility*, Palgrave Macmillan, Houndsmills, 2012; Bertozzi, S., "Schengen: Achievements and Challenges in Managing an Area Encompassing 3.6 million km^2", The Centre for European Policy Studies, Brussels, 2008; Pécoud, A. and Guchteneire, P. (eds.), *Migration without borders: essays on the free movement of people*, Berghahn Books, Paris and New York, 2007; Grabbe, H., "The sharp edges of Europe: Extending Schengen eastwards", *International Affairs*, Vol. 76, Issue 3, 2000, pp. 519-536; Convey, A. and Kupiszewski, M., "Keeping up with Schengen: Migration and Policy in the European Union", in *International Migration Review*, Vol. 29, No. 4, 1995, pp. 939-940.

22 Ruben, Z., *Cultures of Border Control: Schengen and the Evolution of Europe's Frontiers*, University of Toronto, Toronto, 2008 [PhD Thesis]; Anderson, M., "The Transformation of Border Controls: A European Precedent?", in P. Andreas and T. Snyder (eds.), *The Wall around the West. State Borders and Immigration Controls in North America and Europe*, Rowman & Littlefield Publishers, Lanham, 2000, pp. 15-29; Pratt, M. A. and Brown, J. A. (eds.), *Borderlands Under Stress*, Kluwer Law International, The Hague, 2000; Bigo, D., "Frontiers and Security in the European Union: The Illusion of Migration Control", in M. Anderson and E. Bort (eds.), *The frontiers of Europe*, Pinter, London, 1998, 148-164.

23 Neal, A., "Securitization and Risk at the EU Border: The Origins of FRONTEX", *Journal of Common Market Studies*, Vol. 47, No. 2, 2009, pp. 333-356; Wæver, O., "The EU as a security actor: reflections from a pessimistic constructivist on post-sovereign security", in M. Kelstrup and M. Williams (eds.), *International Relations Theory and the Politics of European Integration*, Routledge, London, 2000, pp. 250-289; Bigo, D., "When two become one: internal and external securitisations in Europe", in M. Kelstrup and M. Williams (eds.), *International Relations Theory and the Politics of European Integration, Power, Security and Community*, Routledge, London, 2000, pp. 171-204.

policies for granting visas[24] and asylum[25], and immigration and immigration control.[26]

It was on this epistemological basis that the current view of the complexity of the European space invited us to think about the boundaries that separate territories as well as their absence. In this way, we believe we are contributing to an understanding of the process for implementing the Schengen area and the way in which this has affected and altered the relationships between member states and between them and third countries as well as the influence this has had within the context of the European Neighbourhood Policy.

At the same time, we think it is essential to analyse the changes to the concept of border and border control and to measure the evolution of movements within the Schengen area, which in its turn enables us to understand the relations between territories, states and individuals and to shed light on the various impacts the Schengen agreements have had on these spaces, the people and their societies and their border experiences.

It was also important to include new contributions on the exclusive migration policies put into practice in certain territories and the various movements and initiatives that have arisen as an alternative to the migration policies of Europe and Schengen. In brief, we have sought to understand to what extent the phenomena of human mobility affect the design of the mechanisms for managing the Community territory and vice-versa.

There are therefore various possible levels of analysis in a study about Schengen. We are dealing with a space that has generated controversy

---

24 Hobolth, M. H., *Border control cooperation in the European Union: The Schengen visa policy in practice*, The London School of Economics and Political Science, London, 2012 [PhD thesis]; Bigo, D. & Guild, E., "Policing at a Distance: Schengen Visa Policies", in D. Bigo and E. Guild (eds.), *Controlling frontiers: free movement into and within Europe*, Ashgate Publishing Limited, Aldershot, 2005, pp. 233-263; Meloni, A., "The Development of a Common Visa Policy under the Treaty of Amsterdam", *Common Market Law Review*, Vol. 42, 2005, pp. 1357-1381.

25 Huysmans, J., *The politics of insecurity: fear, migration, and asylum in the EU*, Routledge, New York, 2006; Lavenex, S., *The Europeanisation of refugee policies: between human rights and internal security*, Ashgate, Aldershot, 2001; Collinson, S., "Visa Requirements, Carrier Sanctions, 'Safe Third Countries' and 'Readmission': The Development of an Asylum 'Buffer Zone' in Europe", in *Transactions of the Institute of British Geographers*, Vol. 21, No. 1, 1996, pp. 76-90.

26 Triandafyllidou, A. (ed.), *Irregular migration in Europe: myths and realities*, Ashgate Publishing Limited, Farnham and Burlington, 2010; Broeders, D., "The New Digital Borders of Europe. EU Databases and the Surveillance of Irregular Migrants", *International Sociology*, Vol. 22, No. 1, 2007, pp. 71-92; Ette, A. & Faist, T. (eds.), *The Europeanization of National Policies and Politics of Immigration: Between Autonomy and the European Union*, Palgrave Macmillan, Houndmills, 2007.

and, in an attempt to understand it, we have sought to gather here more clues by bringing together multidisciplinary works that include research from the fields of history, international relations, European studies, anthropology, sociology, political science, psychology and law. The results of the research presented in this book were not based solely on institutional documentation (governmental and Community) but also on a methodology that included field work and ethnographic research as well as interviews carried out in different parts of Schengen Europe with migrants and actors from civil society. The series of texts collected here offer the reader a variety of perspectives. These are interrelated and reveal, first of all, the individual who is on the move (that is, the migrant) and therefore related to the state through the technical and human means that are imposed by the state as a condition for mobility; strategies to circumvent such obstacles are looked at as are the respective technological and legislative responses coming "from above", the consequences of which are well known especially around the border area, as the works that address securitization discourses and practices make clear. Octávio Sacramento reflects on Schengen as a space of selection and exclusion based on his ethnographic research on the Portuguese border. The texts by Burcu Toğral Koca, Alejandra Germán Doldán and Lucía Payero López on Spain's external border analyse the nexus between migration and security. The first aims to show the relationship between border technologies and the infringement of the rights of migrants using Foucault's concept of biopolitics. The last two look at the current body of legislation and the accompanying political discourse which allows summary expulsions at the border, pointing out how international treaties are being violated and highlighting the ethical problems caused by the use of new control instruments and the implementation of an "operational border".

Secondly, at a meso-level (or on the relation between state(s) and intermediary players), Francesca Esposito, José Ornelas and Caterina Arcidiacono's joint research on the experience of daily life inside migrant detention centres shows us the role played by various actors and interests involved in the survival and expansion of detention centres, using the 'Center for Identification and Expulsion' in Ponte Galeria, Italy, as an illustrative case. In its turn, Leila Giannetto's work, which takes the *Charter of Lampedusa* movement as a case study, allows us to see how civil society organizations act in the field of migration policies, distinguishing between those which operate locally and those which do so at the level of the European Union. Cristina Blanco Sío-López presents the debate and negotiations that have developed around the construction of the concept of the "free circulation of persons" using Schengen as a laboratory and aiming to show the importance of the role of citizens through their representatives in the European Parliament.

Finally, taking the direct relationship between state and European Community into account, migration policies and freedom of movement in their role as fundamental pieces for European integration/construction are studied. From a historical perspective, Simone Paoli seeks to answer the question: how and to what extent have the Schengen agreements influenced Italian immigration policy? Then Nicolae Păun and Adrian-Gabriel Corpădean revisit Romania's accession to the Schengen area, describing the demands and scepticism of the Community in general and of political groups and other member states in particular, while on the other hand showing how the topic appeared at the level of civil society and decision-making structures. Taking a broader approach, the work of Ana Isabel Xavier correctly stresses the weight of external "threats" – terrorism, migration, organized crime – when defining the EU's internal security policy.

These three dimensions are divided between the two parts that make up the present work. In the first part are the studies that deal with the challenges faced by the unification of the European space given the diversity of actors, pressure factors (both domestic and external) and powers involved in its administration when what is at stake is the circulation of people (*The free circulation of persons: actors, policies and challenges*). In the second part, more attention is paid to border management devices (*Mobility and border management*). The book opens with a chapter written by Carlos Coelho, a Member of the European Parliament whose work has long been devoted to this matter, on the origins and evolution of the Schengen Area, its compensatory measures and the improvements that need to be addressed.

This work has been made possible solely as a result of the support we received from the start to host the Conference in June 2015. This support came from the following institutions who we would like to gratefully thank: the Portuguese Foundation for Science and Technology (FCT), the Institute of Contemporary History (IHC-FCSH/UNL), the Faculty of Social Sciences and Humanities of the NOVA University of Lisbon, the Migration Observatory (OM), and the European Commission Representation in Lisbon which also financially sponsored publication of this work.

Lisbon, 3 August 2015

Schengen: people, borders and mobility

Carlos Coelho

This year we celebrate abolishing internal borders between Portugal, Spain and the other five founding states. Portugal was at the forefront of the European Integration.

Indeed, twenty years have passed since a fundamental step towards integration was taken. But it was not only an act of political significance. It was a concrete action that citizens could feel directly. Twenty years ago we, the peoples of Europe, got closer to each other.

Such a historical event, of such importance and lasting effects, should no doubt be celebrated. But *au-delà de l'histoire*, why does Schengen remain today so important to Europe?

Why is Schengen so important?

First and foremost because it reminds us that Europe is not only the economy and the internal market. It reminds us that the European Union is not only about free movement of goods, services and capitals. It is also about free movement of people. It is the "ever closer union" in the interest of the citizens. A Union of European Citizenship, a Union that aims to make easier living across this continent. A Europe of and for the citizens.

A Europe for citizens also encompasses security, which is another essential element to understand the importance of Schengen. When internal borders are abolished, external borders need to become stronger; they need to be reinforced in order to guarantee that our citizens and our territory remain safe, because a breach in the external borders weakens the security of the whole Schengen area. Therefore, as the Agreement foreseen from the beginning, "compensatory measures" are required. But because each of the more than 50.000 kilometers of land and sea borders remains under national control, we must ensure that member states trust in the work carried out by each other. And this is the last fundamental pillar of Schengen: Mutual Trust.

As it would become known with the Tampere Programme, Schengen encompasses an area of Freedom, Security and Justice. And whereas it is clear to me that we cannot have one without the other, or damage one to get the other, it is also very clear that without mutual trust we will not have any. Schengen demands, therefore, that police and judicial actors can cooperate, that information can be shared; it demands an impartial and effective evaluation system. For the benefit of external borders, but also for the benefit of internal security. Ultimately, for the benefit of the European citizens.

At this point, however, I should make a declaration of interests. I want to be clear from the outset: I do not believe in aseptic views of reality, especially if you are a representative of the people. Therefore, my views naturally reflect my beliefs. And these can be reduced to this essential idea that Europe is for the citizens and therefore it has to continue to reach out to them as it did in the past through the creation of the Schengen area. This is the Europe I believe in.

Recent events, a bit all over Europe, have led us to believe that the support for the European project is declining. As populist and radical parties increase their electoral results, it would seem that the public debate had become limited to two political strands: those that are against Europe and Schengen; and those which focus only on the internal market, envisaging a Union for economical purposes only.

But looking at what people really think, the conclusion could not be more different. Consistently since 2007 at least[1], Europeans name free movement as one of the most positive outcomes of the European Union. In the Spring of 2014[2], the Euro barometer survey showed that free movement was seen as the most positive outcome. 56% of Europeans think of free movement of citizens as the most positive realisation of the Union, even ahead of peace amongst member states.

This is not to say that we do not face problems, that there is no room for improvement or that citizens do not demand for changes, namely more security.

Our continent has been for centuries a borderland, where territorial boundaries were always much disputed and not always reflecting nations. Therefore, security and identity were always strongly linked to the idea of controlling who enters our territory. Still today, border-crossing controls remain charged with symbolism.

---

1 Standard Euro Barometers 67, 70, 72, 73, 77 and 81 (retrieved from http://ec.europa.eu/COMMFrontOffice/PublicOpinion/index.cfm/Survey/index#p=1&instruments=STANDARD).

2 Standard Euro Barometer 81 (Spring 2014), retrieved from http://ec.europa.eu/citizenship/pdf/spring_eurobarometer_july_2014.pdf).

On the other hand, the economic crisis, the attacks in Paris, foreign fighters, the crisis in the Mediterranean (and now increasingly in the Balkans) have generated a sense of fear, of distrust. This sentiment is the root cause for more protectionism and security.

It is thus not surprising that Europeans value free movement so much, while calling for more control when they feel threatened.

Some of you might still remember what it was like to go to Spain to buy candies or Coca-Cola. How complicated and lengthy it was. When internal borders were abolished, Portuguese and Spaniards felt how crossing the border, for whatever reason, had turned into a simple act, much less bureaucratic and surely faster. But for the countries of the 2004 enlargement, this feeling was something different and filled with hope. For Polish, Hungarians or Czechs and all the others entering the Schengen area, it was recognising them as full members of the European Project. It was a sign of trust. In 2007 I witnessed the borders being opened in several of these countries. Believe me when I tell you that it touched everyone. You could feel the emotion in each and every person; you could feel the renewed sense of freedom.

Likewise, but for the opposite reasons, Romanians and Bulgarians, member states since 2007, feel as second-class citizens because they are still subject to border controls. Their efforts to comply with the Schengen *acquis* produced results; the Commission and the European Parliament have already supported their claim to join, but they remain outside the Schengen area.

My purpose is to underline the importance of Schengen. It is not merely an historical agreement or an historical date. It is a complex system that requires mutual trust. It is made of balanced approaches, as it touches upon very sensitive political issues. But above all, it is the core of the Europe of citizens. Schengen is the core of the area of Freedom, Security and Justice.

My intention is to focus on the following three topics:

- From the origin until nowadays
- compensatory measures
- what is not working.

From the origin until nowadays

Despite having been signed in 1985, Schengen only entered into force 10 years later, in 1995. As stated above, it started outside the EU framework, but it was soon incorporated by the Treaty of Amsterdam in 1997. Even before entering into force, it was accessed by a hand full of countries, amongst which was Portugal. In its origin was the will to a deeper and faster integration than the other member states.

Although the internal market entailed free movement of workers it would not necessarily lead to abolishing the control at the borders. And, unlike their partners, the Schengen States were willing to do so and even more. Already in the Schengen Agreement the preamble read: "resolved to continue the process of creating an ever closer union among the peoples of Europe".

Nonetheless, the first and more evident effect was of an economic nature. Economies become more integrated if products can move more easily, if workers can move freely. The European Commission estimates that the deepening of the internal market over the period 1992-2006 raised EU GDP and employment by 2.2 per cent and 1.3 per cent, representing figures of 233 billion euro and 2.8 million persons respectively.[3] And if it is true that not all of it results from Schengen, it is undisputed its crucial input. This is also reflected, today, in tourism: Europeans do 1.25 billion journeys, yearly, just inside the Schengen area.[4]

But right from the start it was evident that Schengen carried the seed for a Union that wanted to be political as well. With the Maastricht Treaty, in 1992, that seed produced results. The European Union was created and national citizens vested with a second citizenship, comprising political rights of its own: the European citizenship. In the Treaty of the European Union we can still read: "Every person holding the nationality of a Member State shall be a citizen of the Union" and "Every citizen of the Union shall have the right to move and reside freely within the territory of the Member states […]". But Schengen was not about a legal status. It was rather about identity and bringing Europeans together.

As I already said elsewhere[5], the European identity is something hard to define. And, if existent, I believe it to be more evident by opposition, when it is confronted with other external identities. Probably Portuguese remain Portuguese, French remain French but we are closer.

---

3 European Economy, Economic paper, No. 271 (January 2007), European Commission Directorate-General for Economic and Financial Affairs, p. 5 and pp. 55-58 (retrieved from http://ec.europa.eu/economy_finance/publications/publication784_en.pdf).

4 Europe Without Borders – The Schengen area, European Commission Directorate-General for Home Affairs, p. 11 (retrieved from http://ec.europa.eu/dgs/home-affairs/e-library/docs/schengen_brochure/schengen_brochure_dr3111126_en.pdf).

5 Identidade Europeia: Quem são os Europeus de Hoje? (May 2015), Carlos Coelho, Fundação Calouste Gulbenkian (retrieved from http://carloscoelho.eu/texts/view/identidade-europeia-quem-sao-os-europeus-de-hoje-carlos-coelho-responde-na-fundacao-gulbenkian).

Commissioner for Research, Science and Innovation, the Portuguese Carlos Moedas, is the first Commissioner "son" of the Erasmus family. There is an entire generation of young people that never knew what it is to stop between Portugal and Spain or from Paris to Berlin. Today citizens from 26 countries can live, study, or work anywhere they wish. Crossing borders within this area has been made incredibly simple. Schengen brought Europeans together, helped dissipate fear and difference, that so many times in the past led to mistrust.

But there still is work to be done.

In a survey from 2009[6], more affluent EU-15 migrants were often described as "mobile Europeans", while those coming from the new member states were referred to as "immigrants", and could face discrimination regardless of their EU-citizenship status. More recently, in 2012, the majority of Europeans declared to see positively migrants from other member states compared to migrants from third country nationals. In 2013, there were 12 million citizens living in a member state different from its origin[7], compared to only 5 million in 1995.[8]

Despite its evident positive effects, Schengen has been, unfortunately, under enormous pressure: in its external border and internally.

During the last decade, the Mediterranean region – northern Africa, Middle East, Turkey, the Balkans – has been affected by a number of international and regional developments leading to enormous political instability. This has contributed to increase migration flows and asylum pressure, especially to Italy, Greece, Spain, Malta and Cyprus.

In the first trimester of 2015, more than 1.500 people died trying to cross the Mediterranean. This year can very well be the deadliest in 20 years. This brutal reality is clear evidence of the need for immediate response. It is also demonstrates that we are facing a problem that does not concern just frontline Member States, but calls for solidarity from the entire Schengen area.

For the past three years too, Europe was also confronted with a new phenomenon of terrorism and home grown jihadists, the so called *foreign fighters*.

---

6 Free Movement in Europe: Past and Present, (April 2011), Saara Koikkalainen, Migration Policy Institute (retrieved from http://www.migrationpolicy.org/article/free-movement-europe-past-and-present).

7 EU citizenship – statistics on cross-border activities (April 2013), Eurostat (retrieved from http://ec.europa.eu/eurostat/statistics-explained/index.php/EU_citizenship_-_statistics_on_cross-border_activities).

8 20 years of the European Single Market – Main Achievements (2012), European Commission, p. 25 (Retrieved from http://ec.europa.eu/internal_market/publications/docs/20years/achievements-web_en.pdf).

These phenomena led to an increase of populist and simplistic approaches, which appeal to nationalism rooted in insecurity and fear. Also threatening the very existence of Schengen.

Compensatory Measures

As was noted above, the greater freedom which came from abolishing internal borders required, on the one hand, increased security at the external borders and, on the other hand, more cooperation within the Schengen area. These so called "compensatory measures" are, as I mentioned before, both at the core of mutual trust and result from it.

Indeed, the signatories of the Schengen agreement reaffirmed "their objective to facilitate the free movement of persons, while ensuring the safety and security of their peoples, by including provisions on justice and home affairs in this Treaty". This would be mirrored in the Maastricht Treaty, which introduced the three pillars. Justice and home affairs, the lasting third pillar, would see a great increase in instruments due to the incorporation of the Schengen *acquis* in the EU framework by the Amsterdam Treaty.

The most recognizable instrument is the Schengen Information System. SIS is a huge database, which in December 2014 contained 53 million alerts on objects and almost 2 million alerts on people. As an example, these alerts can be to refuse entry to persons who do not have the right to enter or stay in Schengen territory or they can be to find and detain a person for whom a European Arrest Warrant has been issued. Alerts on objects, also as an example, can be stolen aircrafts, firearms and issued documents, amongst many other categories. The system operates 24 hours a day, every day of the week, the whole year and links law enforcement agencies, customs and border guards from all the Schengen states.

As you might know, this is not the only database related to Schengen, although it is the only one foreseen in the Agreement. Others were developed, such as the Visa Information System (VIS), to store visa applications, or Eurodac, used in asylum procedures.

But compensatory measures were not only translated into information systems. Several legal instruments have been approved over time to ensure an efficient, coherent and trustful functioning of the Schengen area. These covered visa and asylum policies, external borders and judicial and police cooperation in customs and criminal matters.

For the Schengen Governance however, the Schengen Borders Code and the New Evaluation Mechanism are particularly important.

What is not working well and needs to be improved

The importance of the Schengen Borders Code and the New Schengen Evaluation Mechanism was already quite evident in 2011, when the migratory pressure was reaching the high levels we are still facing today. Member states, especially in the north of Europe, became increasingly afraid that the Mediterranean countries could not handle the number of migrants coming through their shores. The simplistic approach was to say: close the internal borders.

As mentioned before, solidarity and trust are key in Schengen. Instead of closing borders, we need an holistic approach to migration and asylum and, on the other hand, ensure a higher level of accountability and greater transparency with regard to how the Schengen *acquis* is being implemented and enforced by Member States, in order to ensure maximum compliance.

This is the reason behind the New Schengen Evaluation Mechanism, which entered into force this year. As rapporteur in the European Parliament, it was my intention to shift from the old intergovernmental system of peer review to an EU-based approach where the central coordinating role is given to the European Commission. It was also key to me and the European Parliament that the new mechanism would introduce a clause providing for unannounced visits of experts, and clearer rules for the follow-up to evaluations. We managed to have it and in addition to these improvements, the evaluation process also includes measures aimed to assist member states in fulfilling the recommendations adopted as part of the evaluation process.

It is quite clear to me that the migration problem is much bigger and requires an all-encompassing strategy. This includes other policies such as development and foreign affairs, but it also includes other aspects of Schengen, such the full implementation of the Common European Asylum System. It must address solidarity amongst Member states and also ensure that we tackle the root causes of these movements. However, and this is a big however, we must ensure that we can assess whether member states are complying with what is already in place. The purpose of an evaluation system is to find what is wrong, what is not being well applied. Definitely, not to disguise, hide or forget those failures. Instead, the purpose should be to take action and solve problems, because the purpose of an effective evaluation mechanism is to make our borders stronger and more efficient.

This New Mechanism followed another major change: the second generation of the Schengen Information System. Only operational since April 2013, it intended to accomplish, amongst others, two objectives: increase security at the external borders, namely with regard to terrorism and irregular migration, but also increase the security inside our territories.

To achieve these objectives new features were introduced. Some of which should be highlighted:

- Alerts can now be linked; That is, if a stolen car is found through a random internal control, when accessing the SIS the enforcement officer will be able to see that the car is possibly part of a broader criminal network. Leading to discreet surveillance instead of seizing the car and arresting the suspect. This feature in particular changed the very functioning of the system. It was no longer a hit-no hit reactive vertical system. It became an horizontally integrated, proactive system;
- Another important feature is that now the European Arrest Warrant can also be attached to the person concerned, leading to a faster procedure;
- The number of access points also increased, following the enlarged purpose of SIS. But what a user can see is only what it needs to its field of work. For example in Portugal border guards have access to different elements than the criminal police;
- Lastly, and of crucial importance, the system can store biometric data. It improved the effectiveness of the system for the purposes of organised crime and terrorism, in particular a rising type of criminality: identity theft and forged identity documents. For the same reason, it also helped decreased the so-called "*John Smith*" phenomenon. That is, to wrongly identify someone because he or she has the same name of someone flagged in the system.

This is particularly important to – again – understand the reactions following the terrorist attacks early this year. The fringes, especially, saw again an opportunity to wave the nationalist flag and call for reintroducing internal borders. The major parties, on the other hand, decided to revive data retention, fast-track PNRs and Smart Borders. Forgetting that Schengen is not only security, but also freedom and justice.

In my opinion, we lacked the clarity to understand Schengen. And for several reasons:

(i) we have yet to see the first results from the New Schengen Evaluation Mechanism, which is to say we do not really know whether member states are implementing correctly the Schengen *acquis*;

(ii) but we know already that the SIS II is not yet being used at its full potential, as the Commission has noted time and time again;

(iii) the Schengen Borders Code already foresees the possibility to temporarily reintroduce checks at the internal borders for security reasons;

(iv) lastly, Europol, Eurojust, European Commission, national stakeholders have several times noted that Law enforcement agencies and judicial authorities do not cooperate as much as they should and they could.

Conclusion

In fine, Schengen is about the citizens, their freedom and their security, internally and at the borders. For a balanced approach, both need to be accounted for in the right proportion.

At the very core of Schengen is mutual trust. There is neither freedom nor security without mutual trust and both security and freedom must foster it. We must resist simplistic and populist approaches. For an efficient, functioning Schengen area that is centered in the citizens, we need a balanced approach which most of the time is complex.

As First Vice-President Timmermans recently said, "Schengen is not part of the problem but part of the solution".[9] I entirely subscribe this statement. Schengen has played an essential role in European integration and in bringing Europeans together. It will never be complete, and its balance will always be difficult. It is our duty to preserve it and improve it, as doing so we are improving citizens lives. We are building the Europe of citizens.

This is what I believe in. This is what the European Parliament is fighting for every day. This is what I think the other EU institutions and Schengen member states should be doing also.

---

9 European Parliament, Debate "Preparation of the informal meeting of Heads of State or Government, 12 February 2015" (retrieved from http://www.europarl.europa.eu/sides/getDoc.do?pubRef=-//EP//TEXT+CRE+20150211+ITEM-008+DOC+XML+V0//EN).

Part I

The Free Circulation of Persons: Actors, Policies and Challenges

Part I

Dialogues beyond the 'Fortress Europe'

Tracing back the Genesis and Evolution of the 'Free Circulation of Persons' Concept through EP Schengen Area Debates, 1985-2015

Cristina BLANCO SÍO-LÓPEZ

Abstract: This contribution aims to enhance the mapping and critical analysis of the evolving priorities and policy-making objectives of the EP key players upholding or resisting the building of the Schengen Area and, more particularly, the consolidation of the principle of the free circulation of persons within the EU. As this historical process touches upon the complexities of the construction of transnational identities, it also aspires to provide the complementary methodological viewpoints of history of concepts and critical discourse analysis for the study of socio-political relations and democratic decision-making. Indeed, the unconventional EP debates on this matter can help us to elucidate if free movement of persons was being granted as a subsidiary concession or if it constituted and end in itself, being, therefore, in direct relation with EU foundational propositions and long term hopes based on the principles of solidarity and sustainability. In short, the critical examination of such documentary corpus could play an essential role in empowering EU citizens and residents arguments against any possible involution of the Schengen area into the largely condemned 'Fortress Europe'. Hence, it could also aid to re-encounter that particular version of European integration devoted to transforming stumbling blocks into stepping-stones.

Introduction

"[…] many articulate people seemed to have a sense of high social purpose and it might have been a spring of brave hopes"
Joan Didion

Background and Objectives

Taking into account the 30th anniversary of the Schengen Agreement on 14 June 2015, this chapter aims to analyse the origins, evolution and challenges of the Schengen area from the perspective of key European Parliament (EP)'s players. Moreover, the diachronically examined relevant EP documents will definitely help to further elucidate multilevel motivations, strategies and discourses laying the foundations of the free movement of persons as part of the so-called "four freedoms".[1] Indeed, these sources also contribute to shed light on the symbolic and normative weight of continuities and ruptures in network-led developments, bargaining and consensus building operations concerning the implementation of the Schengen *acquis*, all of which are deeply related to the notion of quality of democracy[2] at the Community level. In this respect, the studied EP documentation offers an invaluable 'behind-the-scenes-view' approach to evolving opinions, dialogues and transfers of ideas between domestic actors, MEPs and key *rapporteurs*, not only from founding member states, but also from subsequent EC/EU candidate and acceding countries. In sum, this piece aims to provide an in-depth historical analysis of the crucial issue of free movement of persons in the EU, which remarkably contributed to define the nature and potentialities of the European integration model within a global context.

Likewise, this chapter also attempts to determine whether the EP is a context and a content shaper regarding this fundamental and future-oriented contribution to the European integration process. Moreover, it tries to elaborate on the diachronic commitment of the Parliament in standing for the quality of democratic provisions, especially concerning the demands for the integration of the Schengen process in Community law under the EP democratic control. In addition, it aspires to illustrate the complex interplay of competences, agents and gaps in EU democracy and to clarify whether the free movement of persons is to be considered as an instrument or as a consequence. In this regard, it also pays attention to the symbolic and semantic weight of the term 'Schengen', with a view to analyse the moulding power of such narrative paradigm in the evolution of EU political cultures and policy choices beyond pre-established frameworks. In conclusion, it seeks to illustrate the role of the EP in the generation and consolidation of a European model that is essentially not limiting but enabling, within a changing framework which perpetually

1 For further analysis on the "four freedoms", please, see Barnard, C., *The Substantive Law of the EU. The Four Freedoms*, Oxford University Press, Oxford, 2013.

2 Refer to Morlino, L., "Legitimacy and the quality of democracy", *International Social Science Journal*, Vol. 60, Issue 196, June 2009, pp. 211-222.

strives to combine ethical imperatives and a positive societal impact mindset.

Methodology

This contribution is based on the historical analysis of EP archival sources from 1985 to 2015, coming from the Historical Archives of the European Parliament in Luxembourg. A special attention is paid to EP debates, since they detail an otherwise invisible dynamism of the diversity of interactions which lies at the foundations of the EU legislative process. They constitute, indeed, a paradigm of networked knowledge and combinatorial creativity[3] able to illustrate the mechanics behind the trends and choices that have a direct impact on the daily life of the EU citizenry.

The chosen methodology firstly integrates a history of concepts[4] approach concerning the analysis of the diachronic evolution of key concepts relative to the Schengen area in EU policy-making from the perspective of the EP. Secondly, this chapter also applies a critical discourse analysis[5] perspective with a focus on institutional discourse, which is understood as a goal oriented discourse that paves the way for the generation of an expected acceptance. In this way, it is said to contribute to the seeming monopoly of legitimate discourse. However, it should also be noted that the defining pluralistic character of EP sources has the effect of projecting a more multifaceted yet accountable sense of legitimacy. For this reason, discourse is not to be considered as pure content, but as a window to the given players' mental or social world.[6] More specifically, the main adopted approach will be that of examining a level of relevance within the subtle realm of EP debates and their paradigmatic expression of intertwined intimate convictions. In addition, it should be specified that the EP documentation on this topic definitely helps to nuance and calibrate the initial EU policy-making propositions and evolving directions of the Schengen Agreements.

---

3 See Wlodzislaw, D., "Intuition, Insight, Imagination and Creativity", *IEEE Computational Intelligence Magazine*, Vol. 2, Issue 3, 2007, pp. 40-52.

4 See Palonen, K., "The History of Concepts as a Style of Political Theorizing. Quentin Skinner's and Reinhart Koselleck's Subversion of Normative Political Theory", *European Journal of Political Theory*, July 2002, Vol. 1, pp. 91-106.

5 Refer to Fairclough, N., *Critical Discourse Analysis*, Longman, London, 1995.

6 Cameron, D., *Working with Spoken Discourse*, Sage Publications, London, 2001, p. 43.

Stepping Stones towards the Schengen Agreement and the Free Movement of Persons

First and foremost, it should be clarified that the precedents to the Schengen Agreements, signed on 14 June 1985, go back deep into the first integration and cooperation experiences of the post-war era. Nonetheless, it is also significant to allude to previous ideas in this direction, dating even from the interwar period, such as the references to the need to eliminate internal borders within the continent, which Coudenhonve-Kalergi already mentions in his works on 'Paneuropa'. These also include proposals on a desirable free movement of students and teachers within a "borderless space".[7]

The Schengen Agreement of 14 June 1985 and the Schengen Implementing Convention of 19 June 1990 – which came into force on 26 March 1995 – constitute a fructification of all these initiatives, despite the fact that the free movement of persons' concept has undergone an important evolution in its contents and implications. More specifically, it was firstly viewed as a means to serve economic objectives at the time of the creation of the European Economic Community (EEC). However, this notion progressively evolved – through the formulation of the so-called "People's Europe" and the later "Citizens' Europe" – towards more socio-cultural and identity-building implications. This seemed to culminate with the Maastricht Treaty (TEU) European citizenship notion, which implies that every EU citizen – that is, the holder of the nationality of an EU member state – has the right to move and reside freely within the territory of the member states.[8]

Challenges and Propositions of the Schengen Agreement and Convention, 1985-1992

In the months following the signature of the Schengen Agreements, the EP experiences a deepening of the discussions on the crucial dimensions of the free movement of persons, such as the abolition of the restriction of travel for local residents at the Community's internal frontiers. It is important to note, in this respect, that EP multilevel players are presented as supporters of the priority of defending these residents on the grounds of their particular situations being deemed incompatible with the stated objectives of the Single Market. As we will see throughout the analysis

7 Refer to International Pan-European Union *fonds* at the Historical Archives of the European Union (HAEU) in Florence: http://archives.eui.eu/en/fonds/181668?item=PAN/EU (last accessed on 20/07/2015).

8 See http://www.europarl.europa.eu/aboutparliament/en/displayFtu.html?ftuId=FTU_2.1.3.html (last accessed on 20/07/2015).

of a rich variety of EP sources in a diachronic perspective, for many key players at the European institutions, the defence of the aims of the internal market seems to be more important than the defence of democratic rights and freedoms *per se*. Very much on the contrary, EP actors will constitute a differential voice in this long-term debate by continuously searching for a balance between the internal market priorities and the preeminence of free movement of persons as an end in itself within the historical process of European integration. Thus, they vehemently attempt to incorporate the deeply ingrained foundational ideals of a 'Citizens' Europe' as part of an enriched *acquis*.[9]

In 1986, and in the midst of key turning points in the history of European integration – such as the signature of the Single European Act modifying the Treaty of Rome and the accession of Spain and Portugal to the Community – EP actors devote their attention to the crucial question of the cost of a non-united Europe in relation to Schengen area debates. Against this backdrop, the EP urges the Commission to make public the actual total cost – including the social costs – of a non-united Europe and to provide the European Parliament with the information necessary to undertake political action to stimulate the Council to arouse public opinion in the Community on this matter.[10] It is then that MEP Martínez Heredia (S-ES) emphasises the need to conciliate the creation of a 'European consciousness' through the press and communications media with the socio-economic development of the Community, while touching upon the interrelated factor of tenable welfare procurement for a 'People's Europe':

> I also agree that is fundamentally competitiveness in economic relations that will make our Community even stronger. But I believe in a People's Europe which cares about the poor, the deprived, the unemployed, those who suffer from the lack of collective solidarity in this Peoples' Europe that so many love to evoke, the one that firmly turns its back on the tragedy everyday subsistence represent for many families. I believe in a People's Europe where our Parliament shows solidarity to those who suffer most or with those who have most to bear.[11]

---

9 On the notion of a Citizens' Europe as recovered and supported by Altiero Spinelli in this period, see Blanco Sío-López, C., "The Battle for the Constitutionalisation of the Union: Parliament, Advocate of a European Constitution (1979-1990)", in Y. Mény (ed.), *Building Parliament: 50 Years of European Parliament History, 1958-2008*, Office for Official Publications of the European Communities, Luxembourg, 2008, pp. 111-116.

10 Resolution of the European Parliament of 14 July 12 June 1986 on the cost of a non-united Europe, OJ C 176/125, 14 July 1986, p. 125.

11 European Parliament debates of 13 September 1988 on a motion for resolution by Mrs. Veil and others on the People's Europe, No. 2-368, p. 51. Motion for a Resolution of

This committed social dimension is also linked to other key elements of the free movement of persons' debate, which include – as MEP Perry (EPP-GB) indicates – the problems arising in connection with security, xenophobia, old age and urban deprivation, which "cannot be ignored in the process of developing an area without internal frontiers".[12] One of the most comprehensive voices in this respect comes from MEP Vayssade (S-FR), who then states that "we want to build Europe for the benefit of the women and men who live here"[13], hence, meaning for all citizens and residents, within an original sense of inclusive European integration community building.

The intersection between freedom movement of persons and a People's Europe became then gradually more focused on the nature and potentialities of social and identity-building elements. From this perspective, the official narrative also included the argument that "the completion of the Single Market presupposes comparable progress in the field of citizens' rights and a People's Europe".[14]

Regarding the interplay between the free movement of persons and the crucial issue of immigration – which exponentially increases its presence in the EP documentation of this period – MEPs from a plurality of views insist in the need to constructively integrate third country immigrants in the Community, an approach holding a positive societal impact we could consider as largely forgotten in our present. Plus, they also reaffirm the need to promote their integration into society by combating all forms of discrimination, racism or xenophobia in accordance with the *Solemn Declaration by the three Institutions* of June 1986. In addition, they stress "the value of the contribution made by immigrants to the building of a multi-national and multicultural European society".[15]

It is also important to mention the observation done in this period regarding the differential asymmetric speed of each of the four freedoms. Indeed, major progress is being made on the liberalisation of capital movements, but these generous concessions are not being matched in freedom of movement for workers or in actions to give substance to the auspicated 'People's Europe'.[16] EP players consider, within such context, that the overestimation of economic integration over a European

---

the European Parliament of 13 August 1988 on a People's Europe, OJ C 674/88, 13 August 1988.

12 *Ibid.*

13 *Ibid.*

14 *Ibid.*

15 Motion for a Resolution of the European Parliament of 8 13 September 1988 on the Citizen's People's Europe, OJ C 497/88262, 8 September/10 October 1988, pp. 40-41.

16 *Ibid.*

sustainable social model could engender the gradual rupture of the links between the European institutions and the citizens, which is also now probably growing wider each day:

> Europe 1992 will be a failure if it offers no more than the implementation of the White Paper on the internal market. The accompanying measures in the social, regional and environmental fields are indissolubly linked. The measures connected with a People's Europe are stagnating. That is a political time-bomb of the first order. The credibility of the whole project is at stake.[17]

Hence, it is important to bear in mind this early warning about an also early disregard for the free movement of persons in favour of the other three freedoms. As a matter of fact, it marks the starting point of a discourse and policy-making conducting thread increasingly oriented towards market priorities in detriment of social and human concerns, a trend which has been exacerbated in the context of our current economic crisis. Very remarkably, the repercussions of such imbalance are deeply interconnected to the need to redefine political and socio-economic models and principles within a *momentum* characterised by a retroactive combination of questioning and resilience.

Following the signature of the Convention implementing the Schengen Agreements in June 1990[18], the Parliament expressed critical views regarding the way in which the negotiations were conducted and concluded. More particularly, it manifested its concern regarding the fact that the Convention was negotiated outside the Community institutions and, thus, it insisted on the fact that the parliamentary and democratic control of its application was not guaranteed.

Another key ground of commitment for EP players regarding the Schengen area in this period was the interplay between the free movement of persons and the tackling of racism and xenophobia at the European level:

> We call on the Commission to draw up proposals for directives on the harmonisation at the highest level of legislation in the Member states against racism and xenophobia and equal treatment of Community and non-Community migrants, in particular as regards the *acquis*ition of social rights and freedom of movement.[19]

---

17 European Parliament debates of 11 October 1989 on the People's Europe, pp. 51-52 the completion of the internal market, No. 3-381, pp. 75-112.

18 See http://eur-lex.europa.eu/LexUriServ/LexUriServ.do?uri=CELEX:42000A0922(02):fr:HTML (last accessed on 20/07/2015).

19 Motion for a Resolution of the European Parliament of 4 October 1990 on the report of the Committee of Inquiry into Racism and Xenophobia, OJ C 1727/90, 4 October 1990.

Also, the challenging issue of the democratic control of the security facets of Schengen encountered a fertile discussion ground in the EP during the 1991 Gulf war. More particularly, it touched upon decisively articulated 'liberty vs. security' arguments, hence, hitting one close to home in our present, despite current forcedly narrative closures of a 'conflict escalation-refugee outcry' feedback loop:

> The EP hopes that the Gulf war will not be used as a pretext for harsher external border controls not justified on grounds of security. It undertakes to ensure that the Gulf war is not a motive of discrimination against non-Community nationals and calls on the governments of the Member states and the other Community institutions to do the same.[20]

From a different perspective, the persistent lack of openness towards the general Schengen procedure was also later condemned not only by MEP Malangré (PPE-DE), the *rapporteur* for the Committee of Legal Affairs and Citizens' Rights, but also by the Dutch Council of State, the screening committee of the French Senate and several resolutions of the European Parliament. The EP then considered that it was not acceptable to simply to say 'yes or no' to an instrument of such far-reaching implications as the Schengen Convention. It is for the same reason that the Parliament then proposed reversing the procedure: to begin with, it maintained that member state' parliaments should be informed in advance about the initiation and progress of talks, and, subsequently, of a proposal for an agreement.[21]

Concerning the increasing overabundance of highly semantically charged notions and definitions in this period, EP players asked: "Are 'serious suspicion', 'serious offence', 'serious danger', and 'danger posed by a person' to be interpreted? The terms 'public policy' and 'internal security' are likewise very broad. There is no uniform interpretation of them within the Schengen states. That is why the Dutch Parliament has asked for definitions to be given in protocols in accordance with the interpretation given to them by Community Law".[22]

Another key issue which gathered major attention in this period is that of the escalating violation of privacy. EP players even refer then to the fact that Schengen is presented as a probable excuse for a systematic classification, profiling and follow-up of the movements of European citizens, an idea which deeply resonates with the generalised, daily and worldwide violations of privacy rights of global citizens nowadays:

---

20 Motion for a Resolution of the European Parliament of 14 February 1991 on the Schengen Agreement, OJ C 0086/91, 14 February 1991.

21 *Ibid.*

22 *Ibid.*

"First the Schengen Information System (SIS) and then the European Information System (EIS): Is Europe collecting information about its citizens on a hard disk?".[23]

On a more general and equally foreboding note, MEP Van Outrive (PSE-BE) then stated that:

> citizens are left out in the cold. The consequences of the lack of cohesion, overlapping and greater internal control, and the financial implications will soon make themselves felt. There is a reason to fear that this exercise will backfire, in view of the already considerable – and growing – aversion of European citizens to Brussels. But the citizens are not alone in being left out on account. Public prosecution departments and courts have not been sufficiently involved in the work either.[24]

Indeed, the cleavage between European citizens and institutions continues to increase now by the day, accentuated by a rooting lack of solidarity in the drafting of efficient yet socially and humanly comprehensive measures to tackle the devastating effects of the current economic crisis. It should also be specified that this is just further sedimenting a detachment already cumulated in previous phases of the European integration process. Actually, this evidences the negative impact of an over-concentration on an economic – or, more accurately on a merely monetary – integration, thus disregarding a social, cultural and environmental dimension, despite the fact of these having been repeatedly and largely demanded by the citizenship.

The post-Maastricht democratic *deficit* and the Schengen area, 1993-1999

This phase is notably characterised by the following key turning points: The 26 April 1994 Bonn Protocol (appliance of asylum protocol); the 26 March 1995 Schengen Convention launch of the end of internal border areas for the original five states, Portugal and Spain and the online launch of the Schengen Information System (SIS). This same year, on 28 April, Austria joins Schengen and, on 26 July, EU members sign Europol Convention. On 19 December 1996, Denmark, Finland and Sweden join Schengen, in a year that, from the EP's documentation view is featured by a critical examination of the preparatory documents of the Intergovernmental Conference of 1996. Regarding this highlight, the EP then demanded that more democracy, or the democratisation of Community acts, was required. Such request was closely linked to the solicitation of more transparency and efficiency in the Union, which were

[23] *Ibid.*

[24] *Ibid.*

also essential objectives of the revision of the Maastricht Treaty on this occasion.

Such requests deeply affected the debate on the four freedoms. Indeed, it is important to note how EP players constantly reiterated and pointed out that the free movement of persons is to be considered the most important of the four freedoms. They also, hence, reminded that this freedom includes the freedom of establishment, as well as the right to work or study in a member state other than the person's country of origin.

Moreover, a multiplicity of pluralist EP actors decisively defended the idea that free movement of persons would not hinder security policy development. Supplementary, they also considered that free movement of persons within the Community would, in no way, hamper action against drugs trafficking and rejected as ill-founded the arguments related to action against narcotics used by some member states to delay the introduction of this freedom.

In this period, and coinciding with the war in the ex-Yugoslavia – and with its nefarious and never sufficiently acknowledged human tragedies – the EP was also used as a sounding board of minority, yet progressively more present, nationalist and xenophobic voices: "We stress the need to harmonise the methods for obtaining nationality by basing them on the parental relationship (*ius sanguinis*) rather than on the place of birth (*ius soli*)".[25]

Apart from a clear xenophobic element, such measures of seemingly eliminating the presence of crime by externalising it were strongly counteracted by the EP by reminding the transnational presence and actions of a deeply rooted organised crime, which, as an effect of globalisation, does not stop at national frontiers, but operates in spite of them.

The EP debates of this period also richly discussed the crucial and multilayered issue of migration, usually from a diversity of intertwined perspectives. For instance, MEP Roth (V-DE) indicated that:

> I should like to express my dismay and indignation at the arsenal of repressive proposals that the immigration Ministers decided in Copenhagen. It takes a particularly mischievous imagination to trace the ideological and political basis of this witch-hunt against non-Community citizens. Particularly shocking is the nearness in time of the Recommendation on Controls and Removal of third-country nationals – the very language is repressive – to Solingen, which has become the newest symbol for the growing deadly racism in the European Community. A responsible policy would be a radical reorientation to a positive signal for our societies that immigration is a positive

25 Motion for a Resolution of the European Parliament of 19 May 1993 on barriers to the free movement of persons within the Community and Schengen Agreement, OJ C 665/93, 19 May 1993.

> reality and that a multi-cultural and multi-ethnic co-existence is not somehow a danger but an enormous enrichment. A co-existence in which all those who live here, work here, and have their lives centred here are granted the same rights. That is not an exaggeration, but the foundation of democracy. What we can see clearly than ever, is the growth of a European Community Police State with all-embracing controls, systematic criminalisation and institutional discrimination against people of different national origin, in which inalienable and civil rights are infringed – an alarming development which lead, as a result, to an apartheid-like division in our society.[26]

In similar vein, the neglecting of the solidarity and diversity dimensions of European integration were then said to have contributed to the fragmentation and erosion of the European socio-political texture, which makes it (also today) ever less capable of humanly responding to humanitarian crises:

> By lumping together legal and illegal immigration, by placing on every immigrant a permanent and systematic suspicion of guilt, we give free rein to the xenophobic violence of some and a clear conscience to the widespread but still inactive racism of others. Human rights must not be a matter of variable geometry. They are universal and immutable. The right of asylum, the right to live with one's family, the right to move about, the international conventions, are not to be interpreted in one way for a period of economic expansion and another for a time of recession.[27]

In line with the previously described ideas, MEP De Piccoli (PSE-IT) indicated that "immigration[28] from third countries cannot be stopped now, nor it will be stopped in the future: we must create instruments for managing it adequately. Controlling immigration must mean a policy of integration based on full recognition of civil and political rights of those who reside legally in the Community".[29] In this regard, there was then a rising fear that legal migration was also being put into question *per se*, as MEP Coimbra Martins (PSE-PT) maintains, with an accent on an increasingly neglected solidarity principle:

> Are these officials trying to prevent illegal immigration or disrupt, discourage and put an end to legal immigration? Do we adopt the laws that the economic and political situation requires, or will the demons of racial purity be released? After all, we are all immigrants and our residence permit is only temporary.[30]

---

26 European Parliament debates of 15 July 1993 on Immigration, pp. 150-165.

27 *Ibid.*

28 Roos, C., *The EU and Immigration Policies: Cracks in the Walls of Fortress Europe?*, Palgrave Macmillan, Basingstoke, 2013.

29 European Parliament debates of 15 July 1993 on Immigration, pp. 150-165.

30 *Ibid.*

Against this backdrop, the EP firmly pointed out that the free moment of persons is not just an integral part of the internal market but also one of the main objectives of the European Union, in accordance with article 7a EC.[31] This entailed also the development of an increasing EP self-assumed mission to avoid the consolidation of a 'Fortress Europe'.[32] Accordingly, the Parliament considered that, in order to achieve the free movement of persons for all the citizens of the Union and for all citizens of third countries legally residing in the Union, it should call on the Commission, the Council and the member states of the Union to finally adopt and put into practice compensatory measures to ensure internal security once border controls were abolished, without turning the Union into a 'Fortress Europe'. It also recalled the vital role which the national parliaments and the European Parliament must play in exercising democratic control as representatives of the citizens of the European Union in a matter which constituted the essence of 'European citizenship'.[33] In the midst of these crucial discussions MEP Pailler (GUE/NGL-FR) then offered one of the finest definitions of 'Fortress Europe' within the examined EP debates:

> Human rights organisations are right to be alarmed and to warn of the dangers. I am opposed to the creation of this 'Fortress Europe', which in enhancing its own security remains deaf to the appeals of the victims of repression and poverty; this discriminatory Europe, which denies immigrants the right to vote in municipal and European elections, despite the recommendations of the Council of Europe; this Europe in which money is free to circulate, while men and women are unable to cross the frontiers of fear and indifference.[34]

This position significantly implied a totally differential approach to the meaning and potentialities of the European integration process, seemingly forgotten in our present. Subsequently, in 1997, Schengen achieves intergovernmental cooperation with thirteen countries. Before that crucial date – and also coinciding with the signature of the Amsterdam Treaty – the EP preparatory documents of the 1996 Intergovernmental Conference[35] relevantly saw the Schengen Agreements as a laboratory: "'Schengen' was originally designed as a 'working laboratory' and its

---

[31] See http://eur-lex.europa.eu/legal-content/EN/TXT/?uri=CELEX:12012E/TXT (last accessed on 28/03/2015).

[32] See Eberhardt, P., "Fortress Europe Revisited", *International Studies Review*, Vol. 9, Issue 4, Winter 2007, pp. 724-728.

[33] Resolution of the European Parliament of 6 April 1995 on the Schengen Agreement and political asylum, OJ C 109/169, 6 April 1995.

[34] European Parliament debates of 6 June April 1995 on Schengen and the right of asylum, No. 4-461, pp. 202-206.

[35] http://www.europarl.europa.eu/igc1996/fiches/fiche25_en.htm (last accessed on 28/07/2015).

incorporation on the Treaty was foreseen – as an integral part of the approach – from the outset".[36]

They also upheld that more democracy, and, as previously indicated, even the democratisation of Community acts, was required. This claim was closely linked to the demands on further transparency and efficiency in the Union, which were already essential objectives of the revision of the Maastricht Treaty. Although there was unanimity on the need to eliminate the Union's democratic *déficit*, there were still differences of opinion at this point "as to the areas in which democracy was inadequate, as well as to the means that must be used to reduce the lack of democracy".[37]

At this point, and taking into consideration social and cultural dimensions, free movement of persons was perceived by EP players in this fashion: "The free movement of persons is relegated to the tomorrow that never comes".[38]

In such context, MEP Schulz (PSE-DE) demanded a renewed emphasis and commitment on free movement of persons: "We do have in the European Union, on the basis of Community law, free movement of services, capital and goods, but we do not have freedom of movement for individuals". Therefore, he presented a critique of intergovernmentalism with a special emphasis on the virtues and potentialities of supranationalism and of the guarantees of EP democratic control.[39]

Concomitantly, MEP Roth (V-DE) alluded then to the revealing concept of 'sugar coating' related to these issues: "The opening of the internal borders was the sugar coating designed to conceal the taste of the new barriers at the external borders of Schengen, and to legitimise the fact that the new Schengen frontiers have been created within the European Union".[40]

He also affirmed that Schengen emerged undemocratically and that it was being operated also undemocratically, eroding the overall quality of democracy in the Union. The way it operated was also

36 Free movement of persons, Justice and Home Affairs: an outline approach, Conference of the Representatives of the Governments of the Member States, 10 February 1997, CONF/3817/97. Historical Archives CIG CIG1996 2080/INST INST-030 0200CIG1996.

37 Briefing of 5 March 1997 on the ICG and the democratic nature of the Union, Secretariat Working Party, Task-force on the 'Intergovernmental Conference'. Historical Archives CIG CIG1996 2010/TFOR TFOR-010 0260.

38 *Ibid.*

39 *Ibid.*

40 *Ibid.*

said to help consolidating a two-class system[41] and even a blueprint for institutionalised discrimination: "The undemocratic way in which Schengen came about and the undemocratic way in which it operates have often be criticised by this Parliament. This is a two-class system, and, as far as I am concerned, it is also the model of a European heartland I really do not want!".[42]

MEP Berthu (I-EDN-FR) again viewed Schengen as a laboratory and launched a question on the purpose of such laboratory, whose answer is still lingering today. He also inferred that Schengen could either be a 'Trojan horse' which is 'sugar coated' – once again – by the ideal of the free movement of persons or a neutral instrument whose meaning is up to us to heighten at the level of a nearly Utopian realm reconnecting it with the founding principles of an 'original' European integration process:

> One might legitimately wonder whether the Schengen Agreements, which have often been described as an experimental laboratory, can be extended to the whole of the Union. But the way to answer that question is to start by learning the lessons of the experiment. Otherwise, what would be the purpose of the laboratory?[43]

The later war in Kosovo certainly stood as a key turning point regarding the EP discussions on free movement of persons and on the Schengen area. More particularly, EP players then considered that the EU's engagement in the Kosovo crisis should mark the start of a genuine common foreign and security policy and called on the European Council to lay the foundations for establishing new structures in line with the requirements set up by the recent Washington conference, i.e. a new 'Marshall Plan' and the strengthening of the West's security structures.[44] The year 1998 marked also the entry into force of the significant EUROPOL Convention in this realm. Against this backdrop, MEP Mohamed Alí (GUE/NGL-ES) equally emphasised the key concept of the 'socio-cultural integration of immigrants':

> In this Schengen area that is being created, there should be a clause making it possible to implement common policies on the socio-cultural integration of

41 For an in-depth analysis of this process and perspective, please, refer to Kostakopoulou, D., "When EU Citizens become Foreigners", *European Law Journal*, Vol. 20, Issue 4, July 2014, pp. 447-463.

42 European Parliament debates of 10 March 1997 on the future of Schengen, Schengen, No. 4-196/7, pp. 6-13.

43 *Ibid.*

44 European Parliament debates of 14 January 1999 on Schengen cooperation, pp. 240-254.

> immigrants, avoiding any discrimination against people or groups due to race, colour or religion or due to national, social or ethnic orientation.[45]

Complementarily, he also warned about the fact that "there is a problem that is not less important in the creation of this Schengen area of freedom and justice: the protection of personal data, which must be guaranteed without exception in any democratic society".[46]

As this phase came to an end, it is important to remember that, in 1999, the Schengen *acquis* became part of EU. The EP also then welcomed the signs of strengthening of the European Union and considered it vital to bring such strong political *momentum* to the Commission, taking advantage of the contextual possibilities then offered by the Amsterdam Treaty.

New challenges to the Schengen *acquis*, 2000-2015

This new phase started out with the 27 March 2000 Justice and Internal Affairs Council adopting an action plan against organised crime, thus implementing previously and constantly noted EP proposals in this regard, particularly in connection with the issue of the democratic sustainability of the Schengen area, as well as in relation with the crucial issue of free movement of persons. This period was also marked by the fundamental turning point of the EU's Eastward enlargement of 2004, which was considered by the then EP President Pat Cox as "the removal of the last brick of the Berlin Wall".[47] More particularly, and focusing on the intersection between EU's enlargement policy and the Schengen area, it is important to note how the relative implementation of the free movement of persons culminated on 21 December 2007, including the formerly known as 'captive nations' (the post-Soviet Central and Eastern European countries, CEECs) on the also discursively defined as 'the other side of Europe'. The accession of Romania and Bulgaria to the EU, as well as the EP's granting of its green light for Bulgaria and Romania to join the Schengen border check-free area were much discussed in this period. MEPs then stated that both countries had met the entry conditions, based on progress reports, but added that the Parliament should be kept informed of additional measures taking into special consideration the geopolitically key Bulgaria-Turkey-Greece area, in order "to cope with

---

45 *Ibid.*

46 *Ibid.*

47 Opening Address by Pat Cox to the *European Parliament's Historic Enlargement Debate* "The future of the enlarged European Union", European Parliament, Brussels, p. 2. http://www.europarl.europa.eu/former_ep_presidents/president-cox/speeches/en/sp0032.htm (last accessed on 28/07/2015).

possible surges in migration pressure".[48] In this respect, rapporteur Carlos Coelho (PPE-PT) then stated that: "we are in a position to welcome Bulgaria and Romania into the Schengen area and I hope that the Council will adopt the same position as soon as they receive our positive opinion. Their citizens should be regarded as fully European citizens, and should not be hostages of populist discourse".[49]

This perspective was, once again, in line with long-term EP pluralist players' decisively defended principles of equality and against the largely condemned 'Fortress Europe'.

In his conclusive analysis, EP President Jerzy Buzek also then stated that:

> Schengen is one of the biggest achievements of the EU. We must not destroy it with rash decisions. The Schengen system is providing the highest standards of border management. Romania and Bulgaria are meeting these standards today hence, we must not delay their integration. I call on the Council to follow the recommendations of the vote expressed today by the large majority of the European Parliament.

Such positive approach is not exempt from demanding challenges to the Schengen *acquis.* These particularly concern Schengen governance after the Lisbon Treaty.[50] In this regard, the EP considered that the governance of the Schengen area was to find the balance between freedom of movement and security in the context of the interdependences of globalisation, which was not exempt of essential ethical dilemmas.[51]

In short, the diachronic EP players' search for a balance between fundamental freedoms and rights and a respectful and non-discriminatory-non-exclusive safety does not exclude ever increasing daunting challenges, even the questioning of ready-made models and one-dimensional systems. Certainly, the legacy of this commitment to revert any foreboding involution of the Schengen area into the largely condemned 'Fortress Europe', could, once again, prove illustrative and helpful to recover original European integration broken links devoted to transform stumbling

48 Bulgaria and Romania ready to join Schengen area, Parliament Press release on Schengen of 8 June 2011. http://www.europarl.europa.eu/news/en/news-room/content/20110608IPR20929/html/Bulgaria-and-Romania-ready-to-join-Schengen-area-says-Parliament (last accessed on 28/07/2015).

49 *Ibid.*

50 http://www.europarl.europa.eu/aboutparliament/en/20150201PVL00008/The-Lisbon-Treaty (last accessed on 28/03/2015).

51 See Huber, K., "The European Parliament as an actor in EU border policies: its role, relations with other EU institutions, and impact", *European Security. Special Issue: Uncertainties at the European Union's Southern Borders*, Vol. 24, Issue 3, 2015, pp. 420-437.

blocks into stepping-stones. Accordingly, we are invited to further explore how representative democracy could still update this current (and rather defective) version of the European integration process by enriching it with seemingly lost yet powerful expressions of fundamental principles, values and norms.

Conclusion

The studied documentary EP collections undoubtedly contribute to visibly re-launch a now much neglected dimension of European integration: The active representation of citizens' perspectives on the effects, potentialities and challenges of the Schengen area and their impact on the socioeconomic risks and opportunities for regions and countries constantly undergoing highly instrumental centre-periphery dynamics. Such perspective could equally be extended to EU foreign policy considerations, taking into account the current visibility of EEAS and the ongoing discussion on the multifaceted value of the European model. Indeed, the free movement of persons constitutes a paradigm that it is being fruitfully studied by other regional integration experiences, especially in Latin America and Asia.

Moreover, the fact that EP actors constantly underline the defining nature of the Shengen area as a laboratory and a testing ground also begets the power to ask which are the purposes and outcomes of such experiment and, more importantly, which is the direction that the European society wants to imprint to such feasibility study, without sidelining, once again, the human rights and the social opportunities factor of free movement of persons.

The examined documents also evidence a trend which could be usefully appropriated by innovative democratic dialogue and cooperation experiences: That of striving to rebalance the increasing preeminence of security considerations, deeply ingrained in a worldview dominated by overarching notions of security, surveillance and control. The EP documents very rightly ask, in this sense, if there is a possible balance between this 'hard power' and 'securitisation-of-politics' integration version and other possible worldviews articulated around fundamental freedoms and rights. After all, we are also reminded in these sources about the fact that the EU is more than a market. Plus, they entail an invitation to re-examine direct experiences of intra and extra-European mobility (so often despised and overlooked) as an opportunity to detect inacceptable cleavages, unjust procedures and mindsets and dysfunctional implementation measures in search for a more humanly empathic common space exempt of routinely painful and irreversibly devastating institutional loopholes. Indeed, EP players diachronically defended the idea that the EU should primarily be an ethically committed political player constantly bringing up the human rights, solidarity and social cohesion dimensions of the European integration process. This could also contribute to re-establish a converging dialogue between citizens and institutions, which now risks being forever lost. Furthermore, we are left to wonder (and act) regarding the crucial question of whether the EU is left to conceptually represent a project of richness and power enhancement for ever restricted corporative elites in times of multilevel crisis, primal questioning and solidly argumented outcries for systemic redefinitions.

In one of the quoted EP debates, the free movement of persons appears relegated to "a tomorrow that never comes".[52] Hence, it is also fundamental to allude to the semantically charged character of this open statement, which also relates to the equally essential questions of the analysed documents, namely: do we want a common Europe where citizens "are being left out in the cold"[53] (and migrants and refugees in the cold waters)? Actually, the daring thoughts contained in the EP documentation on this topic equally reiterate the overlooked value of 'shockwave' and 'ripple effect' concepts, since the more frontiers a society breaks; the more it is prone to dissolve. Last but not least, this corpus of combinatorial policy-making creativity aspires to help unfolding potentialities which could again – or *ex novo* – be voiced and implemented. From a social innovation viewpoint, this could imply the articulation of currently overshadowed and alternative modes of socio-political intelligence. From an interconnected policy innovation and principle tracing perspective, the EP documentation on these crucial matters also constitutes a compelling reminder of the many times unused citizens' participative potential and transformative power.

52 Intervention of rapporteur Van Lancker, European Parliament debates of 10 March 1997 on the future of Schengen, No. 4-496, pp. 6-13.

53 Report of 5 October 1992 on behalf of the Committee of Civil Liberties and Internal Affairs of the European Parliament 288/92 on the entry into force of the Schengen Agreements, *op. cit.*

The EU's security actorness and the area of Freedom, Security and Justice

Assessing the external dimension of the internal rationale*

Ana Isabel XAVIER

Abstract: This chapter aims to contribute to a broader discussion on the European Union's external dimension of the internal security actorness, arguing that the EU has been progressively evolving from politicisation to securitization and militarization in the area of freedom, security and justice (AFSJ). In fact, if we look closely to both the European agenda on Security and on Migration (2015), and compare those newly documents with the 2010 Internal security strategy, the Stockholm Programme, the 2003 European Security Strategy or the 2008 implementation report, the external dimension of the internal security of the EU was deeply strengthen to address the changing security environment. The recent cases of the EUNAVFOR Med and the border management enforcement both from the EU's agencies and member states illustrate this argument. Therefore, we will argue that member states must identify concrete deliverables to translate the security actorness of the European Union into a proper common immigration and asylum policy, which implies a comprehensive approach shaped by a normative conception of solidarity and institutional cooperation.

Introduction

In 1995, the well-known American scholar Joseph Nye wrote that "Security is like oxygen – you tend not to notice it until you begin to lose it, but once that occurs there is nothing else that you will think about".[1] No wonder that security has always been one of the main concerns of States and Institutions, as citizens expect that governmental entities will assure and balance the fundamental rights (freedom and justice) that are entitled to. The European Union's current borderlines (enlarged to

* The author would like to thank the helpful contribution of the peer reviewers for the final version of the chapter.

1 Nye, J. S., "East Asian Security: The Case for Deep Engagement", *Foreign Affairs*, July/August 1995.

Asia and Middle East) pose new challenges to EU's 'actorness'[2] as the effectiveness of its action not only depends on the external promotion of international standards, but in the assurance of security within and outside the 28 member states' borders. As article 2 of the Treaty of the European Union marks: "[t]he Union shall offer its citizens an area of freedom, security and justice without internal frontiers, in which the free movement of persons is ensured in conjunction with appropriate measures with respect to external border controls, asylum, immigration and the prevention and combating of crime".

The area of freedom, security and justice (AFSJ) derives from Title V of the Treaty on the functioning of the European Union and aims to ensure both the free movement of persons and to offer a high level of protection to EU citizens. It includes asylum and immigration policies, police cooperation, and the fight against crime covering policy areas that range from the EU's external borders management to judicial cooperation in civil and criminal matters. Is based on the Tampere (1999-2004), Hague (2004-2009) and Stockholm (2010-2014) programmes and was framed, between 1993 and 2009, by the third pillar – Police and Judicial Co-operation in Criminal Matters (PJCC) before being absorbed into a consolidated European Union structure. In fact, as Monar[3] argues, "[t]he Treaty of the Lisbon reform puts an end to the 'pillar divide' in the external division of the AFSJ by merging the formerly legally separated fields into Title V of the Third Part of the Treaty on the Functioning of the Union (TFEU)".

Through the years, terrorism, organised crime, human beings trafficking, drugs or illegal immigration has been proving that internal and external dimensions of security are not meant to be apart.[4] In fact, the literature review on this topic proves how the external and internal link is not only connected but profoundly interdependent. Pastore[5] believes that "[…] through a series of distinct but connected cultural processes,

---

2 Hettne, B. and Soderbaum, F., "Civilian Power or Soft Imperialism?", *European Foreign Affairs Review*, Vol. 10, No. 4, 2005, pp. 535-552; Sjursen, H., "The EU as a "normative" power: how can this be", *Journal of European Public Policy*, Vol. 13, No. 2, 2006, pp. 235-251.

3 Monar, J., "The EU's growing external role in the AFSJ domain: factors, framework and forms of action", *Cambridge Review of International Affairs*, Vol. 27, No. 1, 014, p. 150.

4 Eriksson, J. and Rhinard, M., "The Internal-External Security nexus – Notes on an emerging research agenda", *Cooperation and conflict: Journal of Nordic International Studies Association*, Vol. 44, No. 3, 2009, pp. 243-267.

5 Pastore, F., "Reconciling the Prince's two 'arms' – internal-external security policy coordination", *Occasional papers 30*, Institute for Security Studies, October 2001, p. 2.

all the main traditional 'internal threats' were re-conceptualised, and the external (extra European) origin or dimension of each of them was greatly emphasised, both in qualitative and in quantitative terms". Also Lutterbeck[6] converge on the uselessness of the distinction between internal and external security: "[o]ne general characteristic of politics in late or post-modernity is often said to be the blurring of the boundaries between the domestic and international realms, due to the fact that political issues are increasingly cross-border in nature and often have both an internal and external dimension. Similarly, a defining feature of security and organised violence in the late – or post-modern era – can be said to be the proliferation of security challenges that can no longer be neatly fitted into the categories of internal and external security, and the increasing blurring of the respective functions and characteristics of internal and external security agencies". Trauner[7] discusses the coherence of the internal-external security nexus under the Lisbon Treaty as well: "[t]he changes introduced by the Lisbon Treaty have the potential to influence the delicate balance between internal security concerns and normative foreign policy aspirations by reiterating the value-based nature of the EU in general and its foreign and security policy in particular".

Therefore, if we agree in the blurring of the internal and external nexus, a holistic approach that assesses the external dimension of the internal security is needed. The 'official' EU narrative tends to accept this relation as interdependent namely in the 2003 European Security Strategy, the 2008 Implementation Report and the 2010 EU Internal Security Strategy in action: "[t]he concept of internal security must be understood as a wide and comprehensive concept which straddles multiple sectors in order to address these major threats and others which have a direct impact on the lives, safety, and well-being of citizens, including natural and man-made disasters such as forest fires, earthquakes, floods and storms".[8] The 2015 European agenda on security agrees:

> In recent years new and complex threats have emerged highlighting the need for further synergies and closer cooperation at all levels. Many of today's security concerns originate from instability in the EU's immediate neighbourhood and changing forms of radicalisation, violence and terrorism.

---

6 Lutterbeck, D., "Blurring the dividing line: the convergence of internal and external security in Western Europe", *European Security*, Vol. 14, No. 2, 2007, p. 248.

7 Trauner, F., "The internal-external security nexus: more coherence under Lisbon?", *Occasional paper 89*, European Union Institute for Security Studies, March 2011, p. 29.

8 Please see European Council, *Internal Security Strategy for the European Union "towards a European Security model"*, Brussels, 2010, available at http://www.consilium.europa.eu/uedocs/cms_data/librairie/PDF/QC3010313ENC.pdf (last accessed on 25/04/2015).

> Threats are becoming more varied and more international, as well as increasingly cross-border and cross-sectorial in nature.[9]

That being said, terrorism, migration or organized crime have been progressively perceived as a non-sociological oriented problem legitimizing extraordinary means to solve that given threat. In other words, topics traditionally solved with a sociological approach have been progressively evolving from politicisation (turned into a political topic) to securitization and even militarization (mobilization of policing and military). In other words, "[...] what has changed in the EU is, first, the explicit mentioning of these internal security preoccupations as objectives of EU foreign policy and, secondly, that police, official from interior ministries and judicial authorities now have a stake in the formulation and the realization of EU foreign policy, together with diplomats and military officials".[10]

In fact, this argument might be enlightened by three recent discussions: the launching of EUNAVFOR MED mission; the deal agreed between England and France on the Eurotunnel; and the fences' construction to avoid the entrance into national European countries. These three examples show how the external dimension of the EU's internal security has been evolving considering all the measures that aim to assure the internal security of the EU both through member states sovereign decisions, and military actions within the common security and defence policy (CSDP) aiming to be undertaken within and out of EU's frontiers, within or out of the EU's institutions umbrella.

To strengthen this argument we will first look at the European strategies between 2003 and 2014 and, afterwards, since 2015. We will then conclude that, notwithstanding the several security strategies where the nexus internal-external is addressed, the EU's capacities in action are in structural need for 'the' strategy that overcomes the dilemma and gap between the current expectations and needs and the instruments available.

---

9 The European Agenda on Security, Communication from the Commission to the European Parliament, the Council, the European Economic and Social Committee and the Committee of the Regions. Strasbourg, 28/4/2015, COM (2015) 185 final.

10 Wolff, S., Wichmann, N. and Mounier, G., "The external dimension of justice and home affairs: a different security agenda for the EU?", *Journal of European Integration*, Vol. 31, No. 1, 2009, p. 21.

The European Strategies towards a comprehensive security framework: 2003-2014

The European Security Strategy (ESS)[11] was presented to the European Council in December 12-13, 2003, after the member states tasked Javier Solana[12] to draft a strategic vision to enhance the internal cohesion and the external dimension of the EU both as a security provider and a global player. Entitled "A secure Europe in a better world" the ESS is a comprehensive document which analyses and defines EU's security environment, gives special attention to the neighbourhood (Balkans, Southern Caucasus and the Mediterranean) and urges the EU to be more active, more coherent and more capable.

The ESS acknowledges the interdependence of the multiple global security challenges, by linking security and development and highlighting the interaction between five key threats: terrorism, proliferation of weapons of mass destruction, regional conflicts, failed states and organized crime. Besides the focus on more diversified, less visible and less predictable threats, Solana also sets two major strategic objectives: build security in the neighbourhood, promoting stability and good governance namely in the Balkans, Caucasus and the Mediterranean; and contribute to an international order based on an effective multilateralism, fostering the transatlantic relationship (NATO) and strategic partnerships (United Nations; OSCE, Council of Europe; ASEAN, MERCOSUR and WTO). With the proper legal framework in terms of humanitarian and criminal international law, whether at the decision making or operational level, Solana appears to have no doubts that the EU needs to focus in prevention and early warning mechanisms to assume the security and development nexus.

In comparison with the 2003 ESS, the ambitions of the EU as a global actor are set aside and underestimated by the normative and peace settler dimension in the 2008 Implementation report.[13] Although it is an implementation report and not a new strategy, the 2008 document succeeds in giving a step forward, both in the update of the threats (climate change, energy security and, as recommended by Portugal, pandemics) and in the

---

11 Please see European Council, *A Secure Europe in a Better World – European Security Strategy*, Brussels, 2003, available at http://consilium.europa.eu/uedocs/cmsUpload/78367.pdf (last accessed on 25/04/2015).

12 High Representative for the Common Foreign and Security Policy in office from 18 October 1999 to 1 December 2009.

13 Please see European Council, *Report of the Implementation of the European Security Strategy: Providing Security in a Changing World*. Brussels, 2008, available at http://www.consilium.europa.eu/uedocs/cms_data/docs/pressdata/en/reports/104630.pdf (last accessed on 25/04/2015).

enlargement of the strategic partnerships to the BRICs, in parallel with the importance of the transatlantic relation and the neighbourhood policy, balancing the east and the south of the 'near abroad'. Five years later, the 2008 Report emphasizes that the threats have become more critical and complex, insisting in the need for the UE to develop an autonomous strategic culture committed with the responsibilities of the international crisis management. When the Treaty of Lisbon enters into force in December 2009 the EU member states had already at their disposal not only a European security strategy that envisaged a comprehensive approach on security, but also a decision making procedure more tailored to the EU's external action.[14]

In turn, the 'EU Internal Security Strategy in action' (ISS)[15] was adopted in February 2010 and approved by the European Council on 25 and 26 March 2010. Regarding the external dimension of the EU's security, the ISS enhances the 2003 European Security Strategy as exposes common threats and challenges and sets a European security model. In fact, the EES and ISS's threats concur and both documents acknowledge the internal and external interdependence enhancing a global security approach with the third countries. The ISS also counterparts ESS in the design of the security model of the EU guided by the principles and values enshrined in the treaties, coordinating existing activities and setting out the guidelines to address the internal and external security challenges. Moreover, identifies common threats and underlines the importance of a concerted action between member states and EU Institutions in order to: dismantle the international crime networks; prevent terrorism, radicalization and recruitment; strengthen the security for citizens and companies in cyberspace; enhance border management security; and build Europe's resilience to crises and disasters.

To address these strategic guidelines, the EU's response aims to be multi-layered and holistic, converging on the internal and external nexus even if "[t]he external projection of *internal* security agencies has generated an increasing overlap, and occasionally open competition, with the policy communities and public agencies traditionally invested

---

[14] The Treaty of Lisbon aimed to reform the EU institutions and improves the EU decision-making process; strengthen the democratic dimension of the EU; reform the internal policies of the EU; and strengthen the external policies of the EU. Regarding the decision-making process within the Council, the Treaty replaces the weighted voting for qualified majority voting. Please see http://eur-lex.europa.eu/legal-content/EN/TXT/PDF/?uri=CELEX:12007L/TXT&from=EN (last accessed on 05/05/2015).

[15] Please see European Council, *Internal Security Strategy for the European Union "towards a European Security model"*, Brussels, 2010, available at http://www.consilium.europa.eu/uedocs/cms_data/librairie/PDF/QC3010313ENC.pdf (last accessed on 25/04/2015).

with the task of ensuring *external* security".[16] In fact, setting a four years shared agenda, EU member states, EU institutions and EU agencies agreed both in a common framework of the threats the EU is facing and in a commitment to use all the resources and instruments to jointly tackle them. In one hand, the ISS was perceived by the agencies, Member states and EU Institutions as the backbone of the external dimension of the internal security of the EU, contributing to strengthen the operational cross-sectorial cooperation among the competent authorities in preventing and fighting multiple threats. The ISS not only defines internal security, identifies strategic objectives and common threats but also highlights concrete responses to those threats. However, on the other hand, its main virtue appeared to be its major weakness: "[w]hile containing some degree of symbolic import regarding the intriguing idea of a European Security Model, that model had little substance and could hardly denote a new strategic identity for the EU. The ISS mainly collected and listed issues and goals that had developed over the previous two decades, with little effort to prioritise tasks, establish coherent action principles, or build a consensual vision".[17]

Probably aware of the need of a step further in the development, monitoring and implementation of the ISS (a priority task of the Standing Committee on Operational Cooperation on Internal Security) the Stockholm programme 2010-2014 – 'An open and secure Europe serving and protecting citizens'[18] establishes the framework for police and customs cooperation, rescue teams, cooperation on criminal and civil affairs, and policy on asylum, immigration and visas.[19] In fact, in addition to the protection of the EU citizens through a comprehensive internal security strategy, the Stockholm Programme emphasises the need to strengthen the police and judicial cooperation (through Europol and Eurojust), and to deepen the activities of the European Crime Prevention Network (EUCPN), the European Police College (Cepol), the Joint Situation Centre (JSC or SitCen) and the European Criminal Records Information System (ECRIS). In what concerns Frontex, this Programme

16 Pastore, F., "Reconciling the Prince's two 'arms' – internal-external security policy coordination", *Occasional papers 30*, Institute for Security Studies, October 2001, p. 2.

17 Bossong, R. and Rhinard, M., "The EU Internal Security Strategy – towards a more coherent approach to EU security?", *Studia Diplomatica*, LXVI-2, 2013, p. 51.

18 Please see https://register.consilium.europa.eu/doc/srv?l=EN&f=ST%2017024%20 2009%20INIT (last accessed on 25/04/2015).

19 As the Title V of the Treaty of Lisbon makes significant changes to relevant provisions of the AFSJ, Stockholm also replaces the Tampere and Hague Programmes adopted by the European Council in Brussels, in December 10-11, 2009. Please see http:// eur-lex.europa.eu/legal-content/EN/TXT/HTML/?uri=URISERV:jl0034&from=EN (last accessed on 10/05/2015).

highlights the operational role of cooperation with countries of origin and transit, namely through the definition of clear rules of engagement for joint operations at the sea.

The agreements with third countries on judicial cooperation and civil law are, indeed, one of the most insisting references of the 2010-2014 Programme. In fact, the chapter dedicated to the external dimension of freedom, security and justice, mentions the Western Balkans, Turkey and the European Neighbourhood Policy as opportunities for future cooperation; Black sea as a strategic area to the stability and security of the region as a whole; and Algeria, Libya, Morocco, Egypt, Afghanistan, Iraq and Bangladesh as readmission agreements to be concluded.

In 8-9 July 2014, in the Informal meeting of the Justice and Home Affairs Ministers' Council, member states agreed that the ISS should be reviewed in 2015 (completing its five year period) and set new strategic guidelines in relation with cybersecurity threats, new forms of organised crime, immigration and illegal human trafficking. In order to give an opportunity to citizens, public institutions, authorities (local, regional and national), international organizations, non-governmental organisations, academic institutions and social partners, to contribute to the new Strategy, the European Commission launched a public consultation on 22 July 2014.

Assessing the external dimension of the EU's internal security

If we agree that the external dimension of the internal security may be defined as all the measures that aim to assure the internal security of the EU but are undertaken in the EU's external frontiers, although under the EU's institutions umbrella, we can now get into detail on the procedures and institutions aimed to assess both dimensions in the EU's architecture. One of the most striking examples is the Common Visa Application Centres. The first one was created in 2007 in Moldova[20] and basically sets an agreement for readmission and visa facilitation between the European community and third countries. The other main measures relate with the field of the police cooperation and technical assistance. In this regard, besides Frontex and Schengen, we should also highlight the Dialogue 5+5 (aims to establish a propitious frame for dialogue and cooperation amongst member countries to tackle issues as security and stability, economic integration and regional migration) and the PNR – Passenger name record (one of the most challenging initiatives as most of

[20] Please see http://europa.eu/rapid/press-release_IP-07-561_en.htm (last accessed on 25/04/2015).

the EU member states had not yet implemented PNR data for the purpose of fighting serious crime and terrorism).

In turn, planned for the spring of 2015, the new European Internal Strategy was foreseen to evaluate both the five years of the 2010 Internal Security Strategy and the 2010-2014 Stockholm Programme, but also to prepare Europe's coming five years (2015-2020) in the AFSJ. In fact, the expectations were clear: the new document should present a comprehensive approach, strengthening the external dimension of the operational cooperation on internal security. Bearing this goal in mind, in 28 April 2015, the European Commission presented a Communication from the Commission to the European Parliament, the Council, the European Economic and Social Committee and the Committee of the Regions entitled 'The European Agenda on Security' (EAS).[21]

The EAS aims to set out how the Union can bring added value to support the Member states in ensuring security, acknowledging that "member states can no longer succeed fully on their own". The 2015 agenda highlights terrorism, organised crimes and cybercrime as the cross-border areas that require an effective and coordinated response at European level through the following key principles: full compliance with fundamental rights; transparency, accountability and democratic control; application and implementation of existing EU legal instruments; and joined-up inter-agency and cross sectorial approach. A fifth principle is related with the coherence of the internal and external dimensions of security:

> [s]ecurity threats are not confined by the borders of the EU. EU internal security and global security are mutually dependent and interlinked. The EU response must therefore be comprehensive and based on a coherent set of actions combining the internal and external dimensions, to further reinforce links between justice and home affairs and Common Security and Defence Policy. Its success is highly dependent on cooperation with international partners. Preventive engagement with third countries is needed to address the root causes of security issues.

In fact, regarding the external dimension of the internal security, the European agenda on security acknowledges the need of the full implementation of the existing instruments at the disposal of all actors involved (EU Institutions and agencies, Member states, Law enforcement authorities, local partners). In what concerns strengthen security at the external borders and ensure operational cooperation across borders, the Agenda suggests, in particular, the deployment of security experts

---

21 European Commission, *The European agenda on Security*, Brussels, 2015, pp. 2, 4, available at http://ec.europa.eu/dgs/home-affairs/e-library/documents/basic-documents/docs/eu_agenda_on_security_en.pdf (last accessed on 20/07/2015).

in EU Delegations in European neighbourhood policy countries and other targeted non-EU countries; explore the potential of a European Police record index system (EPRIS) to facilitate cross-border access to information held in national police records; and establish the European public prosecutor's office to provide a new dimension to the specific issue of protecting losses to the EU budget from criminal activity. Moreover, the Strategy also plans to reinforce Europol`s support functions by bringing together its anti-terrorism law enforcement capabilities in a European Counter-Terrorism Centre within Europol; launch the RAN centre of excellence and extending anti-radicalisation work with Turkey, the Western Balkans, the Middle East and North Africa; and extend the work of the EU Policy Cycle to neighbouring countries.

Likewise, one of the political priorities of the Commission Work Programme for 2015 was planned to be the European Agenda on Migration (EAM). This agenda was pushed for the dramatic situation in the Mediterranean[22] and officially presented on 13 May 2015[23], outlining the immediate measures to respond to the humanitarian crisis and the steps to be taken in the coming years to manage the flow to Europe. Vitorino and Pascouau highpoint the innovation, confirmation and long-term vision of this strategy: "[t]he first innovative aspect concerns the measures announced in connection with the "relocation" and "resettlement" of people seeking or currently receiving international protection. […] Second, the Commission's agenda confirms a trend involving, on the one hand, the need to implement existing legislation and, on the other, the need to improve operational coordination. […] The final part of the agenda, introducing measures for implementation in the longer term, contains the breadth that is missing in the second part. The Commission here introduces those guidelines which, while not yet enjoying the member states' backing, it would like to debate or even to implement".[24]

The EAM thus aims a comprehensive approach, recognising that all tools (civilian and military) and actors (member states, EU institutions, agencies, international organisations, civil society, local authorities and third countries) must be combined to collectively manage such a complex phenomenon. This agenda is paradigmatic on the way migration is mainstreamed into all policy areas, both internal and external, defining

---

[22] The United Nations have recently published that 264,500 migrants have crossed the Mediterranean until August this year, close to 104,000 have landed in Italy and another 160,000 arrived in Greece. Most international efforts have been focused in humanitarian rescue operation.

[23] European Commission, *A European agenda on migration*, Brussels, 2015.

[24] Vitorino, A. and Pascouau, Y., "The EU's migrant strategy: a welcome new impetus", *Tribune Viewpoint*, Notre Europe – Jacques Delors Institute, Brussels, 2015, pp. 1-2.

a new strategic approach to manage better migration in the medium to long term, reducing the incentives for irregular migration; saving lives and securing the external borders; and implementing a strong common asylum policy and a new policy on legal migration.

It is quite interesting because the Stockholm programme already highlighted in 2010 the need for a truly EU approach on migration, mainstreaming migration and asylum as integral parts of EU external policy. This programme foreseen, five years ago, that the challenge was twofold: first, facilitate legal access to the territory of the member states while counteracting illegal immigration and cross-border crime; second, reinforce border controls while protecting vulnerable persons and groups entitled to benefit from asylum and legal migration systems. In fact, the 2010-2014 programme strived for a close cooperation with the UNHCR and the implementation of Regional Protection Programmes, as well as the development and implementation of the Common European Asylum System by the European Asylum Support Office.

However, as Carrera, Gros and Guild[25] argue "[i]n reality, there is a profound gap between those principles [solidarity and fair sharing of responsibility between EU member states] and what actually occurs in the ground. There is little 'burden-sharing' of responsibilities between EU member states, and applying the rule of law in dealing with asylum cases is *de facto* extremely challenging for a majority of them. Burden sharing is limited in almost every respect, but particularly in terms of rescue operations at sea". Hill's "capability expectations gap"[26] is helpful to explore the argument of the structural constrains of the EU as a security provider when facing a growing and dramatic emergency in Europe's external and internal borders. In fact, the recent migration crisis in the Mediterranean has urged a special attention both to prevention, relocation (distribution mechanism for asylum-seekers) and safe and legal resettlement. Moreover, illustrates how the EU has been progressively evolving from politicisation (turning a specific subject into a political topic) to securitization[27] and even to militarization (mobilization of policing and military). Three recent cases can be discussed to enlighten this argument: first, the EUNAVFOR MED mission; second, the agreement between

[25] Carrera, S., Gros, D. and Guild, E., "What priorities for the new European agenda on migration?", *CEPS Commentary*, Brussels, Centre for European Policy Studies, 2015.

[26] Hill, C., "The Capability-expectations Gap, or Conceptualizing Europe's International Role", *Journal of Common Market Studies*, Vol. 31, No. 3, 1993.

[27] Buzan, B., Weaver, O. and Wilde, J. de, *Security: a new framework for analysis*, Lynne Rienner Publishing, Boulder, 1998. According to the authors, securitization is one of the key concepts of the Copenhagen school of International Relations and that generally describes the process of transforming certain subjects as 'security' matters in order to be perceived as such by a persuaded audience.

England and France on the Eurotunnel; third, the fences' construction to avoid the entrance into national European countries.

Starting with the first topic, Federica Mogherini, who serves as High Representative of the European Union for Foreign Affairs and Security Policy and Vice-President of the European Commission in the Junker Commission since November 1, 2014, has always suggested the possibility to deploy missions and operations framed by the CSDP to identify, capture and destroy vessels used by smugglers. EUNAVFOR MED (European Union Naval Force Operation in the Mediterranean) was agreed on 18 May 2015 as a three phase military operation in accordance with the procedures of international law: the first phase will focus in the surveillance and assessment of human smuggling and trafficking networks in the Southern Central Mediterranean; second and third phases aim to search, seize and disrupt the assets of smugglers but depend on the partnership with Libyan authorities upon a security council resolution.[28] This mission counterparts the Operation Triton as a border security operation conducted by Frontex, under Italian control, that began on 1 November 2014 and involves voluntary contributions from Croatia, Iceland, Finland, Norway, Sweden, Germany, the Netherlands, France, Spain, Ireland, Portugal, Austria, Switzerland, Romania, Poland, Lithuania and Malta.[29]

The proof of the progressive securitization and militarisation of this issue is that the staffing and budget of the three agencies directly involved in responding to migratory pressures (Frontex, Europol and EASO) are planning to increase its staffing and budget in 2015. For instance, the Frontex joint-operations Triton and Poseidon will triple its budget to manage the operational border support to member states under pressure and save lives of migrants at sea. In order to establish better information sharing to combat smuggling, Europol will also undertake initiatives to request the removal of internet used by smugglers to attract migrants and refugees. Frontex will join Europol as well in the task of developing profiles of vessels which could be used by smugglers.

---

28 Please see the official website of EUNAVFOR Med mission available at http://www.eeas.europa.eu/csdp/missions-and-operations/eunavfor-med/index_en.htm (last accessed on 20/08/2015).

29 For Brady, Triton "[...] the new joint border surveillance mission is a critical test for the governance and sustainability of the EU's passport-free Schengen area. It will not only be a major operational challenge for the Union's small border agency, Frontex. The support given by individual member states to the mission will show outsiders where the EU is at in terms of delivering an overall border, asylum and immigration policy for the Schengen zone". Brady, H., "Mare Europaeum: tackling Mediterranean migration", *Brief issue 25*, European Union Institute for Security Studies, September 2014.

Moreover, both the deal agreed between England and France on the Eurotunnel and the construction of borders between member states are worth to note as national responses to the recent events. The first case refers to the border policing in Calais to combat illegal migration in the Channel Tunnel and target criminal gangs attempting to smuggle migrants.[30] In the second example, several national governments decided to enforce their national security measures and build fences in an attempt to avoid illegal immigration: more than 100 miles in the border between Hungary and Serbia[31]; another 20 miles between Bulgaria and Turkey; the Evros wall between Turkey and Greece; Ceuta and Melilla as permanent fortresses; and in Frethun and Coquelles sponsored by the British Government.[32] All these situations challenge the security actorness of the EU, urge for the intervention of the EU agencies and open the floor to several ethical discussions. Do those measures actually succeed? According to Parkes, "the burden is exacerbated by the diverse origins of asylum seekers: in May most applicants came from Syria (13,000), Eritrea (5,000), Afghanistan (9,000) and the western Balkans (13,000)".[33]

Therefore, regional Development and Protection Programmes must be set up or deepened in order to foster the cooperation with countries of origin (Syria, Libya, Iraq, the Sahel region, Afghanistan, Yemen) and transit (Egypt, Tunisia, Algeria, Niger and Mali). Existing bilateral and regional cooperation frameworks on migration (Rabat Process, Khartoum Process, the Budapest Process, the EU-Africa Migration and Mobility Dialogue) must be accurately promoted. The role of EU Delegations in the field of migration in key third countries (Egypt, Algeria, Morocco, Tunisia, Niger, Senegal, Sudan, Turkey, Pakistan, Lebanon and Jordan) is crucial as well. But their work in gathering, exchanging and analysing information is only worth it if proceeds in close cooperation with the Immigration Liaison Officers Network (seconded in EU Delegations in those countries) and with local authorities and civil society. At last, border control, starting in North Africa and the Horn of Africa, must be enhanced through the creation of local centres in coordination with the International

30 Please see http://www.bbc.com/news/uk-33982018 (last accessed on 24/07/2015) on the Calais crisis and the prospects of a deal between the UK and France.

31 Please see http://www.bbc.com/news/world-europe-33802453 (last accessed 24/07/2015) on the Hungary's border fence to avoid migrant's entrance in the country coming from Serbia.

32 Please see http://migrantreport.org/britain-follows-hungary-and-builds-4km-fence/ (last accessed on 05/07/2015).

33 Parkes, R., "Asylum flows to the EU: blip or norm?", *Issue 38*, European Union Institute for Security Studies, July 2015.

Organisation for Migration, the United Nations High Commission for Refugees and the local authorities.

To sum up, by addressing root causes, protecting people in need and dismantling smuggling networks, the European agenda on migration is a valuable attempt to provide a comprehensive approach on the external dimension of the internal security of the EU, namely in what concerns Frontex role in the countries of origin and transit. However, at this moment, Frontex has only the ability to coordinate joint return missions but not initiate any on its own, which might result in an unsuccessful operational cooperation in the support to member states. It is therefore bearable that the Commission will soon amend the Frontex legal basis and increase the annual budget and the human resources to reinforce the management of EU's external border. After all, EUNAVFOR Med's mission will be as successful as Frontex's autonomy in the region is strengthened.

Conclusions

The presentation of both the European Agenda on Security and the European Agenda on Migration in 2015 surely represents an interesting opportunity to discuss in what extent the EU external borders challenge the traditional internal and external nexus as well as the area of freedom, security and justice.

To foster the debate on the balance between the efficiency of border crossing and the fight against irregular migration, the Commission seems to plan for 2016 some important decisions. The expectation lies in the amendment of the 'Smart borders' initiative[34], making better use of the opportunities offered by information and technologies systems and creating a record of all cross-border movements by third country nationals. Hence, aiming to secure a high and uniform standard in the control of all aspects of the Union's external borders, the Commission intends to put forward a 'Union Standard for Border Management', exploring the possibility of a 'European System of Border Guards' that could lead to a progressive framing of a 'European Coastguard' through asset sharing, joint exercises and dual use of resources. Also Federica Mogherini has been insisting in a new European foreign policy strategy to be presented next year.[35] In fact, "[…] further to the Commission's "European Agenda on Security" and the Council conclusions of 16 June 2015, work will

[34] This initiative is dated 2011. Please see http://europa.eu/rapid/press-release_IP-11-1234_en.htm (last accessed on 25/04/2015).

[35] Please see EEAS. *The European Union in a changing global environment – a more connected, contested and complex world*, July 2015, available at http://eeas.europa.eu/docs/strategic_review/eu-strategic-review_executive_summary_en.pdf (last accessed

be taken forward on the renewed European Union Internal Security Strategy; full implementation of the orientations on the fight against terrorism agreed at the February 2015 meeting remains a priority; b) the High Representative will continue the process of strategic reflection with a view to preparing an EU global strategy on foreign and security policy in close cooperation with Member states, to be submitted to the European Council by June 2016".[36]

However, the member states have the leading responsibility for security and it is up to them to translate into practical actions and national strategies the overall guidelines of the documents assigned by the Institutions. In fact, an area of freedom, security and justice without internal borders and sustained by a common asylum and migration policy is only possible if member states pool their resources into a truly shared competence, develop an effective sharing and responsibility in rescuing people, provide access to asylum and agree in legal mechanisms for those who want to access Europe and take part of our societies.[37] Law enforcement cooperation and the management of the Union's external borders must be framed in the common acceptance that migration and asylum have different motivations and deserve different procedures.

Therefore, the main challenge still remains: if the European Union wants to succeed not as an 'actor in process' but as a proper security player, member states must embrace the institutional narrative and develop, both at the European and at national level, concerted strategies to proficiently balance freedom, security and justice. That ambition will only succeed if does not collide with the fundamental rights of the European citizens, recognising that the external dimension of the internal security must be deepen to successfully address current threats and challenges. To conclude, if the European Union really wants to engage with the southern flank in a more meaningful way, it should recognise its normative rationale and consider developing reciprocal relations with the origin countries and thus open one more front in its foreign policy. After all, while we celebrate 30 years of Schengen, the prospects to return from militarisation, securitisation or politicisation to

on 05/08/2015); and Biscop, S., "Global and Operational: A New Strategy for EU Foreign and Security Policy", *Governing Europe*, July 2015.

36 Please see European Council meeting (25 and 26 June 2015) Conclusions, page 5, available at http://www.consilium.europa.eu/en/press/press-releases/2015/06/26-euco-conclusions/ (last accessed on 10/08/2015).

37 In the Standard Eurobarometer 83 Spring 2015, 38 of the European Citizens perceived immigration as the most worrying issue of the EU. In the autumn 2014 it was the economic situation the most pressing topic. Please see the first results of the survey, available at http://ec.europa.eu/public_opinion/archives/eb/eb83/eb83_first_en.pdf (last accessed on 25/07/2015).

a classic sociological approach of the migration flows seems so remote as the miles that the 276 113 migrants had to travel by land, air and sea in 2014 (according to the European Commission) with recourse to criminal networks of smugglers and in great danger for their existence and dignity.

The role of Schengen in the Europeanization of the migration policy

The Italian case

Simone PAOLI

Abstract: This chapter analyzes the role played by the Schengen agreements in the radical change of the Italian immigration policy which occurred between the mid-1980s and the early 1990s. On the basis of extensive research in archives, it demonstrates that an important reason that the Schengen countries resolved to act outside the European Community framework and, in this context, to originally exclude Italy was their political determination to press Italy and, ultimately, all the Southern members of the EC into adopting the Northern European approach to the problem of immigration control. On the other hand, it shows that, although it was not the sole explanatory factor, the need to comply with the Schengen membership requirements was the single most significant reason for the shift from a liberal to a restrictive legislation on migration which took place in Italy between the late 1980s and the early 1990s. A majority in both the government and the Parliament did not believe in restrictive measures but they were constrained to adopt them in order to reassure the Schengen members that Italy was able to prevent the entry of unwanted immigrants from the Mediterranean into the Schengen space.

Introduction

During the first forty years after the establishment of the European Communities (EC), European studies primarily focused on the formation and consolidation of the European polity, the main aim being to analyse the reasons why and the ways through which the European political organization was set up. Scholars were more interested in understanding and explaining motives and workings of the political organization that was then emerging in Europe rather than in assessing its effects.

Over the past twenty years, however, researchers have increasingly focused on the consequences of the European integration and not only on its dynamics. In particular, after the ratification of the Maastricht Treaty, which provided new impetus to European integration by widening the scope of the European political organization, Europeanization has been an increasingly investigated political phenomenon; the role played by European institutions and policies in influencing domestic politics has thus become an important object of study.[1]

In the area of migration and asylum, it has been argued that the impact of European integration can be evaluated in relation to whether these effects are direct/intended or indirect/unintended and whether Europeanization is voluntary in the sense of being embraced by key domestic actors or coercive in the sense of being imposed on them.[2]

This approach highlights a variety of potential effects of European integration on migration and asylum policy that will be dependent on: the type of instrument adopted at the European level and, more importantly, the ways in which specific measures are refracted though the territorial, organizational and conceptual borders that mediate the EC's, later the European Union (EU)'s, influence. Seen in this light, European migration and asylum policies may be refracted into domestic contexts in situations where there are labour markets with formal and informal components, differing modes of welfare state organization, distinct traditions of citizenship and social rights, divergent ideas about belonging, entitlement and identity and different foreign policy strategies.[3]

---

1 Graziano, P. R., *Europeanization and Domestic Policy Change. The Case of Italy*, Routledge, London/New York, 2013, pp. 1-20.

2 Most Europeanization studies focus on the countries that were most affected by the European Communities, later the European Union: namely, the member states, especially in the South and in the East, that were newer immigration or transit countries. That said, a minority but significant portion of researches on Europeanization focuses on those member states that were countries of immigration over a longer period of time. These studies reveal how this group of countries have used the European Union as an external venue within which they have sought to attain domestic policy objectives in a new setting where there is a special burden on those states most vulnerable to flows of "unwanted" migrants. See: Geddes, A., "The Europeanization of What? Migration, Asylum and the Politics of European Integration", in T. Faist and A. Ette (eds.), *The Europeanization of national policies and politics of immigration. Between autonomy and the European Union*, Palgrave Macmillan, Basingstoke/New York, 2007. See also: Mastenbroek, E., "EU Compliance: Still a "Black Hole"?", *Journal of European Public Policy*, No. 6, 2005, pp. 1103-1120.

3 See: Menz, G., *The Political Economy of Managed Migration. Nonstate Actors, Europeanization, and the Politics of Designing Migration Policies*, Oxford University Press, Oxford, 2009; Ladrech, R., *Europeanization and National Politics*, Palgrave Macmillan, Basingstoke, 2010. See also: Druláková, R., "Introduction. Europeanization as explanatory concept for European integration in migration policy", in R. Fischer (ed.), *The Europeanization of Migration Policy. The Schengen Acquis between the Priorities of Legal Harmonization and Fragmentation*, Peter Lang, Frankfurt am Main, 2012; Lahav, G. and Luedtke, A., "Immigration Policy", in C. Bretherton and M. Mannin (eds.), *The Europeanization of European Politics*, Palgrave Macmillan, Basingstoke/New York, 2013.

Writing about Central and East European accession states, Sandra Lavenex identifies the onus placed on new member states to adapt to the formal requirements of the EU *acquis* before they could join the club. She suggests that the specific focus of European Union action is on those forms of migration defined as "unwanted" and that this has prompted measures to strengthen border controls with an emphasis on those states seen as vulnerable or as weak links.[4]

Similarly, writing about Spain, Wayne Cornelius argues that the development of migration policy in the late 1980s and early 1990s was almost entirely related to EC membership.[5] On the other hand, Joaquín Arango makes a distinction between the impact of the European Communities on Spanish external border controls and what he calls the "Pandora box" of internal controls and state-society relations; in so doing, he contends that the EC was less influential in shaping Spanish migration policy than Cornelius argues.[6]

In this chapter, we focus on Schengen and the role it played in the change of the Italian immigration policy between the mid-1980s and the early 1990s. In particular, we aim at answering three distinct but intertwined questions: to what extent was the Italian immigration policy influenced by the Schengen agreements?; which were the ways through which the Schengen agreements influenced the Italian immigration policy?; what was the nature and outcome of the complex relationship between external pressures and domestic forces?

In answering these questions, in turn, we will test three main ideas, which underlie this research. Schengen was more important than Brussels in affecting Italian debate and legislation on asylum and migration. Schengen was more influential in shaping the Italian immigration policy than domestic factors.[7] The effects of Schengen were not absorbed by

---

4 See: Lavenex, S., *Safe third countries: extending the EU asylum and immigration policies to Central and Eastern Europe*, Central European University Press, New York, 1999; Lavenex, S. and Uçarer, E. M. (eds.), *Migration and the externalities of European integration*, Lexington Books, Lanham, 2002.

5 See: Cornelius, W. A., "The Uneasy Transition from Labor Exporter to Labor Importer", in W. A. Cornelius, P. Martin and J. Hollifield (eds.), *Controlling Immigration: a Global Perspective*, Stanford University Press, Stanford, 1994; Izquierdo, A. and Cornelius, W. A., *Políticas de control migratorio: estudio comparado de España y EE.UU.*, Edicions Bellaterra, Barcelona, 2012.

6 See: Arango, J., "Becoming a Country of Immigration at the End of the Twentieth Century", in R. King, G. Lazaridis and C. Tsardanidis (eds.), *Eldorado or Fortress: Immigration in Southern Europe*, Macmillan, London, 2000; Arango, J. and Aja, E. (eds.), *Veinte años de inmigración en España: perspectivas jurídica y sociológica (1985-2004)*, Fundació Cidob, Barcelona, 2006.

7 The idea of the supremacy of domestic factors over external pressures is prevalent in literature. See: Einaudi, L., *Le politiche dell'immigrazione in Italia dall'Unità a*

or accommodated within existing domestic arrangements: they were transformatory and, in a sense, coercive.

A painful exclusion: Schengen against Rome (1984-1985)

On 13 July 1984, in Saarbrücken, the French Secretary of State for European Affairs, Roland Dumas, and the Head of the German Chancellery, Waldemar Schreckenberger, signed an agreement, which envisioned the immediate abolition of controls on persons and the easing of controls on vehicles. To compensate for this, it also envisioned the transfer of these controls to external borders; the harmonization of visa policies and legislation on foreign nationals, drugs, arms and passport delivery; and the strengthening of police and customs cooperation.

At that time, Italy had been receiving significant migration flows for at least ten-fifteen years but it did not perceive itself as an immigration country yet; as a consequence, it did not feel any need to adopt and implement a rigorous immigration policy. Moreover, the desire to please origin countries in the Mediterranean combined with an interest in nurturing the large domestic underground economy to create consensus on a *de facto* open-door immigration policy. Between the early 1970s and the mid-1980s, this liberal approach to border control was welcomed by the governments in Northern Europe, since Italy might contribute to ease pressure on them by providing a convenient outlet for unwanted migrants from the South. However, in the mid-1980s, when the decision was made to abolish internal border controls and to establish and strengthen external border controls, the lax immigration policy pursued by the country suddenly became a source of concern.[8]

When the Italian government, at the initiative of the then Foreign Minister, Giulio Andreotti, expressed the intention to reach a Saarbrücken-

---

oggi, Laterza, Roma/Bari, 2007. Even the authors who put more emphasis on external factors argue that reforms did not derive from European Union membership, "though they have all been normatively legitimized with reference to a hypothetical European standard". Giuliani, M., "Europeanization and Italy: a Bottom-up Process", in K. Featherstone and G. Kazamias (eds.), *Europeanization and the Southern Periphery*, Frank Cass, London/Portland, 2001, p. 54. See also: Dell'Olio, F., *The Europeanization of Citizenship. Between the Ideology of Nationality, Immigration and European Identity*, Ashgate, Aldershot/Burlington, 2005; Palidda, S., "Insertion, Integration and Rejection of Immigration in Italy", in E. Guild, K. Groenendijk and S. Carrera (eds.), *Illiberal Liberal States. Immigration, Citizenship and Integration in the EU*, Ashgate, Farnham/Burlington, 2009, pp. 357-372.

8 See: Hreblay, V., *Les accords de Schengen: origine, fonctionnement, avenir*, Bruylant, Bruxelles, 1998; Louette, J.-S., *Les États du Benelux et la France face aux accords de Schengen*, Bruxelles, Centre de recherche et d'information socio-politiques, Bruxelles, 1998; Zaiotti, R., *Cultures of Border Control. Schengen and the Evolution of European Frontiers*, The University of Chicago Press, Chicago/London, 2011.

like agreement with France[9], the Laurent Fabius' government turned the request down. In the opinion of French Interior Ministry officials, Italy's immigration policy was too permissive: this made it the most important transit country for illegal immigration heading for France from Yugoslavia, Turkey and Maghreb and sub-Saharan countries.[10] According to French officials in the Ministry for External Relations, the whole mass of undocumented immigrants who then lived in Italy were potentially ready to cross the Alps into France.[11] In addition, the officers of both the French Ministry for External Relations and the French Interior Ministry were concerned that the abolition of border controls with Italy might encourage an influx of inactive and unemployed Italian persons and, more importantly, favour international terrorism and criminal trafficking into France.[12] Without a readmission agreement with France, cooperation between border guards and, more importantly, a drastic tightening of its own immigration policy, Italy could not hope to form a borderless area with its Northern neighbour.[13]

Soon after the signature of the Saarbrücken Accord, the Benelux countries began to show interest in the project and, at the conclusion of brief negotiations, on 14 June 1985, the French Secretary of State for European Affairs, Catherine Lalumière, the Head of German Chancellery, Waldemar Schreckenberger, the Dutch Secretary of State for Foreign Affairs, Willem Frederik van Eekelen, the Belgian Secretary of State for European Affairs, Paul De Keersmaeker, and the Luxembourgian Secretary of State for Foreign Affairs, Robert Goebbels, signed the Schengen Agreement. Modelled on the Saarbrücken Accord, Schengen provided for the removal of internal border controls, while simultaneously

9 Soutou, G. H., "L'Italie et le 'couple' franco-allemand", in P. Craveri and A. Varsori (eds.), *L'Italia nella costruzione europea. Un bilancio storico (1957-2007)*, Franco Angeli, Milano, 2009, p. 60.

10 ADN [Archives diplomatiques de Nantes], CGF [Consulat général in Florence], 227 PO 1 291, Ministère français de l'Intérieur, *Réflexions sur le contrôle transfrontalier à la frontière franco-italienne*, Paris, 06.1985.

11 ADN, CGF, 227 PO 1 137, Ministère français des Relations extérieures, *Immigration clandestine*, Paris, 25/10/1984.

12 ADN, CGF, PO 1 291, Ministère français de l'Intérieur, *Note relative à l'ouverture de la frontière franco-italienne*, Paris, 05/06/1985; *Ibid.*, Ministère français des Relations extérieures, *Sommet franco-italien. Procédure d'allègement des contrôles aux frontières avec l'Italie*, Paris, 28/05/1985; 227 PO 1 39, Ministère français des Affaires étrangères, *Ressortissants italiens soumis à l'obligation du visa*, Paris, 30/03/1981.

13 ADN, CGF, 227 PO 1 137, Ministère français des Relations extérieures, *Éventuel allègement des contrôles à la frontière,* Paris, 22/10/1984; *Ibid., Cadre général des relations franco-italiennes*, Paris, 19/10/1984; *Ibid., Passages à la frontière Franco-Italienne*, Paris, 18/10/1984.

introducing measures to strengthen external border controls and to ramp up the fight against drug-trafficking, international crime and illegal immigration.

London, Dublin and Copenhagen refused to stop border controls because they did not trust the effectiveness of Southern European countries and wanted to maintain sovereignty in this politically sensitive domain. In addition to these motives, the determination to remain part of the Nordic Passport Union, a borderless area composed of all Scandinavian countries, played a role in Denmark's decision. Similarly Ireland's opposition to borderless areas at the European level came down, in part, to the Republic's desire to remain a member of the Common Travel Area with Great Britain. Athens was, meanwhile, potentially interested. Yet Greece was a newcomer to the EC and an emigration country on the geopolitical periphery, to boot: it would not be invited to join Schengen.[14]

Italy was the only important EC member excluded from the accord.[15]

The Italian Prime Minister, Bettino Craxi, put this item at the top of the agenda in a summit with French President Mitterrand, which took place in Florence on the same day on which the Schengen Agreement was signed.[16] Mitterrand agreed, under pressure from Craxi, on bilateral negotiations aimed at reaching a quasi-Schengen arrangement between Italy and France. Mitterrand was, however, brutally clear that Rome first

---

14 See: Pudlat, A., *Schengen. Zur Manifestation von Grenze und Grenzschutz in Europa*, Olms, Hildesheim, 2013; Idem, "Der lange Weg zum Schengen-Raum. Ein Prozess im Vier-Phasen-Modell", *Journal of European Integration History*, No. 2, 2011, pp. 303-325; Boeles, P., den Heijer, M., Lodder, G., Wouters, K. (eds.), *European Migration Law*, Intersentia, Antwerp, 2009; Karanja, S. K., *Transparency and Proportionality in the Schengen Information System and Border Control Co-operation*, Martinus Nijhoff, Leiden/Boston, 2008; Sciortino, G., *L'ambizione della frontiera. Le politiche di controllo migratorio in Europa*, Franco Angeli, Milano, 2000; Hreblay, V., *Les accords de Schengen: origine, fonctionemment, avenir*, Bruylant, Bruxelles, 1998; Loutte, J. S., *Les États du Benelux et la France face aux accords de Schengen*, Centre de recherche et d'information socio-politiques, Bruxelles, 1998; Bellucci, S., *L'Europa senza frontiere e le nuove misure di cooperazione tra polizie*, Laurus Robuffo, Roma, 1997; Bigo, D., *Polices en réseaux: l'expérience européenne*, Presses de la Fondation Nationale des Sciences Politiques, Paris, 1996; Renault, G., *Schengen. Un modèle pour l'Europe pénale?*, Larcier, Bruxelles, 1995.

15 See: Varsori, A., *La Cenerentola d'Europa? L'Italia e l'integrazione europea dal 1947 ad oggi*, Rubbettino, Soveria Mannelli, 2010; Neri Gualdesi, M., *Il cuore a Bruxelles, la mente a Roma. Storia della partecipazione italiana alla costruzione dell'unità europea*, ETS, Pisa, 2004.

16 ADN, CGF, 227 PO 1 291, Ministère français des Relations extérieures, *Sommet franco-italien (Florence, 13 et 14 juin 1985)*, Paris, 24/05/1985.

needed to strengthen controls on persons trying to illegally enter France through Italy, especially from the Mediterranean region.[17]

Shortly after the summit in Florence, representatives of the Italian Foreign Ministry and the French Ministry for External Relations met. Negotiations lasted for months before coming to an abrupt halt in early 1986: nothing was achieved.

The "great refusal": Rome against Schengen (1985-1987)

Both Italian and French primary sources show that the main cause of the breakdown in negotiations was the Italian government's refusal to meet the requests made by French representatives on behalf of the Schengen states. First, the Italian authorities were reluctant to pay the political and financial cost of removing the geographical limitation contained in the 1951 Geneva Convention from their legislation, in which the status of political asylum was only recognized for "persons fleeing events occurring before 1 January 1951 and within Europe".[18] This request was due to the willingness of the Schengen countries, especially Germany, to share the increasing burden of refugee flows from Africa and Asia.[19] Second, they opposed signing a readmission agreement with France whereby Italy had to readmit irregular migrants transiting from Italy to France.[20] Finally, and more importantly, they were reluctant to make their own immigration legislation conform to the stricter laws adopted by all Schengen states between the early 1970s and the mid-1980s.[21] Rome questioned the

---

17 *Financial Times*, 15/06/1985. See also: ADN, CGF, 227 PO 1 291, Ministère français des Relations extérieures, *Circulation des personnes: Immigration clandestine*, Paris, 05.1985.

18 Introductory note to Office of the United Nations High Commissioner (ed.), *Convention and Protocol relating to the status of refugees, United Nations High Commissioner for Refugees*, Geneva, 2010, p. 2. With the adoption of the 1967 Protocol relating to the status of refugees, the geographical limitation lost much of its significance and it was maintained by a very limited number of states, including Italy.

19 ASFBC [Archivi Storici della Fondazione Bettino Craxi], FBC [Fondo Bettino Craxi], 4A, Ministero Italiano degli Affari Esteri, *Libera circolazione delle persone nella Comunità*, Roma, 11.1986.

20 According to the officials of the Italian Foreign Ministry, the Schengen Agreement "was conceived of, especially by France, as a means of pressuring Italy in order to solve, possibly with profit, the problem of repatriation of illegal immigrants to their countries of origin" [translated by the author]. ASFBC, FBC, 4A, *Libera circolazione delle persone nella Comunità*, Roma, 11.1986.

21 According to the officials of the Italian Foreign Ministry, the real reason why the Schengen countries signed an intergovernmental agreement rather than adopting an EC directive was their conviction that "the other members of the Community (above all Italy) were not sufficiently able to ensure serious control over common external borders" [translated by the author]. ASFBC, FBC, 12B, Ministero Italiano degli Affari

convenience and feasibility of stricter border controls and new penalties on carriers transporting undocumented foreigners[22]; also, Rome staunchly rejected the French call for the introduction of visa requirements for nationals of all emigration or potential emigration countries. While both the French government and presidency regarded visas as effective antidotes to illegal immigration and international terrorism, the Italian government argued for exempting a number of developing countries, especially in the Mediterranean basin, from visa regimes. According to the Italian authorities, the expansion of visa requirements, in addition to being ineffective in dealing with illegal immigration and international terrorism, contradicted the internationalist values of the main national political and social forces. Moreover, it was a hindrance to both tourism to Italy and pilgrimages to the Vatican City and, what was worse, it was an obstacle to the government's Mediterranean strategy.[23]

Prime Minister Craxi and Labour and Social Affairs Minister Gianni De Michelis, in particular, argued that the EC – rather than the Schengen intergovernmental system – was the appropriate framework for dealing with the liberalization of the cross-border movement of persons. In addition, they suggested to replace the Schengen restrictive, security-oriented, approach with a liberal immigration policy and a plan of economic assistance, consistent with the EC moral responsibilities and political and economic interests in the Mediterranean. This attitude went hand in hand with Italy's unspoken need for illegal migrants and with the renewed Mediterranean ambitions of the country, which meant a greater role in the Middle East and the Maghreb region.[24]

This political offensive culminated in the Mediterranean Conference on Labour Market Policies, which was held in Tunis in early 1987 at the suggestion of De Michelis.[25] De Michelis spoke in front of Ministers

Esteri, *Europa dei cittadini. Cooperazione in materia di libera circolazione delle persone*, Roma, 11.1986.

22 ASFBC, FBC, ALL12, Ministero Italiano degli Affari Esteri Seguiti riunione interministeriale sul soggiorno dei cittadini CEE, snellimento controlli frontiere intracomunitarie e proposta tedesca sull'ingresso illegale di extra-comunitari provenienti con navi e aerei, Roma, 14/11/1986.

23 Meloni, A., *Visa Policy within the European Union Structure*, Springer, Berlin, 2006, pp. 38-39.

24 ANF, APR, ACD, 5 AG 4 / CD 135 Dossier 1, Edgard Pisani, *Note pour le Président de la République: Entrevue avec le Président Bettino Craxi*, 03/12/1986. See also: Amri, I., "Le relazioni della Tunisia con l'Europa occidentale in materia di manodopera", in M. Delle Donne and U. Melotti (eds.), *Mediterraneo. Di qua di là dal mare Tunisia Italia*, Ediesse, Roma, 2002, pp. 99-110.

25 Though Gianni De Michelis served as Labour and Social Affairs Minister between 1983 and 1987, from the mid-1980s he was generally considered by European authorities, especially the French, as "the key man of international relations within the

from France, Greece, Spain, Algeria, Egypt, Morocco, Tunisia, Turkey and Yugoslavia, plus representatives from the Arab League, the Arab Labour Organization (ALO), the International Labour Organization (ILO) and the European Community. In that context, he made a sustained effort to reply to the Fortress Europe logic that, according to him, was implicit in Schengen.[26] In particular he supported the establishment of a sort of integrated Euro-Mediterranean labour market, in which Southern surpluses of manpower alleviate shortages of manpower and ageing populations in the North. Also, he proposed to implement economic and social cohesion at the Euro-Mediterranean level, the ultimate aim being to close disparities in socio-economic conditions between the two shores of the Mediterranean.[27]

In the meantime, accordingly, the Italian Parliament approved an immigration law that was not in line with the restrictive legislation adopted and requested by Northern European countries.[28] It introduced restrictive measures on the recruitment of non-EC workers, and penalties

---

Italian Socialist Party" [translated by the author]; between 1989 and 1992, he served as Foreign Minister. ANF, APR, ACD, 5 AG 4 / CD 135 Dossier 1, Vedrine, H., *Note pour le Président de la République*, 27/06/1986.

26 Costa, R., "L'immigrazione verso l'Italia e l'Europa nelle previsioni per i prossimi venticinque anni", in C. Maccheroni and A. Mauri (eds.), *Le migrazioni dall'Africa mediterranea verso l'Italia*, Giuffrè, Milano, 1989, p. 20.

27 ANF, APR, ACD, 5 AG 4 / CD 135 Dossier 1, Vedrine, H., *Initiative italienne sur la Méditerranée*, 07/04/1987. See also: De Michelis, G., *La lezione della storia: sul futuro dell'Italia e le prospettive dell'Europa*, Marsilio, Venezia, 2013; Idem., *La lunga ombra di Yalta: la specificità della politica italiana*, Marsilio, Venezia, 2003. In accordance with this strategy, the government in Rome gave 500 million dollars of assistance to Tunisia in the context of a wider change of priorities and beneficiaries in Italy's policy of cooperation. Calandri, E., *Prima della globalizzazione. L'Italia, la cooperazione allo sviluppo e la Guerra Fredda*, Cedam, Padova, 2013, pp. 251-306.

28 The aim of the act was to legalize and regulate the situation of immigrants in Italy and to gently prevent further illegal immigration rather than to restrict access and cut down inflows. See: Bonifazi, C., *L'immigrazione straniera in Italia*, Il Mulino, Bologna, 2007; Pugliese, E., *L'Italia tra migrazioni internazionali e migrazioni interne*, Il Mulino, Bologna, 2006. See also: Calavita, K., "Italy: Economic Realities, Political Fictions, and Policy Failures", in W. A. Cornelius, T. Tsuda, Ph. L. Martin and J. F. Hollifield (eds.), *Controlling Immigration. A Global Perspective*, Stanford University Press, Stanford, 2004, pp. 366-369; Bonetti, P., "Italy", in B. Nascimbene (ed.), *Expulsion and Detention of Aliens in the European Union Countries*, Giuffré, Milano, 2001, pp. 314-315; Sciortino, G., "Planning in the Dark: the Evolution of Italian Immigration Control", in G. Brochmann and T. Hammar (eds.), *Mechanisms of Immigration Control. A Comparative Analysis of European Regulation Policies*, Berg, Oxford, 1999, pp. 237-239; Hollifield, J. F., "Immigration and integration in Western Europe: a comparative analysis", in E. M. Uçarer and D. J. Puchala (eds.), *Immigration into Western Societies: problems and policies*, Pinter, London/Washington, 1997, pp. 28-30; Zincone, G., "Immigration to Italy: Data and Policies", in F. Heckmann and

for those who favoured illegal immigration or hired illegal immigrants; it also established a voluntary repatriation fund. However, contrary to Schengen countries' expectations, the first Italian law on immigration did not create a system of border controls, refoulement, expulsions and visas comparable to the Schengen countries' ones.[29]

A difficult dilemma: Schengen, yes or no? (1987-1989)

At the fall of the Craxi government in mid-1987, all Italian proposals made at both the European and the Euro-Mediterranean level were put aside, not least because of the cold reaction from the French government. Paris stood against the prospect of relaxing Schengen immigration rules, especially on the Mediterranean front. They refused, too, the idea of associating the strengthening of external border controls with the adoption of assistance plans for third Mediterranean countries.[30] They were convinced, finally, that the migration issue was not to be dealt with in the complex and sometimes chaotic Euro-Mediterranean fora.[31]

At the same time, the government in Rome realized that it was too costly, in both political and economic terms, to stay on the margins of the Schengen club. Not least, there was the danger that Italy might cease to be a transit country, as it was perceived by a large part of its ruling class and public opinion, and become, instead, a receiving country. In addition, the predominance of the "pro-French faction" led by Foreign Minister Andreotti over the "pro-Mediterranean faction" led by Craxi, the ex-Prime Minister and Secretary of the *Partito Socialista Italiano* (PSI), also played a role in the more favourable attitude towards Schengen in the new Amintore Fanfani government.[32] Moreover, after a rebuffed attempt at alliance with Spain, Italy faced the serious risk of being diplomatically isolated in Europe; unlike the Italian Parliament, in fact, the Spanish Parliament was prompt in bringing national immigration legislation in line with the more restrictive legislation of Schengen countries, while

W. Bosswick (eds.), *Migration Policies: a Comparative Perspective*, Enke, Stuttgard, 1995, p. 138.

29 Legge 30 dicembre 1986, N. 943, *Norme in materia di collocamento e di trattamento dei lavoratori extracomunitari immigrati e contro le immigrazioni clandestine* (GU 8, 12/1/1987).

30 Louette, J. S., *Les États du Benelux et la France face aux accords de Schengen*, Centre de recherche et d'information socio-politiques, Bruxelles, 1998, pp. 11-16.

31 ANF, APR, ACD, 5 AG 4 / CD 135 Dossier 1, Vedrine, H., *Méditerranée*, 06/04/1987.

32 The French Ambassador to Italy in the late 1980s and early 1990s considered Andreotti "without any doubts, one of the best friends of France among Italian politicians, one that perfectly speaks our language and truly appreciate and love our culture" [translated by the author]. ADN, CGF, 227 PO 1 291, Pérol, G., *Rencontre du Président de la République avec Andreotti*, 27/09/1989.

remaining reluctant to impose visa requirements on Maghreb and South American citizens.[33]

After a short internal debate the Italian government, inspired by Foreign Minister Andreotti, agreed on asking for admittance to the groups charged with drafting the Convention implementing the Schengen Agreement. The Italian government hoped that the five original Schengen signatories toned down their requests.[34]

Unsurprisingly, the Schengen governments accepted the Italian request for admittance. The aims were to reassure the European Commission and the European Parliament that the Schengen Agreement would eventually include all members of the EC and contribute to a politically and financially convenient externalization of border control activities.[35] The Schengen governments, however, continued to insist that Italy should meet all the conditions and remove the obstacles for acceptance into the Schengen club, starting with the introduction of visa requirements for countries deemed to be problematic, especially in the Mediterranean. There was awareness that Italy would set the precedent for all Southern European states, so there was little room for compromise.[36] In addition, Italian Ministers were excluded from biannual ministerial meetings, which took place in the framework of the negotiations for the Convention implementing the Schengen Agreement. Italian representatives, meanwhile, were admitted as mere observers to technical committees, without any decision-making powers.[37]

After one and a half years of Italian representatives' participation in negotiations, the Italian Parliament discussed the opportunity of entering

---

33 See: Cortés Maisonave, A., "Los antecedentes políticos del codesarrollo: la reinvención del nexo entre la migración y el desarrollo en el sur de Europa", in F. Checa y Olmos, J. C. Checa and A. Arjona (eds.), *Las Migraciones en el Mundo: desafíos y esperanzas*, Icaria, Barcelona, 2009, p. 75; Moreno Fuentes, F. J., "Dissonance between Discourse and Practice in EU Border Control Enforcement. The Spanish Case", in A. Chebel d'Appollonia and S. Reich (eds.), *Immigration, Integration, and Security. America and Europe in Comparative Perspective*, University of Pittsburgh, Pittsburgh, 2008, pp. 262-267.

34 HACEU [Historical Archives of the Council of the European Union], SEC [Schengen Executive Committee], 230487, Ambassade d'Italie à Bruxelles, *Lettre au Secrétariat Général du Benelux*, 13/04/1987; *Ibid.*, Union Économique Benelux, *Demande d'adhésion de l'Italie*, 23/04/1987.

35 Boswell, C., *European Migration Policies in Flux. Changing Patterns of Inclusion and Exclusion*, Blackwell, Oxford, 2003, pp. 100-112.

36 Guimezanes, N., "La Convention de Schengen: une présentation française", in A. Pauly (ed.), *Schengen en panne*, European Institute of Public Administration, Maastricht, 1994, pp. 5-10.

37 Fridegotto, M., *L'accordo di Schengen: riflessi internazionali ed interni per l'Italia*, FrancoAngeli, Milano, 1992, pp. 17-20.

the Schengen system for the first time. Between late 1988 and late 1989, in particular, the Parliamentary Committee on Constitutional Affairs of the Chamber of Deputies conducted an enquiry into immigration and the conditions of foreign nationals in Italy. This highlighted the existence of important political forces opposing the Italian participation in the upcoming Schengen area.[38] There was, it is fair to say, a general failure to understand immigration and its potential implications; in addition, most criticisms depended on a common internationalist ideology and the shared memory of a long migratory past. Also, foreign policy considerations were crucial in shaping the views of Italian Socialists; put simply, participation in the Schengen system seemed at odds with the Socialists' Mediterranean strategy, which included privileged economic and political relations with Maghreb and Middle Eastern countries. Third-Worldism played a decisive part in the critical positions taken by the representatives of the *Partito Comunista Italiano* (PC), meanwhile. The pro-immigration stance of the Catholic Church, finally, was influential in determining the *Democrazia Cristiana*'s (DC) position.[39]

All the members of the government who spoke during hearings criticized the Schengen Agreement and opposed Italian accession as well: with the sole exceptions of the Foreign Minister and, from mid-1989 to mid-1992, the Prime Minister, Andreotti, and the Interior Minister, Antonio Gava. The Labour and Social Affairs Minister, Rino Formica, questioned, for example, Schengen's emphasis on police border controls in the fight against illegal immigration. The Minister of European Affairs, Antonio La Pergola, argued against the decision to act outside the EC framework and to disregard, as he saw it, the interests and opinions of third Mediterranean countries. The Vice-Prime Minister, Claudio Martelli, a Socialist, bluntly attacked the Schengen Agreement head on. In particular, he denounced Schengen as an inhuman and ineffective attempt to establish a *cordon sanitaire* against the South whose poverty was, according to him, in great part attributable to the North. Martelli proposed as an alternative the strategic planning of migration flows at the EC level and in close coordination with the countries of origin: according to this proposal, the

---

38 In addition, all the members of associations and trade unions, including the *Confederazione Generale Italiana del Lavoro* (CGIL), the *Confederazione Italiana Sindacato Lavoratori* (CISL) and the *Unione Italiana del Lavoro* (UIL), who participated in the meetings of the Parliamentary Committee on Constitutional Affairs of the Chamber of Deputies, expressed scepticism and criticism against the Schengen system. BASSETTI, M., "Immigrazione e razzismo in Italia", *Testimonianze*, No. 3-4, 1990.

39 ASILS [Archivio Storico dell'Istituto Luigi Sturzo], FDC [Fondo Democrazia Cristiana], SCONGRN [Serie Congresso Nazionale], 29, Delegazione italiana nel Gruppo del Partito Popolare Europeo, *Mozione dei Deputati Europei DC per il Congresso*, 18/02/1989.

European Community ought to set a flexible and articulated framework within which all its member states, on the basis of their respective socio-economic needs and in a spirit of international solidarity, would plan immigrant quotas and sign bilateral agreements with sending countries.[40] This proposal was clearly intended to satisfy the request for flexible and low-wage workers coming from Italian employers. In addition, it gave space to the Italian government's ambition to play a leading role in the Mediterranean region while, simultaneously, defending the primacy of the EC in international cooperation on migration and asylum.[41]

In this context, the request to impose visas on people coming from Maghreb countries became the most significant obstacle to Italy signing the Schengen Agreement and the upcoming Convention implementing the Schengen Agreement. In an attempt to strengthen diplomatic relations with Maghreb countries, especially Morocco of King Hassan II and Tunisia with its new President Zine El Abidine Ben Ali, the Vice-Primc Minister openly challenged the Schengen countries, by confirming the Italian government's unwillingness to impose visas on persons coming from these states. Martelli, with the support of his party, and hoping to help with the unification of the Maghreb countries, was also actively committed in promoting free movement agreements between the European Community and the plan for an Arab Maghreb Union (AMU), which involved Algeria, Libya, Mauritania, Morocco and Tunisia.[42]

With this in mind, after the well-publicized murder of a South-African refugee, Jerry Essan Masslo, and a consequent, unprecedented, mass rally against racism in late 1989, Martelli introduced a bill to reform Italian immigration policy. He was determined that it would not conform to Schengen norms; according to him, Italy should be particularly careful not to follow the model of France, which he regarded as a country: "shaken by waves of racism and with a foreign population that is five times larger than ours".[43]

---

40 Camera dei Deputati, *Immigrazione e condizione dello straniero. Indagine conoscitiva della I Commissione Affari Costituzionali e Testi normativi conseguenti (novembre 1988-dicembre 1989)*, Ufficio Pubblicazioni del Servizio Informazione Parlamentare e Relazioni Esterne della Camera dei Deputati, Roma, 1990.

41 Martelli, C., *Il merito e il bisogno*, SugarCo, Milano, 1987, p. 194.

42 Mahiou, A., "Problématique de la construction maghrebine", in R. Bistolfi (ed.), *Euro-Méditerranée. Une région à construire*, Publisud, Paris, 1995, pp. 199-211; Daudel, C., "Quelles perspectives entre la CEE et l'UMA?", *Afrique et Asie Modernes*, No. 166, 1990, p. 34; Aliboni, R., "Le Maghreb et la Communauté européenne: vers une nouvelle approche solidaire", *Orient*, No. 3, 1990, p. 87.

43 See: *La Stampa*, 19/12/1989; *Il Giornale*, 20/12/1989. See also: Martelli, C., *Ricordati di vivere*, Bompiani, Milano, 2013.

Italy in Schengen: voluntary or coercive Europeanization? (1989-1990)

After the approval of Martelli's decree law by the Council of Ministers, however, a heated debate began in which the distance between Italian and Northern European immigration regimes became a fundamental argument against Martelli's approach. That was the time when long-standing fears of immigrant invasion from the South combined with more recent fears of a looming immigrant invasion from the East. Significant political forces, including the neo-fascist *Movimento Sociale Italiano* (MSI) and the regionalist *Lega Lombarda* (LL)/Lega Nord (LN), began to openly criticize the liberal approach taken by the Vice-Prime Minister. They caricatured Italy as the soft underbelly of Europe and the open door to the Continent, borrowing from the French and German media and from the political debate in those two countries. Also, governing parties such as the *Partito Liberale Italiano* (PLI) and, above all, the *Partito Repubblicano Italiano* (PRI) protested Martelli's decree law in an attempt to take advantage of middle-class voters' fears and to reach out to the Schengen governments.[44]

The governments of the Schengen countries, in fact, made every effort to persuade both the Italian government and Parliament to accept their views on immigration.[45] The French government and presidency were the most resolute in pressing the Italian authorities. In the words of the then Ambassador of France in Rome, on the eve of the Venice summit between French President Mitterrand and Italian Prime Minister Andreotti due on 4-5 October 1989, "our interest [...] is neither to have a transit country on the Eastern Mediterranean flank, the most vulnerable to demographic pressures [...], nor to have a marginalized country against which we should maintain a *cordon sanitaire* on the Alps, unless we will be able to solve the problem. Negotiations on the Schengen agreements give us a chance – after all, regardless of the outcome of these negotiations. Since Italy knocks at the door, we need to [...] force the Italian government to undertake the necessary reforms to its legislation according to a clear and strict timetable" [translated by the author].[46]

44 Senato della Repubblica italiana, *Atti parlamentari. X Legislatura, Resoconto stenografico*, Roma, 27/02/1990. See also: *Il Manifesto*, 23/12/1989; *Avanti!*, 24/12/1989; *Il Giornale*, 06/01/1990; *Panorama*, 14/01/1990.

45 Contel, M., De Biase, R., "Italy", in S. Angenendt (ed.), *Asylum and Migration Policies in the European Union*, Research Institute of the German Society for Foreign Affairs, 1999, pp. 240-242.

46 ADN, CGF, 227 PO 1 291, Pérol, G., *Rencontre du Président de la République avec Andreotti*, 27/09/1989.

Similarly, the Italian politicians who were most exposed to European influence, such as European Commissioner Carlo Ripa di Meana, publicly agreed with the Schengen countries, who refused to open their borders with Italy unless Italy adopted stricter rules on immigration; this included, naturally, visas on migrants or travellers from Southern Mediterranean countries.[47]

Pressure from Schengen governments, which was added to growing protests from both opposition and government parties and increasingly vociferous complaints from city mayors and professional groups, especially shopkeepers, led to an abrupt change of mind in the two main government parties, the DC and the PSI.[48] This, in turn, led to a dramatic shift from a liberal to a restrictive approach to immigration. Though a majority in both parties remained secretly sceptical about the Schengen system and its underlying philosophy, they decided that the electoral, political and economic costs of self-exclusion were too high.[49]

At the conclusion of the parliamentary debate, the original law decree was radically modified[50], and all the most significant reforms requested as conditions for the country's accession to Schengen were adopted. First, the Italian Parliament abolished the special clauses of the Geneva Convention in which the status of political asylum was only recognized for those from European countries.[51] Second, it strengthened rejection and detention procedures for irregular immigrants, tightened up sanctions for migrant smugglers and traffickers and introduced penalties on carriers transporting the undocumented. Finally, it agreed on visas for those coming from sending countries, including Turkey, the Maghreb and

---

47 *Il Messaggero*, 24/02/1990.

48 See: *Il Giornale*, 15/02/1990; *Secolo*, 15, 17, 20 and 21/02/1990; *L'Unità*, 17 and 23/02/1990; *Il Mattino*, 18/02/1990; *Corriere della Sera*, 18/02/1990; *L'Espresso*, 18/02/1990; *Avanti!*, 20/02/1990; *La Repubblica*, 23/02/1990; *Avvenire*, 24/02/1990; *Il Giorno*, 24/02/1990. See also: Paoli, S., "La legge Martelli su asilo politico e immigrazione: una scelta europea", *Storia e Politica - Annali della Fondazione Ugo La Malfa*, Vol. XXIX, 2015.

49 ASILS, FDC, SCONSN [Serie Consiglio Nazionale], 71, Forlani, A., *Relazione del segretario politico al Consiglio Nazionale della Democrazia Cristiana*, 19-20/02/1990.

50 Decreto Legge 30 dicembre 1989, N. 416, coordinato con la Legge di conversione 28 febbraio 1990, No. 39, recante *Norme urgenti in materia di asilo politico, di ingresso e soggiorno dei cittadini extracomunitari e di regolarizzazione dei cittadini extracomunitari e apolidi già presenti nel territorio dello Stato*, (GU 49, 21/3/1990).

51 It is fair to say that the removal of the geographical limitation was also due to the pressure made by left-wing parties, religious and secular associations, intergovernmental organizations and international non-governmental organizations. Hein, C., "Storia del diritto d'asilo in Italia", in C. Hein (ed.), *Rifugiati: vent'anni di storia del diritto d'asilo in Italia*, Donzelli, Roma, 2010, pp. 33-84.

sub-Saharan African countries.[52] This was at the same time, it must be remembered, that all Schengen countries, immediately after the collapse of Communist regimes and under pressure from Germany, decided to remove Hungary and Czechoslovakia from the Schengen Black List. They also agreed to treat the German Democratic Republic, prior to reunification, as a non-foreign part of Germany, so *de facto* admitting East Germany into Schengen.[53]

It is fair to say that the so-called Martelli Law did not eliminate all differences between immigration legislation in Italy and in most Northern European countries. In addition to a generous regularization scheme, in fact, the law introduced a system of quotas for new immigration, thus leaving the option to allow immigration flows if domestic labour market conditions were suitable.[54] More than this, doubts remained on Italy's willingness and capacity to enforce the law.[55] That said, the governments of the Schengen countries could be satisfied with the reassurances given by the Italian government and Parliament through the approval of the law and the promise, quickly fulfilled, to sign a readmission agreement with France. Consequently, Vice-Prime Minister Martelli was allowed to sign the Schengen Agreement and the Convention implementing the Schengen Agreement on 27 November 1990.

The Italian government, meanwhile, was content with its entry into Schengen after a debate which had risked the country's relations with its Community partners and the government's coalition and natural constituency.

Conclusion

In conclusion, an important reason why the Schengen countries resolved to act outside the EC framework and, in this context, to exclude Italy was their political determination to press Italy and, ultimately, all

---

52 Bade, K., *Migration in European History*, Blackwell, Malden, 2003, pp. 234-240.

53 HACEU, CGFMP [Coordinators' Group on Free Movement of Persons], 3607/1/90, Groupe des Coordonnateurs "Libre Circulation des Personnes", *Conclusions*, 16/02/1990; HACEU, ADGI [Ad Hoc Group on Immigration], SN 2480/90 (WGI 541), Groupe Ad Hoc Immigration, *Réunion*, 29/01/1990; WGI 567, Groupe Ad Hoc Immigration, *Conclusions*, 05/03/1990; WGI 598, Groupe Ad Hoc Immigration, *Conclusions*, 05/04/1990; WGI 612, Groupe Ad Hoc Immigration, *Conclusions*, 15/05/1990.

54 C. Martelli, C., "Introduzione", in A. Saija (ed.), *La normativa sugli extracomunitari. Testo e commento della Legge 28/2/1990 N. 39*, Edizioni delle Autonomie, Roma, 1990, pp. 5-6.

55 Bonifazi, C., "European Migration Policy: Questions from Italy", in R. King, G. Lazaridis and C. Tsardanidis (eds.), *Eldorado or Fortress? Migration in Southern Europe*, Palgrave Macmillan, Basingstoke, 2000, pp. 233-252.

the Southern members of the EC into adopting the Northern European approach to the problem of immigration control. These Southern EC countries would, by this logic, have been transformed into a convenient and efficient first line in the externalization of border controls and a buffer zone against Southern Mediterranean countries.

The Italian government resisted, for a long time, to comply with the requirements to join Schengen; they were perceived, in fact, as detrimental to national demographic, economic and political interests, in addition to being considered as incompatible with national values and traditions.

Initially, the government tried to offer an alternative to the Schengen way, which was supported by most political and socio-economic forces. This plan failed due to the country's diplomatic isolation and the new government's lack of conviction (1985-1987). After the defeat of this strategy, a significant part of the Italian executive began to argue that the political and, to a certain extent, economic costs of staying outside the Schengen Area were too high. This group, led by the Foreign Minister, was able to convince the entire government to apply to join Schengen in the vain hope that the most undesired conditions might be renegotiated. When the Schengen countries made it clear that, for Italy, was a case of take it or leave it, the Italian government and Parliament seemed quite united in opposing the country's entry (1987-1989). Things changed when domestic concerns combined with foreign policy considerations (1989-1990). On the one hand, there was the sudden need to reassure vociferous sectors of the Italian public opinion which, after the collapse of Communist regimes in Central and Eastern Europe, were becoming more and more preoccupied with migration-related problems. On the other, more importantly, there was the urgency to consolidate political and economic relations with European partners, even to the detriment of those with Southern Mediterranean countries; also, there was the need to not be excluded from a significant economic and political initiative at the European level such as Schengen. The Italian government and Parliament, therefore, though reluctantly, agreed on a law that was, in large part, an attempt to comply with membership requirements. A majority in both the government and the Parliament did not believe in restrictive measures but they adopted them in order to reassure the Schengen members that Italy was able to prevent the entry of unwanted immigrants into the Schengen space. In addition to affecting Italian legislation, Schengen was crucial in influencing the national migration debate. In particular, it provided respectability and legitimacy to the anti-immigration discourse; not by chance, between the late 1980s and the early 1990s, the need to adapt the national immigration policy to Schengen became a significant source of inspiration or, alternatively, a cunning argument in the hands of anti-immigration forces.

Romania's Schengen accession bid: a sinuous path

Nicolae PĂUN and Adrian-Gabriel CORPĂDEAN

Abstract: This research falls into the broad category of International Relations and European Studies and encompasses a multidisciplinary perspective on the chain of events that have shaped Romania's still incomplete process of joining the Schengen Area, eight years after its integration into the European Union. From a socio-political point of view, we aim to emphasise the presence of this intricate topic at the level of the civil society and in discourse, by means of speech analyses conducted on prominent decision-makers and other stakeholders. Furthermore, at the institutional level, it is particularly important to attempt to draw a timeline of the events that have become landmarks in Romania's lengthy negotiation process on Schengen membership, with the inevitable twists and turns that have marked relations with the supranational and intergovernmental Community levels in this regard.

Background

Since its accession to the European Union, on the 1st of January 2007, along with its southern neighbour, Bulgaria, Romania has been a strong supporter of the integration process, not only at the political level, but also with regard to popular support and approval of institutional reform. Adoption of the *acquis* has been steady, albeit compared to other states in the east-central area, Romania and Bulgaria fall under the control of the Mechanism for cooperation and verification, an instrument whose purpose is to foster continuous reform in the field of juridical performance, the rule of law, organised crime prevention and the fight against corruption.[1] In recent endeavours, the Romanian and Bulgarian governments have agreed to perform a best practice exchange pertaining to the Mechanism for Cooperation and Verification, in the view of its possible discontinuity. With this particularity in mind, it is to be noted that at present, there are two major elements of the community *acquis* which are not being implemented by Romania – the former refers to the

[1] Heidbreder, E., *The Impact of Expansion on European Union Institutions: The Eastern Touch on Brussels*, Palgrave Macmillan, New York, 2011, p. 153.

adoption of the single currency[2], whereas the latter is its membership of the borderless Schengen Area. Whilst joining the Eurozone represents an obligation assumed by the country through its accession Treaty, and is to be achieved in the foreseeable future, it becomes apparent that Schengen membership, itself obligatory according to the same conditions, is a much more arduous desire at present.

This chapter aims to present Romania's intricate accession bid to the Schengen area, through a multi-angle perspective, encompassing the commitments assumed by this country, the course of reform implemented so as to comply with the considerable volume of provisions, as well as the political attitudes within the EU regarding this endeavour. The context surrounding this topic needs to take into account sinuous elements such as the rise of Euroscepticism in both Old and New Europe, migration and its perception or reflection in political discourse, together with Romania's relations with key partners exhibiting some reluctance to its accession bid to date.

The essential premise from which we shall build our argumentation is a reminder that for Romania, Schengen accession is not meant to be perceived as a political option, or even as a right, as it is formally speaking an obligation assumed through the EU accession negotiations and their outcome. In fact, the Accession Treaty of Romania and Bulgaria, signed on 25 April 2005, through Article 4 of the Protocol on the conditions of accession, clearly stipulates that the adoption of the Schengen *acquis* constitutes an obligation thereby assumed by both states:

> 1. The provisions of the Schengen *acquis*, referred to in Protocol No. 17 to the Constitution on the Schengen *acquis* integrated into the framework of the European Union, and the acts building upon it or otherwise related to it, listed in Annex II, as well as any further such acts adopted before the date of accession, shall be binding on and applicable in Bulgaria and Romania from the date of accession.
>
> 2. Those provisions of the Schengen *acquis* as integrated into the framework of the European Union and the acts building upon it or otherwise related to it not referred to in paragraph 1, while binding on Bulgaria and Romania from the date of accession, shall only apply in each of those States pursuant to a European decision of the Council to that effect after verification in accordance with the applicable Schengen evaluation procedures that the necessary conditions for the application of all parts of the *acquis* concerned have been met in that State.[3]

---

2 White, S., Batt, J. and Lewis, P. G. (eds.), *Developments in Central and East European Politics*, Duke University Press, Durham, 2007, p. 262.

3 *Protocol concerning the conditions and arrangements for admission of the Republic of Bulgaria and Romania to the European Union*, Official Journal of the European Union, L 157/29, 21 June 2005.

The aforementioned provisions render the efforts meant to achieve full compliance with the Schengen *acquis* mandatory in both states, with an evident intent to foster their integration into the free-movement zone and as an incentive to take decisive action in areas where progress remained necessary with respect to justice and security. As it results from the second paragraph of Article 4, the regular evaluation procedure applies to the progress of the two countries in the adoption of the Schengen regulations, with the Council of the European Union exerting its exclusive decision-making role in this respect.[4]

The same Protocol concerning the conditions and arrangements for admission of the Republic of Bulgaria and Romania to the European Union stipulates, at Article 32, the creation of a temporary Cash-flow and Schengen Facility over a two-year period following EU accession, so as to foster the correct implementation of the Schengen *acquis* in matters pertaining to the security of the new external borders of the Union. This certifies the fact that part of Romania's responsibility under the auspices of Schengen compliance is undoubtedly that of protecting the external borders, a criterion with considerable weight in the *acquis*, for which Romania has received 600 million euros from the European Union.[5]

The accession bid includes, from a formal standpoint, a number of five steps that need to be undertaken, including the official statement of preparation and the Schengen evaluation questionnaire, which constitute the preparatory phase meant to assess a country's readiness. The next stage consists of the evaluation visits, intended to follow the pace of implementation and tackle several key priorities individually, namely police cooperation, personal data protection, visas, asylum, drugs, firearms, air, land and maritime borders, and the Schengen Information System (SIS) and Supplementary Information Request at the National Entries (SIRENE).[6] The data collected as such becomes the input of the Schengen Evaluation Working Group within the Council of Ministers and gives rise to the reports on the findings of the evaluation visits, with recommendations about measures and corrections that the state is required to implement. Finally, it is the Justice and Home Affairs Council that

4 Brady, H., *Saving Schengen: How to Protect Passport-Free Travel in Europe*, Centre for European Reform, London, 2012, pp. 8-9.

5 Ceccorulli, M. and Labanca, N. (eds.), *The EU, Migration and the Politics of Administrative Detention*, Routledge, New York, 2014, p. 132.

6 In Romania's case, the latter is in keeping with the *National Strategy for Accession to the Schengen Area for the Period 2008-2011*, 25 November 2008, Official Journal of Romania, No. 832, 10 December 2008.

takes the decision of allowing a country to join the Schengen Area, whilst the European Parliament may only exert an advisory role in this regard.[7]

Looking closely at the steps to be undertaken, it becomes apparent that their outcome yields nothing less than the strengthening of the quality of EU citizenship, through the integrative approach of the data systems that Schengen operates with. The information flows thereby exchanged amongst the participating states render their interdependency and operability greater and reinforce security ties that are not only desirable, but also welcome in the light of current global threats.

The reception of the accession bid within the EU's institutional framework

The technical evaluation process of Romania's accession bid was conducted in situ between March 2009 and December 2010, revealing the country's compliance with the *acquis* in all regards, as stipulated by the aforementioned provisions. The complete implementation of the necessary regulations was certified on 9 June 2011, at the Justice and Home Affairs Council meeting in Luxembourg, in the case of both Romania and Bulgaria, without there being any decision on the completion of the accession process per se and by delaying a "return on the issue" until the end of that year.[8] The European Parliament, through the voice of rapporteur Carlos Coelho, from the European People's Party, had already given a green light to the two countries' accession bid, one day prior to the Council meeting, with 487 votes in favour, 77 against and 29 abstentions[9], thus a consistent majority. Two particularly interesting points of view stemming from Parliament emerged on this occasion, with the former being uttered by Coelho himself:

> We are in a position to welcome Bulgaria and Romania into the Schengen area and I hope that the Council will adopt the same position as soon as they receive our positive opinion. [...] Their citizens should be regarded as fully European citizens, and should not be hostages of populist discourse.[10]

It becomes apparent that the extent to which the EP supports Schengen membership is quite high, albeit this message already points at the desire not to make the decision a bargaining chip for political purposes other

7 Balzacq, T. and Carrera, S. (eds.), *Security Versus Freedom?: a Challenge for Europe's Future*, Ashgate Publishing, Hampshire, 2013, pp. 195-198.

8 Press release, 11008/11, 3096th Council meeting, Luxembourg, 9-10 June 2011, p. 10.

9 *Bulgaria, Romania ready to join Schengen area, says Parliament*, European Parliament, News, 6-9 June 2011, p. 12, available at http://www.europarl.europa.eu/pdfs/news/public/focus/20110526FCS20303/20110526FCS20303_en.pdf (last accessed on 29/04/2015).

10 *Ibid.*

than the technical ones enshrined by the *acquis*. In fact, EP President at the time, Jerzy Buzek, delivered a similar opinion on the same occasion, underlining that:

> Schengen is one of the biggest achievements of the EU. We must not destroy it with rash decisions. The Schengen system is providing the highest standards of border management. Romania and Bulgaria are meeting these standards today – hence, we must not delay their integration. I call on the Council to follow the recommendations of the vote expressed today by the large majority of the European Parliament.[11]

The failure of the Council to act on the two countries' bid attracted another round of support stemming from Parliament, whose resolution from 13 October 2011 exhibits the existence of clear contradictions between the two legislative bodies of the EU in this respect, with only the former participating in decision-making on the matter at hand. The text adopted by Parliament reads:

> "1. Points out that both countries have fundamentally redesigned and reorganised their integrated border management systems by investing substantially in their law enforcement authorities, including the provision of training and the latest technology, and have visibly reinforced their institutional and legal frameworks, a fact which is acknowledged in all the Schengen evaluation reports;
>
> 2. Notes the constant support and solidarity shown by Bulgaria and Romania as reliable partners in south-eastern Europe, along with their continual contribution to border security in this part of the EU;
>
> 3. Underlines that both countries have fully implemented the Schengen *acquis*, which – according to their Accession Treaty and the existing EU legal framework – is the only prerequisite for their accession to the Schengen area;
>
> 4. Urges all Member states to take the decision on enlarging the Schengen area to include Bulgaria and Romania solely on the basis of the Schengen *acquis* and procedures; believes that additional criteria cannot be imposed on Member states which are already in the process of joining the Schengen area;
>
> 5. Reiterates Parliament's support for enlarging the Schengen area to include Bulgaria and Romania, and calls on the European Council to proceed in accordance with the EU Treaty and to take the necessary measures to enable Romania and Bulgaria to accede to the Schengen area;
>
> 6. Calls on all Member states to honour their commitments under the EU legal framework as regards the Schengen accession criteria, and not to give priority to national populism;

---

11 *Ibid.*

7. Instructs its President to forward this resolution to the Commission, the Council and the governments and parliaments of the Member states".[12]

An analysis of this viewpoint is bound to take into consideration the strong formulas adopted by Parliament against the attempt to transform the decision on Schengen membership into a political tool, with the rather surprising use of the phrase "national populism" clearly hinting at several attitudes stemming from national chancelleries, as we shall pinpoint in this research.

Meanwhile, there was one Council meeting where the issue of Romania and Bulgaria's Schengen accession was debated, on 22-23 September 2011[13], and a subsequent European Council appeal addressed to the former on 9 December 2011[14], during the course of which a certain solution appeared to emerge, that of a progressive form of accession, encompassing firstly the air and maritime borders and then the ever challenging land frontiers.[15] In the absence of a decision, the European Council took on its usual role of impetus-provider and on the 2nd of March 2012, its conclusions emphasised the juridical compliance of the two countries with the applicable provisions, prompting a need to reach a decision in this regard. Quoting from part IV of the conclusions:

40. The European Council, recalling its discussions in 2011, reiterates that all legal conditions have been met for the decision on Bulgaria's and Romania's accession to the Schengen area to be taken.

41. The European Council also acknowledges the continuous efforts undertaken by Bulgaria and Romania.

42. The European Council requests the Council, during the intervening period, to identify and implement measures which would contribute to the successful enlargement of the Schengen area to include Romania and Bulgaria.

43. The European Council asks the Council to return to this issue in order to adopt its decision at the meeting of the Justice and Home Affairs Council in September 2012.[16]

---

12 *European Parliament resolution of 13 October 2011 on the accession of Bulgaria and Romania to Schengen*, Brussels, 13 October 2011, 2011/2853(RSP).

13 Press release, 14464/11, 3111th Council meeting, Brussels, 22-23 September 2011, p. 7.

14 European Council Conclusions meeting, EUCO 139/1/11, Brussels, 9 December 2011, published on 25 January 2012, p. 6.

15 Ceccorulli, M. and Labanca, N. (eds.), *The EU, Migration and the Politics of Administrative Detention*, Routledge, New York, 2014, p. 130.

16 European Council Conclusions meeting, EUCO 4/3/12, Brussels, 1-2 March 2012, published on 8 May 2012, p. 14.

The efforts made by the European Council aiming to prompt a decision on the two countries' accession to the Schengen Area failed once again to attain any concrete results, to the extent that it was 25-26 October 2012 before the subject became part of the Justice and Home Affairs Council's agenda, under the Cypriot Presidency of the Council of Ministers. Nevertheless, the two-step proposal was included in the text of the conclusions, rendering it a viable alternative.[17] In spite of the positive plead in favour of accession made by the chair and echoed by Home Affairs Commissioner Cecilia Malmström on various occasions, the situation remained uncertain and added to the frustration expressed by both the Romanian and the Bulgarian governments. To exemplify the aforementioned supportive attitude, it is interesting to take into account the following statement made by Cecilia Malmström at the European Parliament Socialists & Democrats' Conference on 'Upholding Freedom of Movement – An Improved Schengen Governance', held in Brussels earlier that year, on the 8th of February: "Today, the Schengen Area encompasses most of the EU's Member states and a number of 'associated' non-EU States, and I hope that the Council will soon decide that internal border controls with Bulgaria and Romania can finally be lifted".[18]

Once again, further pressure was exerted by the European Council, which, on 13-14 December 2012, uttered a reminder of the compliance of Romania and Bulgaria with the Schengen *acquis*, thus prompting the Council of Ministers to re-examine the case and place it on its decision-making agenda. In fact, the Justice and Home Affairs Council did formally include the item on its agenda in March 2013, if only to once again postpone any attempt at reaching consensus until its December meeting. During the course of the latter, amid clear signals that the same fate was about to unfold, the Romanian and Bulgarian governments opted to draft a joint declaration included in the official minutes of the December 5-6 meeting, urging the member states' governments to reach unanimity on the subject and acquiesce to the formal compliance with the criteria demanded for accession. Nevertheless, the same blunt and laconic formula was included in the Conclusions of the Council, namely: "The Council decided to address this issue again at its earliest convenience with a view to considering the way forward on the basis of a two-step approach".[19] During the course of 2014 and up to date, further support

17 Press release, 15389/12, 3195th Council meeting, Luxembourg, 25-26 October 2012, p. 12.

18 Cecilia Malmström, *The importance of safeguarding Schengen*, SPEECH/12/78, European Parliament S&D Conference on "Upholding Freedom of Movement - An Improved Schengen Governance", Brussels, 8 February 2012.

19 Press release, 17342/13, 3279th Council meeting, Brussels, 5-6 December 2013, p. 11.

for Romania's Schengen accession was uttered by both Parliament and Commission, with an intergovernmental decision still pending.

Political hurdles, international reactions and diplomatic endeavours

With the institutional approach summarised, and the fact of meeting and even exceeding standards rendered secondary by the political context, it becomes essential to analyse the peculiar attitudes and the procrastination that appear to characterise what was originally intended to be a clear-cut effort, so as to comprehend the reasons why a political decision within the community context relies to such a great extent on national will, to the evident detriment of the formal set of procedures reigning over the Schengen decision-making framework. This is all the more important as the provisions pertaining to the governance of the area have been updated and enhanced, some would say, in order to better comply with both the context of increased external migration to the EU and the need to tackle the fears of various member states with respect to the threats to the external borders of the Union. To elaborate, recent addenda to the Schengen *acquis* include a more accurate definition of short stays of non-EU citizens in the Schengen area, as of 2013, the Smart Borders initiative, the FRONTEX cooperation on external borders and the EUROSUR, or European Border Surveillance System information sharing and cooperation tool.[20] To this, one may add the provision that a state can reinstate temporary border controls by invoking public policy or national security concerns[21], although all of the above appears to be unconvincing in the light of the mounting Eurosceptical and anti-immigration attitudes that cannot be taken for granted when assessing the problematic dossier of Romania and Bulgaria's Schengen accession bid.

A particular risk that has manifested itself has been the temptation to turn the Schengen debate into a key bargaining chip, a mere instrument in the hands of populist political parties, used as leverage meant to help attain electoral goals, albeit with some arguments that should not be disregarded by the two governments directly involved, well aware of the fact that consensus cannot be imposed, but negotiated. In May 2011, the first clear signs that the Dutch government would oppose Romania's Schengen membership were given by European Affairs Minister Ben Knapen, tying the decision on the verdict delivered by the Mechanism for cooperation

---

20 Gropas, R. and Triandafyllidou, A., *European Immigration: a Sourcebook*, 2nd edition, Ashgate Publishing, Hampshire, 2014, p. 381.

21 Atger, A. F., *The Abolition of Internal Border Checks in an Enlarged Schengen Area: Freedom of movement or a scattered web of security checks?*, CEPS, 2008, pp. 15-16.

and verification on justice reform.[22] The echoes of such an attitude were encountered in the sceptical views of the Finnish government that took office in June 2011, in a country that witnessed a dramatic rise in popular support directed towards Euroscepticism, chiefly associated with the True Finns Party[23], which won no less than 19.1% of the votes in the 2011 elections.[24] Later that year, however, a more balanced stance adopted by Finnish European Affairs Minister Alexander Stubb favoured the two-step solution for Romania and Bulgaria's accession, beginning with airports and maritime borders and subsequently addressing the more complicated file of the land frontiers.[25] A similar proposal came from French interior minister Claude Guéant, also in June 2011[26], who envisaged the completion of the first step in the autumn of that year, followed one year later by the second, conditioned by the presence of customs officers from other member states.[27] This two-speed accession, though a historical first in the accession process, remains a likely prospect and may give the signal for defusing an imminent demotivation scenario. At the same time, nonetheless, Alexander Vanderee, the spokesperson of the interior ministry of the Netherlands, maintained the country's opposition and conditioned a revision of the latter on enhanced fight against organised crime, a matter pertaining primarily to Bulgaria, and corruption, in both countries' cases.[28]

Ill-timed reactions did not fail to appear from all parties involved, from harsh, albeit partly justified, criticism stemming from Romanian

---

22 See: Press Release *Visit Ben Knapen to Romania*, Embassy of the Netherlands in Bucharest, 12 May 2011, available at http://roemenie.nlambassade.org/nieuws/2011/05/press-release-visit-ben-knapen-to-romania.html (last accessed on 28/04/2015).

23 Interview for Novinite.com (Sofia News Agency), novinite.bg and the Trud daily with Maria Lehala, MP with Perussuomalaiset (True Finns), 9 December 2011, available at http://www.novinite.com/articles/134714/Finnish+Nationalistic+MP+Maria+Lohela%3A+Bulgaria+Isn't+Quite+Ready+for+Schengen (last accessed on 28/04/2015).

24 OSCE, Office for Democratic Institutions and Human Rights, Republic of Finland, Parliamentary Elections 17 April 2011, *Election Assessment Mission Report*, Warsaw, 21 July 2011, p. 23.

25 Pop, V., *Finland drops veto against Schengen enlargement*, EUObserver, 14 November 2011, available at https://euobserver.com/justice/114273 (last accessed on 28/04/2015).

26 In terms of bilateral politics, some frictions were occurring at the time between the Romanian and the French governments over the issue of Roma migration, albeit the former do not pertain de jure to the Schengen debate per se.

27 Ruscior, C., *România are vocația de a intra în Schengen*, Radio France Internationale Romania, 18 April 2011, available at http://www.rfi.ro/articol/stiri/politica/romania-are-vocatia-intra-schengen (last accessed on 28/04/2015).

28 *Olanda își menține opoziția față de aderarea României și Bulgariei la Schengen*, Euractiv, 16 November 2011, available at http://arhiva.euractiv.ro/uniunea-europeana/articles%7CdisplayArticle/articleID_23761/Olanda-isi-mentine-opozitia-fata-de-aderarea-Romaniei-si-Bulgariei-la-Schengen.html (last accessed on 28/04/2015).

Foreign Minister Teodor Baconschi and President Traian Băsescu, to peculiar trade disputes or boycott calls and, on the other side, from the Partij voor de Vrijheid (Party for Freedom) leader, Geert Wilders, and its overtly, widely-criticised anti-immigration website. The context rendered evident, in Romania's case, a sense of profound discomfort, along with a risk of demotivation that is inherent when such a project appears to fail albeit its indicators have not only been met, but actually exceeded.

Several dilemmas have emerged amid such tensions, whose effects are rather unpredictable and definitely worthy of a thorough assessment by all parties involved. One of these refers to the desire expressed by the Romanian government, to separate the evaluations provided by the Mechanism for Cooperation and Verification from the vote on the country's Schengen accession, which, albeit correct from a procedural standpoint, does little to add weight to the credibility of the anti-corruption commitments that Romania should stand firm on. Indeed, while the mechanism itself should bear little importance in assessing Schengen compliance, it has proven to exert a function of strengthening the rule of law, an incentive for justice performance, political restraint and media vigilance, all of which are to be desired in a developing democracy. The other dilemma implies separating the accession bid of Romania from that of Bulgaria, amid suspicions that the latter is holding back the former – an apparently risky endeavour, which may well turn into a successful attempt orchestrated by Eurosceptics and meant to antagonise two neighbouring countries otherwise working towards the same goal. Let it be said that the peril revolving around separating the two states in endeavours germane to EU-related goals is by no means a novelty, as discussions on this matter had emerged, to no avail, even amid the two countries' negotiations with Brussels on EU membership.

The current prospects still appear to be somewhat gloomy, given more recent reactions by French Foreign Minister Laurent Fabius, who expressed concern, following a United Nations General Assembly meeting in New York, on the 26th of September 2013, over border security in the event that Romania and Bulgaria were allowed to join the Schengen area. "People coming from outside Europe could enter Romania and Bulgaria and then freely enter the rest of Europe" – in the words of Fabius, amid tense relations with Romania owing to immigration-related disputes.[29] Recent endeavours by new Romanian President Klaus Johannis are meant to win the support of the French government, in the light of an improved diplomatic climate and with pertinent justification. In effect, the migration

[29] *France against Romania, Bulgaria joining Schengen zone*, Reuters, 30 September 2013, available at http://www.reuters.com/article/2013/09/30/us-france-roms-idUS BRE98T08120130930 (last accessed on 28/04/2015).

card is quite likely to have been overrated amid the Schengen objections, as in previous occasions, to the extent that Romania indeed does not constitute a main route for migrants, as the current context has clearly shown.

Another significant obstacle was raised by the stance of Germany with regard to the Schengen bid of the two countries, as Interior Minister Hans-Peter Friedrich explained in March 2013, citing concerns about anything from corruption to human trafficking and abusive immigration. The Christian Social Union politician stressed that "the right of free movement gives all people in Europe the opportunity to come to another country for work, for education, but it is not allowed to come only to Germany or Great Britain to get social security and added: that is the reason why we want to send people back, and this is what we have to regulate in our European law… There is no problem when people are coming to Germany for work, that is what we want in Europe, but we don't want people coming only to have social security".[30] Recent events on the Romanian political and judicial stage[31] have prompted a major shift in Germany's attitude, though, to the extent that in March 2015, Foreign Minister Frank-Walter Steinmeier praised the country's progress and ensured that Berlin would support its Schengen bid. In his own words:

> I know that Romania has made remarkable efforts in recent years. I know the latest Cooperation and Verification Mechanism, report highlights the progress made, especially in terms of strengthening the independence of the judiciary […]. We are willing to support the discussion process in an open way.[32]

This represents one of the prominent positions favouring Romania's efforts, in keeping with other benevolent attitudes that may prove to be helpful in reopening discussions within the Council, such as the one conveyed by Italy's ambassador to Romania, Diego Brasioli, or, more recently, by the Council Presidency holder, Latvia's ambassador to the country, Ilgvars Klava. The latter expressed his optimism with regard to an imminent decision in this regard and stated:

> We are working together on the security issues and on everything that means airports and the movement of some people who have criminal and terrorist intentions. Therefore we must work together on these security issues, but

[30] *Germany mulls Schengen veto on Bulgaria and Romania*, BBC, 4 March 2013, available at http://www.bbc.com/news/world-europe-21653092 (last accessed on 28/04/2015).

[31] Such events include the election of a new President, Klaus Johannis, as well as the numerous arrests and convictions in high-level corruption cases.

[32] *Romania's Schengen Bid Wins German FM's Support*, Balkan Insight, 10 March 2015, available at http://www.balkaninsight.com/en/article/germany-to-support-romania-s-access-to-schengen (last accessed on 28/04/2015).

they shouldn't be used as a pretext or as an excuse for not continuing the expansion of the Schengen area.[33]

His views were mirrored by Romanian Foreign Minister Bogdan Aurescu, who, in the light of his much more tactful approach to Schengen negotiations, added: "We believe that a Romania inside the Schengen area, de jure, not only *de facto*, represents nothing but an added value, especially in the current internal security context"[34] – a veiled but well-timed reference to the geopolitical role played by the country amid the stringent concerns over Russia's stance in the region.

In guise of conclusion

While it remains difficult to thoroughly assess all potential scenarios that may unfold in the very near future with regard to Romania's Schengen accession bid, several points need to be outlined in the light of such findings as the ones presented above.

Firstly, it is clear that the exclusively intergovernmental mechanisms persisting in EU decision-making in the post-Lisbon context remain severely reliant on the political stance and inevitable interests of governing parties throughout the Union and their occasional will to meet increasingly Eurosceptical demands. The political discourse attached to such attitudes often fails to take notice of realities and turns to hasty allegations, such as the evident overstatements around the migration routes that allegedly cross the Romanian territory.

Secondly, protracted discussions, repetitive formulas and apparently unjustified delays in the Schengen accession endeavour, irrespective of the support granted by such entities as the European Parliament and Commission, trigger an inevitable sense of demotivation and the clumsy political statements that come forthwith. However, recent evolutions on the Romanian political stage have yielded a more elaborate diplomatic approach, whose results have turned positive, prompting us to express some optimism as to the time frame of an accession process that Romania cannot afford to lose any degree of interest in.

Thirdly, the possibility of resorting to a precedent-setting two-step approach to Romania's Schengen membership is becoming a likely scenario and could deliver some degree of satisfaction, if one is to take

---

33 *Latvia's Ambassador, on Romania in Schengen: Decision reaching during Latvian Presidency, realistic possibility*, Agerpres, 21 January 2015, available at http://www.agerpres.ro/english/2015/01/21/latvia-s-ambassador-on-romania-in-schengen-decision-reaching-during-latvian-presidency-realistic-possibility-13-24-35 (last accessed on 28/04/2015).

34 *Ibid.*

into consideration the fact that, in terms of airport and sea security, the country has been exceeding the requirements for a few years now. Once set in motion, this will inevitably lead to full participation and the benefits comprised therein, including enhanced mobility, trade flows, visa uniformity and a justified sense of furtherance of the integration process in a country that maintains its commitment to it and does not resort to any form of political support directed towards Eurosceptical movements.

The Charter of Lampedusa

Organised civil society in the EU multi-level system of governance

Leila GIANNETTO

Abstract: Great opportunities for civil society organisations (CSOs) to participate in the everyday work of EU governance have been opened by the Treaty of Lisbon. However, not all civil society organisations are able to fulfil EU funding requirements or to gather enough resources to engage with EU institutions. This creates a division between professionalised CSOs that operate at the EU level and CSOs that operate mostly at the local level. Against such background this chapter aims to answer the following question: is the multi-level European Union creating a multi-level civil society? In order to answer to this question, the present study focuses on the recently born European movement *La Carta di Lampedusa*, advocating for migrant rights. Interviews, participant observation and document analysis are employed to analyse perceptions and preferences of the members of this movement with regard to EU level advocacy coalitions and the future of their "bottom-up" movement. A new cleavage of ideological nature is identified, indicating a rupture between CSOs working at local and EU levels.

Introduction

Great opportunities for civil society organisations (CSOs) have been opened by the Treaty of Lisbon to participate in the everyday work of EU governance. Article 11 TEU now states that, first of all, citizens and "representative associations" voices shall be heard by EU institutions in "all areas of Union action"; secondly, EU institutions shall be transparent and open in the dialogue with "representative associations and civil society"; and, finally, the European Commission "shall carry out broad consultations with parties concerned", when the EU is about to take action in any specific field. However, the need for more participation of civil society at the EU level had already been acknowledged in the 2001 Commission's White Paper on Governance[1], with the recognition of the

[1] See Armstrong, K. A., "Rediscovering civil society: the European Union and the White Paper on Governance", *European Law Journal*, Vol. 8, No. 1, 2002, pp. 102-132; see also Ruzza, C., *Europe and civil society. Movement coalitions and European*

development of new modes of governance such as the Open Method of Coordination. These new forms of governance aim at engaging civil society in the policy-making process – from the input side[2] –, but only within specific fields and with a purely consultative role. Other "entry points" for civil society into the practices of EU governance are the European funds; these have been allocated over time to civil society organisations that are active in the European Union, sparking a debate over the steering of civil society in times of shortages of private and national funding.[3]

However, not all civil society organisations are able to fulfil the EU requirements for funding or to gather enough financial, human and organisational resources (i.e., policy goods) to engage in a dialogue with EU institutions. Furthermore, Braun (2012) identifies in the ability to shape coalitions and to be well positioned within them another important requirement for CSOs to gain access to EU actors. This creates a division between CSOs that operate at the EU level and CSOs that operate mostly at the local level and are cut out from the system of funding and dialogue promoted by the EU. So, are we witnessing the creation of a multi-level civil society that is adapting to the EU multi-level governance structure?

In order to answer to this question, the present study focuses on the CSOs active in migration policies area and more specifically on the perceptions of the participants in a recent movement called *La Carta di Lampedusa* or the Charter of Lampedusa (hereinafter also 'the Charter'). This movement was established in response to the tragedies that took place at the Schengen borders in October 2013, when boats carrying hundreds of migrants capsized off the Lampedusa coasts (Italy). The participants were interviewed about their perceptions regarding advocacy coalitions working at the EU level and their preferences for the future of their bottom up movement. The chapter is structured in three sections: the first describes the role of civil society in the EU, providing a brief account of theoretical approaches and history; the second analyses in greater detail the challenges and opportunities opened by the Treaty of Lisbon for CSOs operating in the field of migration policies; the third and final

---

governance, Manchester and New York, Manchester University Press, 2004; and Heidbreder, E. G., "Civil society participation in EU governance", *Living Reviews in European Governance*, Vol. 7, No. 2, 2012.

2 See Smismans, S., *Civil Society and Legitimate European Governance*, Edward Elgar, Cheltenham, 2006.

3 See Mahoney, C., Beckstrand, M. J., "Following the Money: EU Funding of Civil Society", paper prepared for 11th bi-annual *European Union Studies Association* conference, Marina del Rey, CA, US, 23-25 April 2009; European Economic and Social Committee (EESC), *The Impact of the Crisis on Civil Society Organizations in the EU. Risks and Opportunities*, EESC/COMM/12/2012, Brussels, 2012.

section considers the case of *La Carta di Lampedusa* and its approach towards the dialogue with EU institutions and, more specifically, with CSOs operating at the EU level.

On the role of civil society in the EU governance system

In the last two decades, the study of civil society has seen a "revival"[4] in the European Union due to a number of factors: the crisis of representation, the rise of the executives, the difficulties in establishing a strong link between EU institutions and European citizens, and, finally, the growing perception of the Union's democratic deficit.[5] The concept of civil society in itself is difficult to define: the history of civil society dates back to the Greek and Latin culture.[6] The original concept of *koinonia politikè* (Aristotele), or *societas civilis* (Cicero) described by Perez-Diaz as the "classical" approach to civil society[7] was all-encompassing: the organisation of the lives of the freemen of the *polis*, in a unified society[8], was synthesised in this expression. By the Middle Ages the term become secularised, separating the religious sphere from the sphere of civil society.[9] However, while "the Aristotelian notion did not allow for our distinction between state and society"[10], in more recent times, following the contribution of Locke, Hegel, de Tocqueville and Weber, and again after the demise of totalitarianism, civil society has increasingly been defined by contraposition to the state, as a separate organising principle. Another distinction was made by Parsons, in the twentieth century, in order to better specify our idea of civil society: the latter shall be considered not only distinct from the state but also from the economic sphere.[11] Within this restricted definition, civil society appears as the sum

4 See Cohen, J. L., Arato, A., *Civil Society and Political Theory*, MIT Press, Cambridge, 1999.

5 See Warleigh, A., "Europeanizing civil society: NGOs as agents of Political Socialization", *Journal of Common Market Studies*, Vol. 39, No. 4, 2001, pp. 619-639; Ruzza, C., *op. cit.*; van Deth, J. W., "European Civil Society: The Empirical Reality in the Multi-Level System of the EU", in B. Kohler-Koch, D. De Bièvre, W. A. Maloney (eds.), *Opening EU-Governance to Civil Society – Gains and Challenges*, CONNEX, Mannheim, 2008, pp. 326-348; Piattoni, S., "Representation as delegation: a basis for EU democracy?", *Journal of European Public Policy*, Vol. 20, No. 2, 2013, pp. 224-242.

6 See Cohen, J. L., Arato, A., *op. cit.*

7 Perez-Diaz, V., "Civil Society: a multi-layared concept", *Sociopedia*, Vol. 21, No. 3, 2011, pp. 433-455.

8 See Armstrong, K. A., *op. cit.*

9 See van Deth, J. W., *op. cit.*

10 From Cohen, J. L., Arato, A., *op. cit.*, p. 84.

11 From Perez-Diaz, *op. cit.*, p. 6.

of all the voluntary associations[12] that are present in the public sphere, with a variety of ends: religious, political, cultural, environmental, etc.

The definition of civil society that is referred to in this chapter is inextricably linked to the specific focus of this research – i.e., the multi-level governance of the European Union – as given by Finke: "civil society is composed of voluntary groups, organizations and associations which articulate the variety of societal voices in the EU multi-level system".[13] The actors that form civil society according to this definition have always confronted the state on specific policy issues; however, with the delegation of competences from states to the European institutions, some of the normative claims that were previously addressed to the state level by advocacy groups, organisations and associations shifted to the European level and adapted to the new practices of policy-making.[14] This phenomenon has also been touched upon within the framework of the "governance turn in EU studies".[15]

Civil society groupings, in particular at the European Union level, have come to be addressed as stakeholders, or interest groups, representing more or less 'diffused interests'.[16] The European Commission has strongly supported the participation – mainly via consultation procedures – of CSOs in the policy-making process of the European Union exactly because of the interests that these organisations represent, in a system that, since the Maastricht Treaty, has been deemed to be in a 'democratic deficit'. In an era of representation crisis, civil society organizations have been described in the literature as a means of 'bringing the citizen back in', acting as the missing link between EU citizens and EU institutions.[17] In view of this, the Commission emphasised the positive role that CSOs might have on the overall democracy of the EU governance first of all by gradually introducing the concept of 'civil dialogue'[18], then through

12 Parsons defines an association as "a corporate body whose members are solidary with one another, in the sense of having a consensual relation to a common normative structure" in Cohen, J. L., Arato, A., *op. cit.*, p. 130.

13 From Finke, B., "Civil Society Participation in EU governance", *Living Reviews in European Governance*, Vol. 2, 2007, p. 21.

14 See Ruzza, C., *op. cit.*

15 See Kohler-Koch, B. and Rittberger, B., "Review article: the 'Governance turn' in EU studies", *Journal of Common Market Studies*, Vol. 44, 2006, pp. 27-49.

16 See Olson, M., *The Logic of Collective Action: Public Goods and the Theory of Groups*, Harvard University Press, Cambridge, 1965.

17 See Warleigh, A., *op. cit.*, p. 620; and Mascia, M., *La Società Civile nell'Unione Europea*, Marsilio Editori, Venezia, 2004.

18 See Smismans, S., "European Civil Society: Shaped by Discourses and Institutional Interests", *European Law Journal*, Vol. 9, No. 4, 2003, pp. 482-504.

the words of Romano Prodi in 2000[19] and finally through the White Paper on Governance of 2001. The latter, in particular, highlighted the positive effects of the engagement of EU institutions with civil society – i.e., closing the gap between European citizens and EU governance or between "society and transnational governance"[20] – and established the provision for more institutionalised processes of consultation (e.g., Open Method of Coordination).

Associations, that "range from narrow specific to broader encompassing interests and from advocacy groups to member based umbrella organisations"[21], have taken different forms: non-governmental organisations (NGOs), advocacy groups, social movements, epistemic communities, trade unions, employers' organisations; consumers' and entrepreneurs' associations, but also research institutes and universities. However, the study carried out by Kohler-Koch and Quittkat[22] has evidenced that in the EU arena, practitioners and officers widely consider general interest groups[23], and to some extent trade unions, to be part of civil society, while business interest associations and professional organisations are less easily associated with such definition. Their study evidences once more how difficult it is to define univocally civil society, but concludes that the latter is considered by the vast majority of the interviewees – chosen by Kohler-Koch and Quittkat among the research community – as a very weak political actor, but a social actor that is "institutionalised or in the process of being institutionalised"[24], and which is active in the life-world.

Since the "revival" of civil society, the literature has been concerned with two main functions of civil society: first of all, improving the legitimacy of the EU representation system by focusing on an enhanced participatory democracy (input-oriented approach), thus possibly helping overcome the 'no demos-no democracy' thesis[25], and

---

19 As reported by van Deth, according to Commissioner Romano Prodi: "EU decision-making processes 'called for a civic participation in all stages of the policymaking process'", in van Deth, J. W., *op. cit.*, p. 327.

20 From Armstrong, K. A., *op. cit.*, p. 114.

21 See Kohler-Koch, B., Quittkat, C., "What is civil society and who represents civil society in the EU. Results of an online survey among civil society experts", *Policy and Society*, Vol. 28, No. 1, 2009, pp. 11-22; quote from p. 12.

22 *Ibid.*

23 General interest is defined as an interest "in the pursuit of a public good (such as social stability, environmental sustainability) or a universal value (such as human rights)" in Kohler-Koch, B. and Quittkat, C., *op. cit.*, p. 13.

24 From Kohler-Koch, B. and Quittkat, C., *op. cit.*, p. 15.

25 See Smismans, S., *op. cit.* in footnote 18; Fung, A., "Associations and Democracy: between theories, hopes and realities", *Annual Review of Sociology*, Vol. 29, 2003,

secondly, contributing to "effective governance and problem-solving" (output-oriented approach).[26] Before the Commission's White Paper on Governance was delivered, the European Economic and Social Committee highlighted the prominent role that civil society organisations have in the EU: not only promoting participation and efficiency, but also providing a space of learning, "public awareness" raising and education[27], thereby becoming "schools of democracy".[28]

Moreover, lines of funding were established at the EU level in order to foster CSOs in their role of service providers and policy implementers: the first and most significant of them, which was created with the Treaty of Rome, is the 'European Social Fund'. Policy implementation by CSOs is a field of study for the so called Third Sector approach. In a system highly dependent on subsidiarity, in which welfare policies' implementation is increasingly privatised[29] and has to be adapted to the specific features of every member state, EU level CSOs create trans-boundary networks and engage in competitions to accede to EU funding, thus following the policy guidelines established by the European Council every 7 years. It must be noted that this process has been criticised in the literature for allegedly creating a system whose intention is "to shun 'uncivil society' in favour of harnessing 'civil' society towards the (unchallengeable) objectives of the Union".[30]

The present study focuses on the sociological definition of a 'European civil society' as it has evolved to confront a multi-level EU system of governance. Armstrong in 2002 has defined the European civil society as formed by "multiform, multidimensional and multi-level actors". The analysis in this chapter focuses on whether the various levels of governance – i.e., the European, the national and at the local levels – have shaped a multi-layered system of organised civil society, among which tensions might arise particularly in times of crisis. In order to tackle this issue, the organisation of civil society in the field of migration policies in the EU is studied in the next section.

pp. 515-539; Saward, M., *The Representative Claim*, Oxford University Press, Oxford and New York, 2010.

26 See Warren, M. E., *Democracy and Association*, Princeton University Press, Princeton, 2001; Finke, B. *op. cit.*; Heidbreder, E. G., *op. cit.*

27 See European Economic and Social Committee (EESC), *The Civil Society organised at European Level*, proceedings of the First Convention on the Civil Society organised at European Level, EESC, Brussels, 1999; Warleigh, A., *op. cit.*

28 From van Deth, J. W., *op. cit.*, p. 335.

29 See Finke, B., *op. cit.*

30 From Armstrong, K. A., *op. cit.*, p. 129.

Civil society and migration policies in the EU

Migration policies in the EU system of governance are fully-fledged multi-level: they are indeed shaped by EU institutions (EU level), whose competences are included in the Treaty on the Functioning of the EU (Title V) establishing and regulating the Area of Freedom Security and Justice (AFSJ); they are also shaped by member states' governments (national level), that both implement EU Regulations, Directives and Guidelines, and provide for the policy-making of the non-communitarised competences (e.g., part of the policy on borders management); they are, finally, shaped by local authorities (local level) that implement both national and European measures. As a consequence, the field of migration policies encompasses a wide range of social actors, operating at different territorial levels and with different functions.

The Stockholm multi-annual Framework Programme, which has been operating from 2009 until the end of 2014, has a specific provision for the role of civil society within the AFSJ. Paragraph 1.2.8 of the Stockholm Programme establishes that EU institutions should "hold an open, transparent and regular dialogue with representative associations and civil society" and the Commission should define mechanisms to make this dialogue effective and useful. For the post-2014 era, Art. 68 of the Lisbon Treaty provides that the European Council is responsible for setting the strategic guidelines for the Justice and Home Affairs field: on 26-27 June 2014, the European Council met in Brussels and delivered these strategic guidelines; in the guidelines, no mention is made of the role of civil society in this field.[31]

In the migration field, the functions of civil society organisations can be generalised as follows: service provision, advocacy, policy formulation, implementation and monitoring.[32] Each of these CSOs functions appeal to different levels of governance and require different skills, knowledge and resources. Moreover, depending on the functions undertaken, CSOs might need to create trans-boundary (or transnational) networks. Table 1, drawn mainly from Banulescu-Bogdan's 2011study, combines CSOs functions with their level of action, thus describing how CSOs interact within the governance system of migration issues in the EU.

---

[31] See European Council, *Conclusions*, EUCO 79/14, 27 June 2014, available at http://www.consilium.europa.eu/uedocs/cms_data/docs/pressdata/en/ec/143478.pdf (last accessed on 12/04/2015).

[32] See Banulescu-Bogdan, N., *The Role of Civil Society in EU Migration Policy: Perspectives on the European Union's Engagement in its Neighborhood*, Migration Policy Institute, Washington DC, 2011; and Thiel, M., Uçarer, E. M., "Access and Agenda-Setting in the European Union: Advocacy NGOs in Comparative Perspective", *Interest Groups and Advocacy*, Vol. 3, 2014, pp. 99-116.

Table 1. Typology of Civil Society Organisations working in the migration policy field

Function	Description	Level of action
Service provision	Groups that provide operational assistance to migrants (e.g., basic needs, legal services, integration aid)	Local level
Advocacy	Groups that advocate for specific migration-related issues and principles	EU and transnational levels[33]
Policy formulation	Groups invited to participate in negotiations during the official stages of policy-making	EU level
Implementation and Monitoring	Groups that are subcontracted to supplement or evaluate government policies	EU, transnational and local levels

Source: author's own elaboration, adapted from Banulescu-Bogdan[34], with reference to Thouez.[35]

According to Thouez[36], it is precisely this fragmentation – due to both the different functions that are performed and the different levels of governance that are involved – that makes CSOs less effective in this field with respect to others, such as environmental and human rights protection[37], especially when using their resources to shape policies through advocacy and dialogue. However, human rights protection and promotion has become one of the numerous aspects addressed by CSOs working in the field of migration. Service provision was considered to be

---

33 As Ruzza evidences "While it would be tempting to identify the centre [of advocacy coalitions' networked structure] with EU-level social movement organisation, this is not necessarily the case. Coalitions incorporate people based both in Brussels and other EU institutional centres, and people based in member states", from Ruzza, C., *op. cit.*, p. 35. In Table 1 the centre of the network is taken into consideration, which is where the main function of the CSO is performed in the case of advocacy CSOs having a networked structure. The *transnational level* of action differs from the EU level: organisations and associations working across the borders of the Member states of the Union – defined as "umbrella groups" in Banulescu-Bogdan – do not necessarily interact with the *EU level* (even though they may apply for EU funding), but create "a stronger collective voice and a broader global reach", from Banulescu-Bogdan, N., *op. cit.*, p. 4.

34 Banulescu-Bogdan, N., *op. cit.*, p. 4.

35 Thouez, C., "The role of civil society in the migration policy debate", *Global Migration Perspectives*, Vol. 12, October 2004.

36 See Thouez, C., *op. cit.*

37 See Ruzza, C., *op. cit.*, and Ruzza, C., "Civil Society Actors and EU Fundamental Rights Policy: Opportunities and Challenges", *Human Rights Review*, Vol. 15, 2014, pp. 65-81.

the core function of civil society dealing with migration related policies and it was performed mainly by religious associations[38]; nowadays, advocacy groups addressing human rights issues are rising in number thanks to the increase both in opportunities to enter the process of policy-making – opened by the EU and discussed in the previous section – and in the volume of migration flows. The case study presented in the following section concerns an organisation that belongs precisely to the group of advocacy CSOs promoting migrants' rights, while also being an umbrella organisation[39] for small and local associations scattered on the territory of the EU (transnational).

Ruzza evidences that there are some advocacy coalitions (movement-inspired) that remain strongly linked to the movements that originated them and others that, while becoming more institutionalised, lose grip on their base.[40] This chapter aims at taking a step further and analyses the decision of a new movement of whether to engage with the professionalised advocacy coalitions working at the EU level to promote their stances at the EU level, particularly in the human rights field. In view of this, the case study presented in the next section focuses on the attitudes of the participants to a new movement – i.e., the Charter of Lampedusa – towards the resourceful CSOs advocating for human rights at the EU level.

The case study: *La Carta di Lampedusa*

3 October 2013 has become a notorious date in the minds of human rights activists, while at the same time bringing to the limelight a significant disregard for migrants' human rights at the borders of the Schengen Area.[41] The Lampedusa disaster[42], in which hundreds of people lost their lives[43], has led to the creation of an advocacy movement aimed at writing and supporting a new charter of rights, named *La Carta di*

38 See Thouez, C., *op. cit.*

39 See Banulescu-Bogdan, N., *op. cit.*

40 See Ruzza, C., *op. cit.*

41 Amnesty International, *The Human Cost of Fortress Europe. Human Rights Violations against Migrants and Refugees at Europe's borders*, Amnesty International Ltd., London, 2014, available at http://www.amnesty.org/en/library/info/EUR05/001/2014/en (last accessed on 09/07/2014).

42 For a description of the tragic event see http://www.bbc.com/news/world-europe-24380247 (last accessed on 25/11/2013).

43 This shipwreck has been tragically exceeded in numbers on 18 April 2015, when an estimated 700 people died in the strip of sea that lies between Libya and Italy. For an overview of the facts of the night between 18 and 19 April 2015: http://www.economist.com/news/europe/21648896-another-boat-capsizes-between-libya-and-italy-europe-debates-migration-policy-worst-drowning-yet?fsrc=nlw|newe|20-04-2015|; http://www.bbc.com/

Lampedusa, or *the Lampedusa Charter*, which was signed on the Italian isle in 2014.[44]

The increasing migration flows and the changing perception of migration in the EU marked the creation and evolution of a common policy for the management of the external borders of the Union, explicitly targeted at stopping irregular migration from the outset.[45] The goals and policy instruments for the management of migration flows have been condensed in pluriannual framework programmes since 1999. The latest is the Stockholm Programme (2009-2014), which has been replaced at the end of 2014 by the guidelines discussed in the last summer meeting of the European Council (26-27 June 2014) and mentioned in the previous section. The focus of the new program is specifically on "tackling irregular migration resolutely", along with "optimising the benefits of legal migration and offering protection to those in need" and "managing the EU's external borders efficiently".[46]

Before and after the Lampedusa disaster of 2013, thousands of migrants have been reported to die while trying to reach the shores of the EU[47]; UN Special Rapporteur for Human Rights, François Crépeau, in July 2013 said: "I regret that within the EU policy context, irregular migration remains largely viewed as a security concern that must be stopped. This is fundamentally at odds with a human rights approach, concerning the conceptualization of migrants as individuals and equal holders of human rights".[48] The Charter of Lampedusa was born in response to this framework and in light of the perceived failure of EU (top-down) border control policies.[49]

---

news/world-europe-32371348; http://america.aljazeera.com/articles/2015/4/19/up-to-700-feared-dead-after-migrant-boat-sinks-off-libya.html (last accessed on 27/04/2015).

44 Full text available at http://www.lacartadilampedusa.org/printer_version.html (last accessed on 20/04/2015).

45 See Huysmans, J., "The European Union and the Securitization of Migration", *Journal of Common Market Studies*, Vol. 38, 2000, pp. 751-777.

46 See footnote 31.

47 See International Organisation for Migration, *Fatal Journeys. Tracking lives lost during migration*, International Organization for Migration, Geneva, 2014, available at http://publications.iom.int/bookstore/free/FatalJourneys_CountingtheUncounted.pdf (last accessed on 15/04/2015).

48 United Nations Human Rights, "EU border management: protecting the rights of migrants", 22 July 2013, available at http://www.ohchr.org/EN/NewsEvents/Pages/ProtectingRightsOfMigrants.aspx (last accessed on 11/10/2013).

49 Allegretti, P., Armento, M., "La Carta di Lampedusa: Utopia o Nuovo Corso?", paper presented at the conference *Transiti, barriere, libertà: cercare rifugio nel Mediterraneo e in Europa*, ESCAPES, University of Milan, 10-11 April 2014.

The Charter of Lampedusa is the synthesis of months of networked remote work by local associations, migrants and individuals advocating for migrants rights.[50] The Charter, indeed, has been envisaged and discussed tentatively during two web conferences[51], and then written and commented on-line through a 'DokuWiki', an open source technology powered by Wikipedia. Therefore, it constitutes an explicit attempt at using web resources to collectively write a grassroots source of law.[52] The final meeting in Lampedusa, which took place between 31 January and 2 February 2014, was attended by more than seventy associations[53], all of which signed the Charter.

In the preamble, the Charter is defined as a "constituent grassroots process"; the preamble also states that "[a]ll the groups and individuals who undersign the Charter of Lampedusa commit to putting it into practice...whether or not the Charter obtains recognition by current state and/or supra-state institutions",[54] thus stressing the remoteness of the signatories from the European top-down approach to migration. Moreover, one of the catchphrases of the participants to the Charter is: "Costruiamo l'Europa dal basso!"[55] In order to analyse the meaning of this slogan and the attitude of the participants of the Charter of Lampedusa towards CSOs working mainly at the EU level, a questionnaire with open-ended questions was distributed to the national mailing list of the Charter, videos and documents were analysed, and two meetings of

50 A complete list of the signatories is available at http://www.lacartadilampedusa.org/adesioni_eng.html (last accessed on 13/06/2014).

51 Meltingpot Europa, the association that first conceived the idea of a new Charter of migrant rights, organized the first web conference on 29 November 2013 and the second on 15 January 2014. The two web conferences were attended by civil society organisations spread in 70 different cities around Europe and North Africa.

52 Meltingpot Europa, "La prima assemblea per la Carta di Lampedusa", 1 December 2013, available at http://www.meltingpot.org/La-prima-assemblea-per-la-Carta-di-Lampedusa.html#.U75czPl_srU (last accessed on 20/01/2015).

53 Meltingpot Europa, "Lampedusa Charter, a new pact for a new European citizenship. The Lampedusa Charter calls for transnational action", 9 February 2014, available at http://www.meltingpot.org/Lampedusa-Charter-a-new-pact-for-a-new-European-citizenship.html#.U8uTp_l_srU (last accessed on 09/02/2015).

54 The text of the Charter is available at http://www.lacartadilampedusa.org/The%20Charter%20of%20Lampedusa_EN.pdf (last accessed on 21/06/2014).

55 Translation: "Let's build Europe from the bottom up!" (Nicola Grigion during the protest "Noborderstrain", 20/21 June 2014, symbolically held on the World Refugee Day); see also GlobalProject, "#NoBordersTrain: la nostra Europa non ha confine", 2014, available at http://www.globalproject.info/it/in_movimento/noborderstrain-la-nostra-europa-non-ha-confine/17397 (last accessed on 21/06/2014).

Trento-based associations adhering to the Charter[56] were attended by the author as a participant observer.

The Charter of Lampedusa is not clearly defined in terms of how many organisations are involved in its support, nor in how many people take part to the movement. The widespread perception is that the Charter has a rather undefined size, ranging from 10 to more than 100 organisations participating and from less than 50 to 1000 people actively involved. The first promotional meeting in Trento was attended by a number of 50 to 100 people, while the second, aimed at planning actions following the signature of the Charter, saw a significantly smaller turnout, with less than 50 people attending. The signatories to the Charter are generally small associations active at the local level, providing services for refugees, asylum seekers and migrants, and include also a number of *centri sociali*[57] and scholars and citizens that are sensitive to migrants, refugees and asylum seekers' conditions in the EU. The Charter of Lampedusa is spearheaded by the Italian-based association 'Melting Pot Europa', whose website describes the Charter as "the result of discussions and debates participated by 250 hundred people, coming from collectives, associations, self-managed and occupied social spaces, movements, from Italy but also from Hamburg, Berlin, Belgium, Portugal, Turkey, Austria, Switzerland and Tunisia".[58]

The participants to the Charter of Lampedusa, partly interviewed face-to-face and partly surveyed on line, share a strong belief that the Charter needs to be developed, promoted and delivered as a grass-roots project. NGOs and, more generally, resourceful CSOs working at EU level are not perceived as part of the process of creation and promotion of the charter neither through their capability to lobby the EU nor through their possibility to work in close collaboration with EU institutions. This is evidenced not only by questionnaire answers and the participant observation to the two meetings of the Charter of Lampedusa held in Trento, but also by the videos of the proceedings of the signature of the Charter and the articles produced before and after.[59] Answering the question: "Would you like the Charter of Lampedusa to remain a grass-roots' movement/project?", one of the respondents effectively summarized the opinion given by the majority of the participants:

---

[56] The two meetings were held in Trento (Sala Circoscrizionale S. Giuseppe/S. Chiara, via Giusti 35, Trento) on 22 January and 19 February 2014, before and after the signature of the Charter of Lampedusa.

[57] The verbatim English translation of the term is "social centres". For a description of this mainly Italian reality see: Mudu, P., "Resisting and Challenging Neoliberalism: The Development of Italian Social Centers", *Antipode*, Vol. 36, 2004, pp. 917-941.

[58] See footnote 52.

[59] All the material produced is available at http://www.globalproject.info/it/tags/carta-di-lampedusa/community/3 (last accessed on 21/06/2014).

"Obviously yes. The Charter is a document that states a somewhat shared view about migration related issues, and its power is mainly based on the fact that it was written with a participative and fairly horizontal approach. It makes sense if it continues to be a tool to activate as many people as possible, stimulating their self-organization and their awareness". Another respondent to the questionnaire answered more conciliatorily to the same question, arguing that the Charter was born as a grass-roots project but its evolution is impossible to forecast and there is hope that it might become an official source of law one day.

The questionnaire evidenced two other interesting issues related to the perception of CSOs operating at the EU level. First of all, concerning the future of the Charter, the respondents unanimously indicated that there is the need to enlarge the network of local associations all over Europe to promote the actions and message of the movement at the European level while at the same time neglecting the possibility to involve resourceful CSOs or exploit the possibilities provided by EU funds. Secondly, a question on the perceived advantages or disadvantages connected to the cooperation with CSOs working at the EU level has shed light on the general suspicion towards these entities. The reasoning behind this suspicion is that EU level CSOs are feared to exploit migrants' woes for economic purposes, to be unable to endorse radical demonstrations and messages due to their position, and to be influenced by their source of funding (i.e., EU institutions).

The data collected show that the Charter of Lampedusa was conceived form the very beginning as a grass-roots transnational movement, antagonising the EU approach to border management. The Preamble of the Charter reads: "The Charter of Lampedusa is a pact achieved mainly through a constituent grassroots process". Further on, the Preamble also reflects the movement's disillusion towards top-down EU policies of border control, and therefore the necessity for a new approach: "All the groups and individuals who undersign the Charter of Lampedusa commit to putting it into practice…whether or not the Charter obtains recognition by current state and/or supra-state institutions". The willingness of this transnational movement of local CSOs to advocate for migrant rights by implementing a new Charter of rights, independently from EU acceptance, highlights an ideological position that is irreconcilable with advocacy at the EU level.

Concluding remarks

The European elections of 25 May 2014 have uncovered the strength of European citizens' disaffection towards the European Union. Eurosceptic parties had "spectacular gains"[60] in every member state of the Union and their slogans urged the EU to take action and set an agenda to review its policies. This chapter has investigated if a similar disaffection towards the EU is echoed also at the level of civil society: is there a cleavage between civil society organisations lobbying at the EU level and (networked) civil society organisations that operate mostly at the local level?

Even though the single case study presented does not permit clearly generalizable conclusions, this study has evidenced the ideological distance perceived by the participants to the movement *La Carta di Lampedusa* from the CSOs that cooperate with EU institutions. Such distance and suspicion can be interpreted as signs of a segmentation of CSOs in Europe, and therefore of the creation of a multi-level civil society. Moreover, the ideological divide between local and EU level CSOs could be interpreted as an additional criteria guiding CSOs' selection of their level of activity, adding to the other two that were described in this chapter: the different functions that CSOs perform, and the different resources, or public goods, that CSOs manage to mobilise. It remains open for future research to investigate whether the ideological cleavage identified in this work is a way for local level CSOs – with few resources and transnationally organised – to express "sour grapes" towards EU level CSOs and institutions, originating precisely from their lack of access.

[60] For an overview on the European Parliament elections of 2014, see http://www.bbc.com/news/events/vote2014 (last accessed on 29/05/2014).

Part II

Mobility and Border Management

Schengen and the security obsession

Selective citizenship, exclusion and the ironies of control

Octávio SACRAMENTO

Abstract: This text debates the functioning of the Schengen area as a paradox that is ultimately discriminatory. The agreement is based on the idea of the free circulation of certain categories of people, while at the same time pointedly rejecting a wide range of mobilities that are deemed undesirable. Thus two images clash: on the one hand, a world (or at least a subcontinent) of flows; on the other, the reality of human mobility that while global, is highly contingent and restricted. Put another way, the very same borders that have been opened to certain qualities of people and economic interests, at the same time have been closed to many poor and ethnic minorities, both of whom are more or less implicitly presented as constituting a threat to European security. The main goal of my reflection is to try to understand the Schengen area as a site of selective citizenship, where multiple forms of social exclusion are practiced and where the security mechanisms for the management and the control of transits generate effects that, paradoxically, tend to intensify the problems that the authorities wish to combat.

Introduction

It is often said that a more globalized and flexible world is in course, full of mobility and connections. The permeability of borders, transnationalisms, and the fluidity of contemporary social life are all emphasized while, on the other hand, we tend not to pay due attention to the political economy of the global circulation of people. If the notion of cross-border freedom of movement serves to encapsulate a privilege enjoyed by some people (e.g. economic and intellectual elites) and certain things (e.g. capital), it is important not to forget that for many persons life revolves much more around immobility than mobility. The Schengen area is a paradigmatic example of the paradoxical coexistence of unrestricted mobility and the denial of that same freedom. At one and the same time it is the expression of a borderless Europe and a fortress Europe: it is based on the easing of restrictions on the internal borders of member states and on the fortification of their external perimeter; it is predicated upon (and sometimes even promotes, as in the case of the Portuguese golden visa programme) the mobility of certain citizens and, at the same time, wages a war without quarter against a wide range of others, who are seen as unwanted visitors.

By reflecting on the ambiguity of Schengen, the present text aims to address, from a critical standpoint, the increasingly frequent image of an overflowing world, and its concrete reflection as evidenced by the hardening of border restrictions against migrant flows emanating from certain geographical origins, typically comprising the poor and/or belonging to ethnic groups currently or habitually considered a threat to European stability. The main objective of this analysis is to reflect on Schengen as a space that is characterized by its selective citizenship and exclusion, its obsession with security and its extensive transit control mechanisms that, together, produce multiple perverse, contradictory and ironical collateral effects. The analysis is not entirely theoretical. It is empirically inspired and, partially, based on three experiences of ethnographic research relating to themes that intersect with the functioning of the Schengen area and demonstrate many of its pernicious consequences: the detention of *illegal* immigrants in Portugal, cross-border prostitution in the Iberian context, and romantically-inspired transatlantic mobility between Europe and Brazil.[1] Furthermore, my reflection develops and updates discussions started on previous texts[2] and questions border controls in an era of global mobility in a wider European context.

Securitism and selectivity

With the birth of Schengen Agreement in 1985, and its incorporation in the European Union (EU) law via the 1997 Amsterdam Treaty, a so-called "Area of Freedom, Security and Justice" was established covering a number of European states. As a result of the subsequent admission of new EU members, the area today constitutes an extensive geographical

---

1 The first was supported by Portugal's Borders and Immigration Service (SEF), the second by the Portuguese Foundation for Science and Technology (FCT), and the third was my PhD project, supported by the FCT (SFRH/BD/60862/2009). The preparation of this text, in turn, benefited from the support from the CETRAD, a research centre at UTAD evaluated and financed by the FCT (UID/SOC/04011/2013). Besides these institutions, I want to thank the contributions of Chris Gerry and Filomena Morais in the translation of the text into English.

2 Sacramento, O., Ribeiro, M., "Vidas Embargadas: A Institucionalização Temporária de Estrangeiros *Ilegais* em Portugal no Contexto das Actuais Políticas de Imigração", in P. Silva, O. Sacramento and J. Portela (eds.), *Etnografia e Intervenção Social: Por Uma Praxis Reflexiva*, Colibri, Lisbon, 2011, pp. 141-172; Sacramento, O., Ribeiro, F. B., "Procurando Entrar na Fortaleza da Terra Prometida: Translocalização da Intimidade e Mobilidade Migratória Feminina do Nordeste Brasileiro Para a Europa", *Proceedings of the X Congresso Luso-Afro-Brasileiro de Ciências Sociais*, University of Minho, Braga, 2009, pp. 1209-1217.

bloc of 26 European countries (*Schengenland*)[3] between which systematic control of internal borders has been abolished (*de-bordering*). In contrast, with the aim of reinforcing common safety, an integrated strategy of intensive surveillance of external borders has been developed, imposing increasingly restrictive migratory policies and introducing ever-more sophisticated mechanisms of detection and extradition of those immigrants considered illegal (*re-bordering*). In this process we can detect profound changes on the (de)territorialisation and management of the borders. With the constant aim of strengthening and optimizing the flexibility and coverage of EU surveillance of its external perimeter, several policies and mechanisms have been developed to control foreign citizens at the limits and inside the Schengen area, as well as to dissuade potential immigrants in their main countries of origin and the principal points of migratory transit.[4] The capacity of select, screen, control and, if necessary, penalize citizens of third countries wishing to avail themselves of Schengen's area of free circulation is increasingly strong. The principal protagonists in this process have been the European Agency for the Management of Operational Cooperation at the External Borders of the Member states of the EU (Frontex) and an interactive network of administrative structures and their respective data-bases, in which four registration and monitoring systems should be emphasized: the Schengen Information System (SIS II), the fingerprinting system known as European Dactyloscopy (Eurodac), the Visa Information System (VIS) and the European Border Surveillance System (Eurosur). In addition to these systems, the establishment of an all-embracing research and risk assessment agency (ECIPS-European Centre for Information Policy & Security) has extended cyber-borders in an almost metaphysical way both within and outside the European area, making control virtually omnipresent.

The vertiginous rise of Schengen's securitism received a further boost after the 9/11 attacks, the political repositioning, and the spiral of social panic around terrorism that, since then, has taken shape. The terrorist risk, often exploited in an exaggerated manner, provided (and still provides) the fundamental argument and justification for policies supposedly aimed at making Europe safer for its citizens. Beneath the policy generalities,

---

3 For a more detailed assessment of the history of Schengen and its institutions, principles, functioning and impact see, among others, Bacas, J., Kavanagh, W. (eds.), *Border Encounters: Asymmetry and Proximity at Europe's Frontiers*, Berghahn Books, Oxford, 2013; and Zaiotti, R., *Cultures of Border Control: Schengen and the Evolution of European Frontiers*, University of Chicago Press, Chicago, 2011.

4 Broeders, D., "The New Digital Borders of Europe: EU Databases and the Surveillance of Irregular Migrants", *International Sociology*, Vol. 22, No. 1, 2007, pp. 71-92; Lechevalier, A., Wielgohs, J. (eds.), *Borders and Border Regions in Europe: Changes, Challenges and Chances*, Transcript Verlag, Bielefeld, 2013.

there lurk social representations of a truly fantastical nature, in which poor immigrants from the South assume the role of "folk devils" that pose a constant and deadly threat to European security.[5] The war against terrorism is thereby linked to the promotion of internal security and to the repression of immigration: "'irregular immigration' is being subsumed into a European legal setting that treats it as a crime and a risk against which administrative practices of surveillance, detention, control and penalisation are necessary and legitimized".[6] The criminalization of the immigrants and the imposition of a new geography of security onto the European map can be readily seen in public discourse and practices on migration, in which a logic of defence and combat reigns, as well as in the exaggerated use of detention and subsequent extradition of immigrants whose situation contravenes EU regulations.[7]

In this framework of hyper-surveillance of borders and flows, the Schengen area operates in a particularly selective way, being more welcoming or more restrictive depending on whether it is people or capital that is in transit, on the direction in which migrants move (e.g. South to North, East to West), on the time dimension of mobility (e.g. temporary or permanent), on their gender and/or on their social or symbolic profile. Its borders are not the same for everyone, nor are they experienced by everyone equally. Clearly, a tourist or a businessman entering Schengen, particularly if coming from a geopolitically high-ranking country, will not encounter the same problems nor feel the same terror as an unskilled female migrant arriving from somewhere on the world periphery. Generally, borders respond differently to the distinct "mobility regimes"[8] that, for example, tourists and migrants represent: since tourist mobility is desirable, borders fade from view, while migratory movements (especially from the South) tend to be seen as a potential threat, and therefore borders reimpose themselves deploying the detailed scrutiny and rigorous constraints designed to block the establishment of undesirable "ethnoscapes".

[5] Saux, M. S., "Immigration and Terrorism: A Constructed Connection", *European Journal on Criminal Policy and Research*, Vol. 13, No. 1-2, 2007, pp. 57-72.

[6] Guild, E., Carrera, S., Balzacq, T., "The Changing Dynamics of Security in an Enlarged European Union", *CEPS Research Paper*, No. 12, CEPS, Brussels, 2008, p. 2.

[7] Giorgi, A., "Immigration Control, Post-Fordism, and Less Eligibility: A Materialist Critique of the Criminalization of Immigration Across Europe", *Punishment & Society*, Vol. 12, No. 2, 2010, pp. 147-167; Ribeiro, M., Baptista, A., Ribeiro, F. B., Sacramento, O., *UHSA: A Experiência Portuguesa da Instalação Temporária de Imigrantes*, SEF, Lisbon, 2007.

[8] Schiller, N., Salazar, N., "Regimes of Mobility Across the Globe", *Journal of Ethnic and Migration Studies*, Vol. 39, No. 2, 2013, pp. 183-200.

In contrast to the almost impenetrable barrier they pose to poor citizens or to those whose ethnic origins are seen as connoting some type of security threat, borders evaporate for citizens from more privileged nationalities or classes, and for economic interests that – paradoxically – in many cases constitute a more real and present threat to national sovereignty.[9] The border's selective permeability – just like a membrane that identifies, classifies, filters and allows in only whom and what it wants – also expresses the profound material and symbolic asymmetries that have hierarchized at a supranational level virtually all forms of mobility, relations and citizenships.[10] I was able to witness such global hierarchies in the ethnographic fieldwork I conducted on international mobility and the configuration of intimacy between European men and Brazilian women.[11] European men who spend their holidays in Brazil find the country welcoming – its door wide open – mainly due to their specific consumption patterns and accompanying purchasing power. In stark contrast, when seeking entry into Europe, any Brazilian women with whom a tourist may have developed a durable relationship, is faced with a fortress Europe that only at great cost will allow them in, even though it needs them as cheap multifunctional labour. The fear and the dissuasion that Schengen inspires are eloquently expressed in the following excerpt of an interview I conducted in Natal, Rio Grande do Norte, in the Brazilian Northeast:

> I made it into Portugal. I was scared to death, because people talk about Portugal… they say that it's the border… that is the border to everything. The border for entering all those countries. So, if you can't get safely into Portugal, it's no good. So, for me it was like this: I made it into Portugal, I made it past the police there, and I was very well treated, thank God. I was so scared that I prayed a lot, because it was my first time. Oh my God, I prayed a lot! […] I was very scared (Brazilian woman, 34 years old).

Globally, international tourist and migratory movements reflect the contrasts produced by the selective permeability of the Schengen borders –

---

9 Alvarez, R., "The Mexican-US Border: The Making of an Anthropology of Borderlands", *Annual Review of Anthropology*, Vol. 24, 1995, pp. 447-470; Weber, S., "D'un Rideau de Fer à l'Autre: Schengen et la Discrimination dans l'Accès à la Mobilité Migratoire", *Géocarrefour*, Vol. 84, No. 3, 2009, pp. 163-171.

10 Cunningham, H., Heyman, J., "Introduction: Mobilities and Enclosures at Borders", *Identities: Global Studies in Culture and Power*, Vol. 11, No. 3, 2004, pp. 289-302; Kearney, M., "The Classifying and Value-Filtering Missions of Borders", *Anthropological Theory*, Vol. 4, No. 2, 2004, pp. 131-156; Sarró, R., Mapril, J., "'Cidadãos e Súbditos': Imigração, Cidadania e o Legado Colonial na Europa Contemporânea", *Revista Migrações*, No. 8, 2011, pp. 27-34.

11 Sacramento, O., *Atlântico Passional: Mobilidades e Configurações Transnacionais de Intimidade Euro-Brasileiras*, ISCTE-IUL, Lisbon, 2014 (PhD thesis).

indeed, of all frontiers in the rich world – in an ambiguous game of opening and closing of doors that dictates the volume and the composition of the population flows involved. The result is a configuration in which transients are subject to classification and selection and free circulation coexists with restrictions on mobility. In this system, while some are in constant movement, many others emulate such mobility only in their imagination and dreams, relating to their desired destinations only through images in the media. Terms such as the "gated globe" (frontiers on a world scale), or the "gated continent" (referring specifically to Europe)[12] accurately describe the discriminatory nature of many contemporary borders. Similarly, and in opposition to the image of a harmonious world burgeoning with interconnections, these terms remind us of the need to always bear in mind the political economy of mobility – an analytical perspective that tends to be crowded out amid all the metaphors of fluidity, hybridity and double consciousness.[13] Given that the great majority of people are part of the "sedentary masses", these metaphors for a world in perpetual motion are exaggerated[14] and therefore need to be critically assessed – at least for as long as the world maintains its militarized borders, its immigrant detention camps, its extradition of *illegals*, and continues to prosecute a multifaceted strategy aimed at *nipping in the bud* the migration projects of ordinary citizens.

The perverse side effects and ironies of control

The muscular suppression of international migration that characterizes the *modus operandi* of the Schengen area generates perverse side effects

---

12 Respectively, Cunningham, H., "Nations Rebound?: Crossing Borders in a Gated Globe", *Identities: Global Studies in Culture and Power*, Vol. 11, No. 3, 2004, pp. 329-350; and Carr, M., *Fortress Europe: Dispatches from a Gated Continent*, The New Press, New York, 2012.

13 Metaphors referring to a world in motion, liquid, post-national, cosmopolitan, ecumenical and hybrid. See Bauman, Z., *Liquid Modernity*, Polity Press, Cambridge, 2000; Beck, U., "The Cosmopolitan Society and its Enemies", *Theory, Culture & Society*, Vol. 19, No. 1-2, 2002, pp. 17-44; Elliott, A., Urry, J., *Mobile Lives*, Routledge, London, 2010; Inda, J., Rosaldo, R., "Introduction: A World in Motion", in J. Inda and R. Rosaldo (eds.), *The Anthropology of Globalization: A Reader*, Blackwell, Oxford, 2002, pp. 1-34; Hannerz, U., "Fluxos, Fronteiras, Híbridos: Palavras-Chave da Antropologia Transnacional", *Mana*, Vol. 3, No. 1, 1997, pp. 7-39; Schiller, N., Darieva, T., Gruner-Domic, S., "Defining Cosmopolitan Sociability in a Transnational Age. An Introduction", *Ethnic and Racial Studies*, Vol. 34, No. 3, 2011, pp. 399-418.

14 Friedman, J., "From Roots to Routes. Tropes for Trippers", *Anthropological Theory*, Vol. 2, No. 1, 2002, pp. 21-36; Salazar, N., "Ethnographies of Mobility: What's in a Name?", in N. Bon, Š. Kalčić and N. Rogelja (eds.), *Ethnographies of Mobility*, ZRC Publishing House, Ljubljana, 2013, pp. 18-27; Werbner, P., "Global Pathways. Working Class Cosmopolitans and the Creation of Transnational Ethnic Worlds", *Social Anthropology*, Vol. 7, No. 1, 1999, pp. 17-35.

that, ironically, are frequently contrary to the objectives that the European institutions seek to achieve. The majority of symbolic interactionism's labelling theorists highlight that reinforcement of control does not necessarily mean that a particular problem will be mitigated; indeed, it may even encourage the emergence of hitherto unexpected and unpredicted problems.[15] The implementation of Prohibition ("dry law") in the US during the 1920s is a classic example of how an attempt to rigidly control and restrict any sort of activity – in this case the manufacture and consumption of alcoholic beverages – may call into being an even more explosive set of problems. Social control aimed at eliminating certain types of behaviour tends to be "paradoxical" and ironic, often generating a vicious spiral of multiple negative effects. This is evident not least of all in the sphere of immigration, where "[…] strict new laws have compounded the problem as well as created others (e.g., a massive increase in detained immigrants, racial discrimination, denials of due process, and various human and civil rights violations)".[16] These are some of the effects that I will now try to briefly exemplify.

One of the most obvious and immediate effects is the social stigmatization and exclusion that results from the decisions taken in the commanding heights of *Schengenland*. This may be observed in the more or less subtle way in which immigrant communities become the scapegoats for a series of problems, particularly those relating to security. The labels used to refer to immigration almost always reflect this tendency. The common use of terms that breed fear (e.g. *avalanche*, *illegal*) and of metaphors of warfare (e.g. *fight against*, *combat*, *defence*) promote the reconfiguration of immigrant status and identity as being directly related to danger and criminality[17]; a representation that in turn evokes generalized suspicion and promotes social tensions. Thus the Schengen institutions, while contributing to the stigmatization of immigrants and the social panic over immigration, simultaneously try to calm public concern by proposing a Europe that would be in a stage of semi-siege, and whose citizens would become increasingly enmeshed in a biopolitical net. These institutions have adopted a repressive strategy so dysfunctional that it has itself become a relevant cause of the problem they were created to solve.

---

15 Becker, H., *Outsiders: Studies in the Sociology of Deviance*, Free Press, Toronto, 1966; Lemert, E., *Human Deviance, Social Problems, and Social Control*, Prentice Hall, New Jersey, 1972.

16 Welch, M., "Ironies of Social Control and the Criminalization of Immigrants", *Crime, Law & Social Change*, Vol. 39, No. 4, 2003, pp. 319-337, p. 327. See also Shields, P., "Electronic Networks, Enhanced State Surveillance and the Ironies of Control", *Journal of Creative Communications*, Vol. 1, No. 1, 2006, pp. 19-38.

17 Balzacq, T., and Carrera, S. (eds.), *Security Versus Freedom? A Challenge for Europe's Future*, Ashgate, Aldershot, 2006.

Furthermore, since its strategic aim is the spatial and social exclusion of extremely vulnerable people, it stands in contradiction to – and risks undermining – the European project of creating a cosmopolitan, pluralist, and inclusive society in which basic human rights are both respected and actively defended.

The widespread production of migratory exclusions seems to be ideologically driven by the wish to maintain and if possible reinforce the numerous borders of inequality (e.g. political and administrative, ethnic, poverty-related) of a world that is hierarchically organized. Crossing these borders, successfully or otherwise, exposes immigrants in general and, more particularly and extremely, those who find themselves in an irregular situation, to immediate stigmatization and social marginalization. Thus ostensively hyper-vigilant Europe is converted into an "exclusion factory".[18] Immigrant detention camps and extradition centres proliferate. They are to be found almost everywhere in the Schengen area and its neighbouring countries, with the largest located on the southern border, on the Mediterranean coast[19], and constitute the most violent example of the exclusion processes imposed on those that personify the challenge to the ideological dispositions of mainstream identity and mobility policies.[20] These "encampments"[21] summarize in a particularly cruel way the *atopic* condition of the immigrant: placeless, displaced and unclassifiable.[22]

The growing security shield of the Schengen area, in addition to the huge physical and symbolic violence brought upon the immigrants, in particular the so-called illegals, serves to drive underground what is by its very nature an already opaque phenomenon. The whole ethos of ever-tightening security results in the growth of criminality that has to be suppressed, the increased vulnerability of people in precarious situations,

---

18 Engbersen, G., "The Unanticipated Consequences of Panopticon Europe. Residence Strategies of Illegal Immigrants", in V. Guiraudon and C. Joppke (eds.), *Controlling a New Migration World*, Routledge, London, 2001, pp. 222-246; Linke, U., "Fortress Europe: Globalization, Militarization and the Policing of Interior Borderlands", *Topia-Canadian Journal of Cultural Studies*, No. 23-24, 2010, pp. 100-120.

19 See Migreurop, namely his map of the principal spaces of detention in the Schengen area and in neighbor countries: http://www.migreurop.org/IMG/pdf/Carte_Atlas_Migreurop_8012013_Version_anglaise_version_web.pdf (last accessed on 15/04/2015).

20 Underlying these exclusion processes there seems to be the idea that the world can only be safer and more stable if we eliminate or at least control situations that might attenuate or complexify the borders' order system that regulate identities and inequalities. See Amoore, L., "Biometric Borders: Governing Mobilities in the War on Terror", *Political Geography*, Vol. 25, No. 3, 2006, pp. 336-351.

21 On this concept, see Harrell-Bond, B., "Can Humanitarian Work with Refugees be Humane?", *Human Rights Quarterly*, Vol. 24, No. 1, 2002, pp. 51-85.

22 Bourdieu, P., "Um Analista do Inconsciente", in A. Sayad, *A Imigração ou os Paradoxos da Alteridade*, EDUSP, São Paulo, 1998, pp. 9-12.

and a reduction in access to social support. Irony of ironies, the hardening of migration policies ends up increasing the traffic of people and subsequent illegalities that these policies were formulated to combat. With the rising restrictions on entry into the European continent, "an increasing number of migrants have to resort to specialized migration-agents and an increasing number of this kind of organization start to dedicate themselves to this activity [...]".[23] Thus what used to be a problem of *illegal* immigration has become one of human trafficking, to which are directly or indirectly connected other forms of criminal activity, involving the harbouring of those who have outstayed their welcome and/or providing help to those trying to legalize their irregular status.

Once inside the receiving country, the consequences of Schengen mechanisms for immigrants may be, likewise, quite negative; not only do they come under police surveillance but, if found to have infringed the regulations, may find themselves investigated and even detained prior to extradition. It is in this context that we see the spread of what several authors have termed "foggy social structures"[24]: key needs on the part of immigrants are satisfied, each via its own distinctive, more or less organized, informal market (e.g. for employment, for renting a house, acquiring documentation) which, albeit illegally, allows immigrants to hide their irregular situation or ensure the legality of their arrival and residence. In the document market, it is quite common, for example, to arrange a marriage to a European citizen, in which both parties agree to marry for mutual convenience: the latter for financial reasons, the former to acquire legal authorisation to live in the Schengen area.[25] This is just one example of the many underground institutions, with no legal framework, that have established themselves downstream of these international migratory flows, in response to a specific conjuncture

---

23 Peixoto, J., Soares, A., Costa, P., Murteira, S., Pereira, S., Sabino, C., *O Tráfico de Migrantes em Portugal: Perspectivas Sociológicas, Jurídicas e Políticas*, ACIME, Lisbon, 2005, p. 59. Also in North America, for example, we can verify a significant increase and sophistication of the criminal organizations dedicated to the traffic of persons between the borders of Mexico and the US, using routes and strategies that often are the cause of death of trafficked people. See Guerette, R., Clarke, R., "Border Enforcement, Organized Crime, and Deaths of Smuggled Migrants on the United States-Mexico Border", *European Journal on Criminal Policy and Research*, Vol. 11, No. 2, 2005, pp. 159-174; and Nevins, J., "Dying for a Cup of Coffee? Migrant Deaths in the US-Mexico Border Region in a Neoliberal Age", *Geopolitics*, Vol. 12, No. 2, 2007, pp. 228-247.

24 See, for example, Bommes, M., Sciortino, G. (eds.), *Foggy Social Structures: Irregular Migration, European Labour Markets and the Welfare State*, Amsterdam University Press, Amsterdam, 2011.

25 Grassi, M., "Formas Migratórias: *Casar com o Passaporte* no Espaço Schengen. Uma Introdução ao Caso de Portugal", *Etnográfica*, Vol. 10, No. 2, 2006, pp. 283-306.

characterized by Schengen's exaggerated levels and structures of control.

Many of these institutions are in some way linked to informal migratory networks. The latter often provide the social capital that is so important to immigrants as they begin their migratory project and, once in the host country, to live in the protective shadow of their own ethnic communities, benefiting from the help of their fellow countrymen and families.[26] This kind of support and the service provided by the "foggy social structures" creates social invisibility and significantly hampers surveillance, detection and detention by the police. However, the quartet of information systems (SIS II, Eurodac, VIS and Eurosur), mentioned above, is so powerful and pervasive that it can generate identity data not only on specific immigrants but also on their social contexts, which may undermine the anonymity and invisibility their supporting networks provide. Nevertheless, the vicious circle of perverse effects prevails: the intensification of control systems increases dependence on ever more sophisticated and underground organizations, making it difficult for immigrants to access basic services and thereby forcing them to levels often as far below the norms of human dignity as those they left in their countries of origin.

Despite the extensive barriers erected by European countries and by the generality of the developed countries worldwide, people devise ingenious solutions to evade detection or manage to fulfil the criteria for legal status. A study on female prostitution in the Iberian borderland region, in which I participated, uncovered the multiple strategies developed by foreign sex workers (in particular those from Latin America), who enter Europe as tourists in an attempt to circumvent the tight immigration control at airports and ensure their entry into the Schengen area. The measures recommended by them for success in this endeavour include:

> *(i)* avoiding the airports known to have become particularly "difficult", such as Lisbon for those coming from Brazil, or Madrid (Barajas) for those coming from other South American countries; *(ii)* choosing routes that involve several stages or stopovers; *(iii)* dressing, as far as possible, as a tourist but without attracting attention by ostentatiously brandishing cameras, maps and documents; *(iv)* travelling first class; *(v)* carrying letters, invitations and addresses of European nationals that you have supposedly come to visit;

[26] Engbersen, G., "The Unanticipated Consequences of Panopticon Europe. Residence Strategies of Illegal Immigrants", in V. Guiraudon and C. Joppke (eds.), *Controlling a New Migration World*, Routledge, London, 2001, pp. 222-246.

(vi) carrying the amount of money legally stipulated to cover expenses; and *(vii)* carrying a return ticket.[27]

In many cases, this kind of "cat and mouse game" has resulted in an increase in the strategies and counterstrategies of catastrophic effects.[28] Mediterranean waters are constantly stage for the most shocking consequences of this dialectic between fortress Europe and the "wretched of the earth"[29] from the African continent seeking alternatives to poverty and misery. Writing this lines I glance at the newspaper and there it is, the oft-repeated news of yet another disaster in the Mediterranean involving immigrants from Sub-Saharan Africa trying to reach Europe: "[...] after leaving Libya, a boat full of immigrants sank. [...] More than 400 people have disappeared in the shipwreck. They are presumed dead. [...] At the weekend, the Italian coast guard and navy rescued around 6.000 people".[30] Only a few days later another tragedy occurred, this time of even greater proportions and one of the worst ever recorded in Mediterranean waters: "Several hundred people have died in the Mediterranean when a boat carrying around 700 migrants foundered between the coast of Libya and the Italian island of Lampedusa. During the rescue operations only 28 survivors were picked up".[31] From January to mid-April 2015, a further 900 immigrants died crossing the Mediterranean.[32] In 2014, 3.072 people lives were lost and since the year 2000 the toll has been around 22.400.[33] These tragic events show us the profoundly perverse effects of the obsessive recourse to repression in the Schengen area's strategy to manage the incoming flows of economic migrants fleeing poverty at home.

---

27 Ribeiro, M., Silva, M. C., Schouten, J., Ribeiro, F. B., Sacramento, O., *Vidas na Raia: Prostituição Feminina em Regiões de Fronteira*, Afrontamento, Oporto, 2007, p. 260.

28 Broeders, D., Engbersen, G., "The Fight Against Illegal Migration: Identification Policies and Immigrants' Counterstrategies", *American Behavioral Scientist*, Vol. 50, No. 12, 2007, pp. 1592-1609.

29 The term was coined by Fanon, F., in his book *The Wretched of the Earth*, Grove Press, New York, 2004 [1961]; entitled *Les Damnés de la Terre* in the original French version.

30 Guimarães, M. J., "400 desaparecidos em naufrágio de barco com migrantes que tentavam chegar a Itália", *Jornal Público*, 15 April 2015, p. 48.

31 Martins, A., "700 náufragos na 'maior tragédia de sempre no Mediterrâneo'", *Jornal Público*, 20 April 2015, pp. 2-4.

32 According to UN Refugee Agency: http://www.unhcr.org/552e603f9.html (last accessed on 17/04/2015).

33 Brian, T., Laczko, F., *Fatal Journeys: Tracking Lives Lost During Migration*, International Organization for Migration, Geneva, 2014.

Final remarks

Schengen is a transnational political construction that is eminently security-focused and highly selective. In the name of a Europe of "Freedom, Security and Justice", internal customs barriers have been lifted, while control of the perimeter of Europe's common space has been intensified and almost total digital surveillance of movements within and beyond its borders has been deployed. The main objective is to establish, whether according to strictly economistic criteria or due to supposed security reasons, a rigorous distinction between those who are made welcome and those who are branded as undesirables in *Schengenland*, between those who are seen as (potential) citizens and those who are labelled as illegal. Under the present political economy of mobility, the efforts of the Schengen countries are aimed at blocking the mobility projects of those who lack capital and privileges and/or have a cultural background with which Europe does not feel comfortable. Political borders function to reinforce economic and ethnic boundaries, serving also to establish exclusions and social hierarchies at a global scale.

Europe nevertheless needs the very people that own border management strategy deprecates and drives away. It needs them for sectors of activity that suffer labour shortages so that it can cope with depopulation trends in some of its territories and renew its overall demographic vitality. Paradoxical as it may seem, these same people are extremely useful as *illegals*. In actual fact, a system that limits the free movement of people and can variably regulate incoming migratory flows is vital to the European economy.[34] These flows are constituted mainly by people who are extremely vulnerable, susceptible to the imposition of labour regimes unfavourable to their own rights and interests, and willing to accept wages that reflect the convenience of their employers. The economic prosperity in Europe is also a result of that.

The strategy recommended by Schengen, promoting security as the overriding priority, is becoming trapped in a web of denial with increasingly dramatic effects. It has seriously underestimated the deeply negative impacts that its security measures have or will have on justice, freedom and on other fundamental rights. It appears to scorn the humanist ideals of which the Old Continent is so proud, and to reject the necessary

---

34 Through its labour recruitment procedures at home and in its neighbouring countries, the apartheid regime in South Africa was able to "turn the tap on and off" in accordance not only with the fluctuating demand for foreign labour (in the mines and farms) but also the conjunctural need to placate domestic political unrest. See, for example, Tati, G., "The Immigration Issues in Post-Apartheid South Africa: Discourses, Policies and Social Repercussions", *Espace, Populations, Sociétés*, 2008/3, pp. 423-440 (online version, last accessed on 20/04/2015 at http://eps.revues.org/3496).

model of a "cosmopolitan Europe"[35], constantly enriched and renewed by the cultural diversity it attracts. It neglects the violent stigmatisation and increasing alienation generated around migratory flows, making unviable the regulatory controls that member states seek to impose. And it forgets that the reinforcement of control contributes to the increase in human trafficking and related crimes, as well as exposing migrants to life-threatening situations. This is the price to pay for the construction of a safer Europe, one may say. However, it seems that the more tightly Schengen closes its fist, the more sand runs through its fingers. The more secure Europe and the rest of the developed world *want* to become, the less security they are able to achieve. It is a tragically ironic situation, fuelled by the constant spectre of terrorism.

[35] Beck, U., Grande, E., *Cosmopolitan Europe*, Polity Press, Cambridge, 2007.

Changing Dynamics of "Migration Management"

The "Border" between the EU and Africa

Burcu Toğral Koca

Abstract: Having long-coastal borders with African countries, the EU together with Southern European member states has introduced securitarian border control practices. Backed by discourses linking African immigration to criminality, terrorism, and socio-economic problems, technologized and militarized border control practices have become the cornerstones structuring the EU's border regime. In analyzing these developments, this article, first, develops an analytical framework regarding the migration/security nexus through building upon Foucauldian approaches to biopolitics. This sociological stance offers a critical way to deconstruct how border control practices are formulated as strategies of containing and filtering certain group of migrants including irregular and poor migrants, asylum seekers and refugees. Second, through building upon document analysis, empirical application of this analytical background is carried out with a special focus on border control practices developed by the EU and Spain. Finally, the article highlights the ethical and political consequences of these securitization practices in relation to the human rights of migrants.

Introduction

In the last decades, migration has come to be framed and administered as a security issue by the EU and its member states and this securitization process has increasingly appeared in public discourses and academic research. Parallel to this development, there have also emerged critical voices and literature against this securitization process and its impact on the issue of migration.[1] One of them analyses the migration/security nexus in the context of a biopolitical distinction between 'developed'

1 See among others, Bigo, D., "When Two Become One: Internal and External Securitizations in Europe", in M. W. Kelstrup (ed.), *International Relations Theory and the Politics of European Integration. Power, Security and the Community*, Routledge, London, 2000; Bigo, D., "Security and Immigration: Toward a Critique of the Governmentality of Unease", *Alternatives*, Vol. 27, No. 1, 2002, pp. 63-92; Huysmans, J., *The Politics of Insecurity: Fear, Migration and Asylum in the EU*, Routledge, London /New York, 2006; Balzacq, T., "The Policy Tools of Securitization: Information

and 'underdeveloped' species-life.[2] Following Foucault, this biopolitical distinction enables to administer life at the aggregate level of population and entails a regularity power.[3] This biopolitical governance comprises devices, techniques "used to ensure the spatial distribution of individual bodies (their separation, their alignment, their serialization, and their surveillance) and the organization around those individuals, of a whole field of visibility. They were also the techniques that could take control over bodies".[4] Through drawing from the existing literature on the securitization of migration and combining it with a Foucauldian approach on bipolitics, the aim is, here, to trace this biopolitical governance and its linkage to the process of securitization. In other words, the article seeks to map the technologies of control/ security which are employed to "render visible, categorize, discipline, contain, and exclude the transgressive and mobile other".[5]

In doing this, first, the article discusses the migration-security nexus in the EU's migration regime. Then, by using document analysis of governmental/non-governmental and legal sources and the relevant literature, the conceptual and analytical discussions are made more tangible with a specific attention to the EU/Spain's militarized and technologized border control practices targeting African immigration in the Mediterranean. Focusing on African immigration and related practices provides a suitable laboratory framework to deconstruct the process of securitization as a technology of biopolitics. This is mainly because; African countries – together with Middle Eastern ones – constitute the major source of irregular migrants for Europe. Particularly, the so-called boat people, namely those trying to enter Europe by sea, have been framed as one of the major 'challenge' in political and public agenda for a long time. There has been growing concern about the tragic deaths occurring in the Mediterranean. The 'Arab Spring' has added new dimensions to this debate and provoked new instruments in dealing with the so-called 'boat people'. For these reasons, there needs to be more analysis on the European policies towards African immigration in

Exchange, EU Foreign and Interior Policies", *Journal of Common Market Studies*, Vol. 46, No. 1, 2008, pp. 75-100.

2 Duffield, M., *Development, Security and Unending War: Governing the World of Population*, Polity Press Cambridge, 2007.

3 See Foucault, M., *Discipline and Punish. The Birth of the Prison*, Penguin, Harmondsworth, 1991; Foucault, M., *Society must be Defended. Lectures at the Collège de France, 1975-76*, Picador, New York, 2004.

4 Foucault, *Society must be Defended...*, p. 242.

5 Vasquez, M. A., "From Colonialism to Neo-Liberal Capitalism: Latino/A Immigrants in the U.S. and the New Biopolitics", *Journal for Cultural and Religious Theory*, Vol. 3, No. 1, 2012, p. 82.

order to trace the current securitization practices and their implications on human rights.

The Security-Migration Nexus and the African Immigration

As stated above, migration has increasingly transformed into a security question in the EU. In effect, it is widely asserted that this securitization process has developed parallel to the intensification of the EU integration process.[6] Especially, following the establishment of the Single Market and Schengen Regime, which resulted in the abolition of internal border controls, it is contended that migration has turned into a security issue. This is linked to the assumption that removal of internal borders would result in a 'security deficit', since a Europe without internal borders could be abused and become "a haven for criminals and illegal immigrants".[7] The September 11 and subsequent attacks in Europe have added new dimensions to these ongoing developments and prompted the political and academic discussions on this securitization process. This study claims that securitization process is informed by the practices integrating migration into a security framework emphasizing policing and defence.[8] More precisely, here, practices refer to "an identifiable social and technical 'dispositive' or device embodying a specific threat image through which public action is configured in order to address a security issue".[9] In other words, these practices "by [their] very nature and or by [their] very functioning transform the entity (i.e. subject or object) [they] processes into a threat".[10] They "convey the idea to those who observe them, directly or indirectly, that the issue they are tackling is a security threat".[11] Hence, such a sociological approach to the securitization privileges the role of practices in framing and administering migration as a security threat contrary to the Copenhagen School's focus on 'speech acts' as the vector of the securitization.[12]

---

6 See Huysmans, *op. cit.*; and Karanja, S. K., "The Schengen Co-operation: Consequences for the Right of EU Citizens", *Mennesker og rettigheter Årgang*, Vol. 18, No. 3, 2000, p. 217.

7 Karanja, *op. cit.*, p. 217.

8 Huysmans, *op. cit.*

9 Balzacq, *op. cit.*, p. 79.

10 *Ibid.*, p. 80.

11 Leonard, S., "EU Border Security and Migration into the European Union: FRONTEX and Securitisation Through Practices", *European Security*, Vol. 19, No. 2, 2010, p. 237.

12 The concept of securitization was, first, introduced by the so-called Copenhagen School of Security Studies. Waever, one of the protagonist of this School, states that securitization is the successful construction of an issue as an 'existential threat' to the designated referent object through 'speech acts' of securitizing actors, which justifies

However, this securitization process does not mean that migration as a whole has been securitized or the intention is to contain all types of mobility. As put forward by Rumford, migration practices or "borders are not singular and unitary and are designed to encourage various kinds of mobility, particularly for certain categories of immigrants, migrant workers and students".[13] Undeniably, today, nationals of some privileged countries belonging to the 'developed' West enjoy the freedom of movement without much of an interruption and without being imprisoned within any kind of borders (either territorial or non-territorial). Rich tourists and highly skilled/semi-skilled labour force meeting market demands have still been welcomed by the EU/member states. The securitized group of migrants is likely to be asylum seekers, refugees, and undocumented immigrants or to come from African and Middle Eastern countries. They are the 'human surplus'. In other words, they constitute the "volume of humans made redundant by capitalism's global triumph... [they are] the superfluous, supernumerary and redundant population – the excess of the rejects of the labour market, and the refuse of the market-targeted economy, over the capacity of recycling arrangements".[14] They are designated as a threat to cultural identity, welfare state and internal security of the EU and/or 'developed' West.[15] Therefore, they came to be dealt with harsh measures of biopolitics. These measures refer to the technologies of controlling and containing excessive freedom employed with the aim of regulating the 'human surplus,' 'threatening others'. This biopoliticization of the borders also points to the "filter function of border controls".[16] Or as described by Walters the main effect of this biopolitical structure is the "filtering and protection of the national population, the regulation of the

---

extraordinary security policies – e.g. using conscription, secrecy, and other means only legitimate when dealing with 'security matters' (see Waever, O., "The EU as a Security Actor: Reflections from a Pessimistic Constructivist on Post Sovereign Security Orders", in M. Kelstrup and M. C. Williams (eds.), *International Relations Theory and the Politics of European Integration*, Routledge, London, 2000). Later, the concept of securitization has gained a theoretical status and been revised and reinterpreted. For example, as in case of this study, those following a Foucauldian approach, such as Bigo from the Paris School of Security Studies, Huysmans and Balzacq have applied a sociological understanding and focused on the role of practices rather than 'speech acts' in the process of securitization.

13 Rumfold, C., "Theorizing Borders", *European Journal of Social Theory*, Vol. 9, No. 2, 2006, p. 157.

14 Bauman, Z., *Liquid Times: Living in an Age of Uncertainty*, Polity Press Cambridge, 2007, pp. 28-29.

15 See Huysmans, *op. cit.*

16 Den Boer, M., "Moving Between Bogus and Bona Fide: The Policing of Inclusion and Exclusion in Europe", in R. Miles and D. Thränhardt (eds.), *Migration and European Integration: The Dynamics of Inclusion and Exclusion*, Madison [N.J.]/ Pinter Publishers/Fairleigh Dickinson University Press, London, 1995, p. 92.

movement of things and risks, and the collection of revenue".[17] In this context, securitization as a regime of biopolitics is a strategy separating 'wanted' individuals/groups/states from the 'unwanted', 'dangerous' ones. To put it differently, this securitization of migration strives to contain and exclude 'dangerous' others in order to "secure the Western way of life".[18] As will be detailed in the following pages, a more "humanitarian" discourse, such as saving and improving lives of migrants, is also invoked in order to mask the very political and securitarian character of migration control practices informing this biopolitical governance.

If one has a closer look at the EU and member states' migration practices, it is clearly seen that they clearly signify these tendencies and are endowed with security and policing aspects aiming at controlling, sometimes, excluding and containing certain group of migrants. Surveillance and risk analysis constitute corner stones of these migration practices in differentiating 'risky' bodies from the 'un-risky' ones. Current visa policies with their discriminatory and exclusionary approach towards certain group of migrants, detention and deportation practices, which clash with basic human rights, reflect this approach as well. Further, various data bases, biometric technologies, electronic fences, sophisticated radar systems or military-like devices exemplify that border control practices are culminated by high-technological devices, which were previously used for military purposes. Besides, increasing role granted to police, para-military bodies, intelligence services or security experts demonstrate how security logic prevails in the field of migration. Following the September 11, convergence of migration practices with anti-terrorist measures represents another sign of this biopolitical governance aiming at controlling and filtering populations. Last but not least, integration practices cemented by culturalist and racialized discourses are likely to deal with migrants as 'threatening others' that should be rehabilitated, tamed and normalized to be included into the 'developed' world. In short, these techniques or measures are seeking to regulate and control migrants both inside and outside 'borders' dividing "not land, but populations".[19]

---

17 Walters, W., "Mapping Schengenland: Denaturalizing the Border", *Environment and Planning: Society and Space*, Vol. 20, No. 5, 2002, p. 572.

18 Duffield, *op. cit.*, p. 2. As Duffield further depicts "the opposite of containment is the unsecured circulation of surplus population that external poverty, instability and associated social breakdown continually threaten" (*Ibid.*, p. 184).

19 Buur, L., Jensen, S. and Stepputat, F., "The Security-Development Nexus", in L. Buur, S. Jensen and F. Stepputat (eds.), *The Security-Development Nexus: Expressions of Sovereignty and Securitization in Southern Africa*, Nordiska Afrikainstitutet, Uppsala/ Hsrc Press, Cape Town, 2007, p. 6.

Of those techniques/measures, militarized and technologized border control practices employed by the EU and Spain provide a suitable framework to illustrate the functioning of this security architecture in the Mediterranean. This is mainly because especially Spain – together with other Southern European states, such as Italy, Malta, and Greece – has become the major transit/destination country for African immigrants due to its geographical situation since the early 1990s. To put it differently, African immigration constituted one of the decisive elements pushing Spain's transformation from an emigration into an immigration country. In fleeing deep socio-economic and political problems at their home countries, first, North African immigrants, including Moroccans, Tunisians and Algerians, and later Sub-Saharan immigrants have increasingly relied on irregular means to enter Spain. One important point is that the routes these migrants use have continuously been shifting in response to intensified surveillance and control measures developed by the EU/member states. For example, from the beginning of the 1990s, the Straits of Otranto and the Straits of Gibraltar have been the two key entry points for irregular immigrants along the EU's southern borders.[20] Given the expansion of surveillance measures along these Straits, migrants started to resort to other routes, for example to Ceuta and Mellila and later to Canary Islands.

In response to these irregular entries, Spain and the EU have continuously developed various techniques from the early 1990s. In order to keep away African immigrants and their 'threatening' effects from European territory, new strategies of biopolitics were put into place. These practices also aim at turning neighbouring countries into 'buffer zones' for the very well-being of European countries. Especially North African countries have had to strengthen their own migration regulations, establish deportation centers and camps, sign readmission agreements, as well as tighten controls at physical borders in exchange of financial aid or in the face of political pressure of the EU. Therefore, in controlling and securitizing African immigration, the EU and member states have integrated third countries into their security architecture and biopolitical regime through externalizing the securitization practices. As it is not possible to look into all these practices in the course of this article, the following pages focus on the major turning points and resultant militarized and technologized practices informing the EU's and Spain's migration regime.

[20] Lutterbeck, D., "Policing Migration in the Mediterranean", *Mediterranean Politics*, Vol. 11, No. 1, 2006, p. 61.

Militarized Border Control Practices

As Lutterbeck analyses, one outcome of the "growing preoccupation in European countries with irregular migration and (supposedly) related transnational challenges from across the Mediterranean has been a considerable expansion and intensification of policing and law enforcement of activities in and across the Mediterranean sea".[21] Lutterbeck calls this process militarization of migration control characterized by an "increasing mobilization of both paramilitary police and military security forces, as well as a resort to a growing amount of military-style hardware in preventing irregular immigration and cross-border crime".[22]

At the EU level, the most visible and significant face of this militarization process is the introduction of the European Agency for the Management of Operational Cooperation at the External Borders of the Member states of the European Union, titled under the acronym Frontex (hereafter also referred to as the Agency). Having been established on 26 October 2004 and become operational in May 2005, the Agency, indeed, institutionalized the European border management regime and turned into one of the main body in the fight against 'irregular' immigration. Its budget and human resources have grown rapidly.[23] The Agency's institutional and operational settings signify a clear securitization of migration and include main tenets of the biopolitics. First, in all its pursuits, the main task of the Agency is to control and contain 'unwanted' border crossings by 'irregular' immigrants, asylum seekers and refugees on sea, land and air borders; thereby to ensure the internal security of the EU. In doing this, the Agency has been conducting joint operations in cooperation with member states as well as with source or transit countries for 'irregular' migrants and asylum seekers. These joint operations include apprehension, disembarkation, deportation practices, transfer of 'irregular' migrants into detention centers, and have a clear securitarian character. To be more precise, such sort of cooperative actions among states, especially those conducted at sea borders, "have been traditionally been deployed to address more traditional security issues, such as military attack from a third state, piracy or drug trafficking".[24] Besides, involvement of actors with para-military status from member states in these joint operations

---

21 *Ibid*, p. 60.

22 *Ibid.*, p. 64.

23 For example, while Frontex got 89.2 million euros in 2014, the European Asylum Support Office (EASO) received only 15.6 million euros for the same year (Uluslararası Af Örgütü (Amnesty International), *Kale Avrupası'nın İnsani Bedeli: Avrupa Sınırlarında Göçmen ve Mültecilerin Karşılaştıkları İnsan Hakları İhlalleri*, Amnesty International Ltd., London, 2014, p. 17).

24 Leonard, *op. cit.*, p. 240.

reveals how militarization and securitization of migration controls are intensified by the practices and institutional structure of the Frontex. Similarly, the Agency is in charge of assisting member states through technical and operational means in cases where a rapid crisis-response is required. This assistance can be provided either by establishing a cooperation between two or more member states or through involvement of experts from the Agency to help member states tackle these 'crisis' situations. This framework has become much more sophisticated with the changes laid down by the Regulation 863/2007 amending the Agency's founding Regulation. The most significant 'novelty' introduced with this amendment is the establishment of the Rapid Borders Intervention Teams (RABITs):

> for the purposes of providing rapid operational assistance [...] to a requesting State facing a situation of urgent and exceptional pressure, especially the arrivals of the external borders of large numbers of third-country nationals trying to enter the territory of the Member State illegally.[25]

It is stated that member states "may ask for the support of the RABITs under particular *threat* from illegal migration".[26] Member states' contribution and participation to the RABITs became mandatory with the Article 4 of the Regulation. It is further important to note that with the Regulation, members of the team were allowed to carry arms and use force with the authorization of the host member state (Article 6 (6)). Against this backdrop, the framework, which utilizes the wording of 'crisis' and 'threat' mandatory character of the participation as well as the composition of the team equipped with military-devices represent another securitarian sign of Frontex. Furthermore, Frontex came to work in close cooperation with the security and intelligence-based bodies, such as EUROPOL, the European Anti-Fraud Office OLAF, EUROJUST, the Union Satellite Centre EUSC, the EU's intelligence body Joint Situation Centre (JSC), the Police Chief's Task Force and Interpol. More importantly, the Agency expands this structure into transit and source countries by cooperating with their intelligence services. Javier Quesada, head of the Risk Analysis Unit, made this clear with the following words:

---

25 European Parliament and the Council of the European Union, *Regulation (EC) No 863/2007 of the European Parliament and of the Council of 11 July 2007 establishing a mechanism for the creation of Rapid Border Intervention Teams and amending Council Regulation (EC) No 2007/2004 as regards that mechanism and regulating the tasks and powers of guest officers*, OJ L 199/30, 31.7.2007.

26 *Ibid.*, emphasis added.

We started creating intelligence communities in third countries in the Western Balkans, at the eastern borders of the EU member states and now in Africa. And we intend to continue developing these communities.[27]

The Agency, indeed, represents itself as an intelligence-based body to control and manage 'risks' and 'threats' in its official statements. Keeping in mind that the concept of 'intelligence' has traditionally pointed to the information gathered in the face of threats to national security[28], "the use of this concept, rather than more neutral concepts such as 'data' or 'information', already contributes to securitizing asylum and migration in the EU".[29] Besides, the rationale structuring its risk analysis model represents a preventive approach. Laitinen, the head of the Agency, reveals this very well as follows:

> We assess what is the likely that threatens the external borders, border security, and EU citizens from outside. In other words, criminal pressure, in terms of illegal migration, human trafficking, and so on, not disregarding other types of organized crime and fighting international terrorism.[30]

This discourse represents a clear "security continuum"[31] established among different phenomenon, such as crime, 'irregular' immigration, human trafficking and terrorism and, thereby, provoking criminalization of 'irregular' immigration under a risk assessment model. Further, it fits well to what Bigo describes as "a proactive logic which anticipates the risks and the threats, locating the potential adversaries even before they have consciousness of being a threat to others."[32] Another contentious issue is that this intelligence-based risk analysis is built upon the necessity of ensuring secrecy of operations. The Decision of the Management Board of 21 September 2006 maintains that:

> In order to safeguard the ability of to carry out its tasks, special attention should be paid to the specific requirements of Frontex as a specialized body tasked with improving the integrated management of the external borders of the member states of the EU. Therefore, full account of the sensitive nature of

27 Frontex, *Beyond Frontiers, Frontex: The First Five Years*, Offset-Print, Michałowice, 2010, p. 65.

28 Gill, P. and Phythian, M., *Intelligence in an Insecure World*, Polity, Cambridge, 2006, p. 1.

29 Leonard, *op. cit.*, p. 242.

30 Neal, A. W., "Securitization and Risk at the EU Border: The Origins of FRONTEX", *Journal of Common Market Studies*, Vol. 47, No. 2, 2009, pp. 348-349.

31 Bigo, D., "The European Internal Security Field: Stakes and Rivalries in a Newly Developing Area of Police Intervention", in M. Anderson and M. den Boer (eds.), *Policing Across National Boundaries*, Pinter, London, 1994, p. 164.

32 Bigo, D., "Frontier Controls in the European Union: Who is in Control?", in D. Bigo and E. Guild (eds.), *Controlling Frontiers. Free Movement Into and Within Europe*, Ashgate, Burlington, 2005, p. 86.

tasks carried out by Frontex, in particular in relation to operations at borders and border related data should be taken.[33]

At this point, the justification follows from the argument that collected data, details of operations and sources of information should be kept in secrecy in order to secure the success of operations.[34] However, this secrecy impedes not only principles of transparency and democratic accountability, but also prevents public from taking an active stance against possible breach of fundamental rights and rule of law. As contended eloquently by Carrera "by applying the secrecy rule the very source of legitimizing the operation cannot be at all contested, reviewed and in the end made democratically accountable".[35] Furthermore, this operational setting and the practices of the Agency, particularly joint operations, are also controversial from a legal point of view as well.[36] To be more precise, Frontex operations are likely to prevent asylum seekers from lodging their claims in European countries. Those seeking protection are indiscriminately treated as part of "irregular" and "economic" immigrants or the so-called "mix flows". Turning migrants back across the borders without taking into account their possible claims for asylum, impedes the principle of *non-refoulement*. This is mainly because, as put forward by the United Nations High Commissioner for Refugees (UNCHR), *non-refoulement* principle, also requires "non-rejection at the border" meaning that persons cannot be sent back to a country where there is a possibility of persecution, torture and other forms of ill-treatments.[37] In a similar vein, Papastavridis contends that "the application of the [principle

33 Frontex, "Decision of the Management Board laying down practical arrangement regarding public access to the documents of the European Agency for the Management of Operational Cooperation at the External Borders of the Member states of the European Union (Frontex)", 2006, available at http://www.europarl.europa.eu/document/activities/cont/201005/20100531ATT75236/20100531ATT75236EN.pdf (last accessed on 14/06/2008).

34 Carrera, S., "The EU Border Management Strategy: FRONTEX and the Challenges of 'irregular' Immigration in the Canary Islands", *CEPS Working Document*, 261, 2007, p. 14.

35 *Ibid.*

36 See Baldaccini, A., "Extraterritorial Border Controls in the EU: The Role of FRONTEX in Operations at Sea", in B. Ryan and V. Mitsilegas (eds.), *Extraterritorial Immigration control: Legal Challenges*, Martinus Nijhoff, Leiden, 2010; Gil-Bazo, M. T., "The Practice of Mediterranean States in the Context of the European Union's Justice and Home Affairs External Dimension", *International Journal of Refugee Law*, Vol. 18, No. 3-4, 2006.

37 Debenedetti, S., "Externalization of European Asylum and Migration Polices", paper presented at the 2nd Session of the Florence School on Euro-Mediterranean Migration and Development, 15-30 June 2006, European University Institute, Florence, 2006, p. 23.

of *non-refoulement*] appears to be especially problematic in the majority of [joint operations conducted by the Frontex] since it is very likely that the persons onboard the intercepted vessels would be forced to return their countries of origin, where they may be subject to torture or inhuman or degrading treatment".[38]

Despite these problems, the Agency's operations have been justified with a reference to the 'moral obligation' of the EU to "prevent, not least to end the suffering and dying on the high seas"[39] and become one of the most important tools against African immigrants. Spain, Italy, Malta and Greece have increasingly relied on Frontex in preventing irregular movements from Africa. For example, "the first real test of [Agency's] capacities came with its operational actions in the Canary Islands in 2006".[40] In the face of increasing numbers of irregular arrivals from Africa in Canary Islands, which was framed as an "immigration crisis", and as "a massive invasion of illegal immigrants" in political and media discourses, Maria Teresa Fernández de la Vega, former first deputy prime minister, called for a meeting with the Ministers of Interior, Labour, Defence and External Relations to discuss the issue.[41] After the meeting, Spanish authorities decided to intensify their efforts in "providing for more internment centers and reinforcing the surveillance and border security of the Spanish and African coasts. [Further they] requested the assistance of Frontex…to provide a 'solution' to that migratory crisis".[42] In response, Frontex launched the operations, called Hera I, in July 2006, and Hera II, run from August to December 2006, in order to deter irregular immigration from African countries, including mainly, Mauritania, Senegal, and Cape Verde, to the Canaries. Experts from France, Portugal, Italy, and Germany also involved in these operations.[43] Despite the supranational character of the Agency, these operations were based on bilateral agreements between Spain and African countries. Most importantly, they were not made public; their contents remained secret.[44] As detailed already, this secrecy was justified to secure the success of operations.[45]

---

38 Papastavridis, E., "Fortress Europe" and FRONTEX: Within or Without International Law?", *Nordic Journal of International Law*, Vol. 79, No. 1, 2010, p. 75.

39 Welcome to Europe, "Frontex in the Mediterranean: The border is the problem", 2014, available at http://w2eu.net/frontex/frontex-in-the-mediterranean (last accessed on 02/02/2014).

40 Mir, M., *Managing the EU's External Frontiers: Lessons to Be Learned from FRONTEX's Action in the Canary Islands*, Challenge, Paris, 2007, p. 1.

41 *Ibid.*, pp. 1-2.

42 *Ibid.*

43 See Carrera, *op. cit.*

44 Mir, *op. cit.*, p. 4.

45 Parkes, R., "Joint patrols at the EU's southern border", *SWP Comments*, 21, pp. 1-2.

Apart from Frontex operations, Spain has developed its own militarized border control practices. As Lutterbeck points out:

> One aspect of this process of border militarization along the Mediterranean frontiers of both Italy and Spain has been the increasing deployment and expansion of semi-military security forces, namely police forces with a military status, to deal with undocumented immigration by sea. In general terms, these are internal security or police forces which, in contrast to 'ordinary' police forces, have a number of military characteristics, for example in terms of organization, equipment or formal affiliation.[46]

In the process of this securitization, the Guardia Civil has become the leading actor in controlling 'irregular' immigration from Africa since 1990s. The Guardia Civil was established in 1844 and, originally in charge of dealing with more 'traditional security concerns', including restoring and maintaining internal security, fighting 'domestic' terrorism, as well as later foreign peace-keeping missions. In fact, it can be defined as a "paramilitary police force [reporting] both to the interior and defence ministries" with an official status as an "armed institution of military nature".[47] Furthermore, it has been equipped with "a considerable amount of military-style armory, such as light-infantry weapons".[48] Starting from the early 1990s, it turned into one of the principal bodies implementing and interpreting the law on migrants, including expulsions and detention.[49] During 1990s, the agency was active along the Strait of Gibraltar. In the following years, parallel to the shift in routes for irregular entries, Ceuta and Melilla became its main areas of concern. Ceuta and Melilla are the two enclaves of Spain having autonomous status, located on the north coast of North Africa surrounded by Morocco. Their importance regarding irregular migration became obvious, because of being the only Spanish territories located in the mainland Africa. In this respect, the Civil Guard enhanced its policing efforts targeting these two cities. This militarization process intensified and reached its peak from the 2000s onwards. Between 2003 and 2008, the number of police forces dealing with migration and border control was increased by 53.4%.[50]

---

46 Lutterbeck, *op. cit.*, p. 65.

47 *Ibid.*

48 *Ibid.*

49 Human Rights Watch, *Discretion Without Bounds: The Arbitrary Application of Spanish Immigration Law*, Human Rights Watch, Vol. 14, No, 6, 2002, p. 4.

50 European Migration Network, "Annual Policy Report on Migration and Asylum: Spain, European Migration Network", 2010, available at http://emn.intrasoftintl.com/Downloads/prepareShowFiles.do;jsessionid=5C09DDB49FBFCB749B69BCC521B7AAED?entryTitle=02.%20Annual%20Policy%20Report%202010 (last accessed on 05/01/2011), p. 21.

This militarization of border controls has strengthened in cooperation with African countries as well. For instance, in 2003, Spain and Morocco agreed on patrolling of Spanish borders; accordingly, joint Hispanic-Moroccan border patrols were established in 2004.[51] These patrols involved the troops from Maritime Service of Civil Guard and members of the Royal Moroccan police.[52] Besides, under this agreement, Morocco was granted 400 million euros covering the next three years in exchange of its 'effective' cooperation.[53] Similar agreements were applied to Algeria in the late 2000s through the creation of specialized police cooperation teams.[54] Even though the 'fight against irregular immigration' was the dominant theme structuring these cooperation, Joffe adds that, "Spain has strengthened the links between its security services and those in Morocco and Algeria" with the view that 'terrorism suspects' also come from these two countries.[55] In such a context, 'irregular' immigration was integrated into a wider securitization framework. Last, but not the least, Government Decree of 31.08.2006 established a special coordination mechanism, called Canary Islands Regional Coordination Centre (Centro de Coordinación Regional de Canarias). It came to be run by various actors, including "police corps attached to the Foreign Service, air-sea groups belonging to the Armed Forces and Frontex, the national police forces, customs services and a wide range of reception services for immigrants responsible to the Canary Islands Government's Maritime Safety and Rescue Service and to the Red Cross, as well as other agencies that provide humanitarian aid".[56] The main aim of this mechanism is, as stated by governmental authorities, to fight against irregular immigration. According to Artega, "its mission represents a new generation of security; one that goes beyond what can be defined as purely internal or external, national or international, civilian or military".[57]

---

51 Lutterbeck, *op. cit.*, p. 72.

52 Argerey, P. and Hurtado, I., *The European Migration Policy: Its Approach Towards the Mediterranean Countries*, San Pablo CEU University, Madrid, 2006, p. 13.

53 See Cabras, A., *Migration in the Mediterranean Region*, NATO Parliamentary Assembly, Brussels, 2009.

54 European Migration Network, *op. cit.*, p. 22. Similarly, backed by the financial support of the EU, Spain launched similar joint operations with Mauritanian security forces in patrolling its coastal borders and sealing off the port of Nouahibou in May 2006 (Joffe, G., "The European Union, Democracy and Counter-Terrorism in the Maghreb", *Journal of Common Market Studies*, Vol. 46, No. 1, 2008, p. 166.

55 *Ibid.*, p. 166.

56 Artega, F., *Maritime Illegal Migration Towards the European Union: The Command and Control Centre in the Canary Islands (Centro de Coordinación Regional de Canarias – CCRC) (ARI)*, Elcano Royal Institute, Madrid, 2007, p. 2.

57 *Ibid.*, p. 6.

Technologized Border Control Practices

Parallel to the creation of 'Schengenland', the EU and member states have put enormous emphasis on the technological means to secure the external borders. For example, establishment of various databases, such as Schengen Information System (SIS), Eurodac, Visa Information System (VIS), introduction of biometrics into the EU passports, goal for creating 'synergies' between existing and future databases or the Passenger Name Record (PNR) agreement with the US, electronic fences, are all, signifying the technologized migration control practices. Indeed, this process has accelerated following the September 11 and subsequent attacks in Europe, as politicians and security experts have been able to find a suitable ground to justify these policies with a reference to 'terrorist threat'. As Ceyhan eloquently contends that following the September 11, "more and more governments seek to adopt new technologies of identification in order to securitize identities and identification means and monitor the movements of people inside a given state as well as across borders".[58]

As to the EU level practices, one of those technological means is the VIS. Being established with the Council Decision of 8 June 2004, the VIS aims to prevent "the use of fraudulent documents; to improve visa checks; to improve identifications of individuals for the application of provisions in relation to Dublin II and the return procedure; to enhance the administration of the common visa policy; to prevent 'visa shopping' by ensuring the traceability of every individual applying for a visa and to strengthen EU internal security".[59] When the VIS was first introduced, the EU put special focus on North African and Near Eastern countries. In 2005, it was decided to give priority to North African and Near Eastern countries for the collection of biometric data to be entered in the VIS with a reference to "risk of 'illegal' immigration, threats to internal security and feasibility of collecting biometrics".[60] Such a discriminatory and repressive approach signifies that by relying on the VIS:

---

58 Ceyhan, A., "Policing by Dossier: Identification and Surveillance in an Era of Uncertainty and Fear", in D. Bigo and E. Guild, *op. cit.*, p. 209.

59 Balzacq, T. and Carrera, S., "The Hague Programme: The Long Road to Freedom, Security and Justice", in T. Balzacq and S. Carrera (eds.), *Security versus Freedom? A Challenge for Europe's Future*. Ashgate, Aldershot, 2006, p. 22.

60 Council of the European Union, *Press Release, 2696th Council Meeting Justice and Home Affairs*, 14390/05 (Presse 296). Brussels, 1-2 December 2005. This was later extended to all third-country nationals applying for Schengen visas (see European Parliament and Council of the EU, *Regulation (EC) No 767/2008 of the European Parliament and the Council of 9 July 2008 concerning the Visa Information System (VIS) and the exchange of data between Member states on short-stay visas (VIS Regulation), OJ L 218/60, 13.8.2008*.

> the Union classify countries according to risk potentials and categorize citizens of certain countries as potential criminals even before reaching the territories of the Union. Indeed, anyone willing to travel to the EU who is in need of visa, would need to provide biometrical data to relevant authorities, as well as several other personal documents ranging from details of bank accounts to properties owned.[61]

Another important technological mechanism having implications over African immigrants is the introduction of the European Border Surveillance System (Eurosur) following a 2008 initiative of the European Commission. As part of a 'software' component of the Integrated Border Management, Eurosur is "an information-exchange system designed to improve management of the EU external borders" and "enables near real-time sharing of border-related data between members of the network, consisting of Schengen countries and Frontex".[62] Being part of a $410 million package, the system makes possible the use of drones, high-resolution cameras, satellites and spy planes to detect migrant vessels at sea. Frontex is, here, granted an important role "for the surveillance of the pre-frontier area, which includes the Mediterranean Sea as well as ports and the coast of North African countries using drones".[63] Eurosur became operational in December 2013[64] and has three main objectives:

> To reduce the number of irregular migrants entering the EU undetected; to reduce the number of deaths at the maritime borders by saving more lives at sea, and to increase the internal security of the EU as a whole by contributing to the prevention of cross-border crime. It will apply to the surveillance of all

---

61 Benam, Ç., "Internal Security and the New Border Management Model of the EU: Migration-Security Nexus", PhD Thesis, Middle East Technical University, 2011, p. 182.

62 Frontex, "EUROSUR", 2014, available http://frontex.europa.eu/intelligence/eurosur (last accessed on 01/10/2014).

63 European Council on Refugees and Exiles, "EUROSUR questioned in the European Parliament", *ECRE Weekly Bulletin*, 29 June 2012.

64 It is stated that Lampedusa tragedy "pushed forth the activation of the Eurosur" (Triandafyllidou, A. and Dimitriadi, A., "Governing Irregular Migration and Asylum at the Borders of Europe: Between Efficiency and Protection", *Imagining Europe*, No. 6, 2014, p. 2). As stated in one of the analysis of the EP, this tragedy 'put trans-Mediterranean migration back on top of the political agenda' (Manrique Gil, M., Barna, J., Hakala, P., Rey, B. and Claros, C., "Mediterranean Flows into Europe: Migration and the EU's Foreign Policy", http://www.europarl.europa.eu/RegData/etudes/briefing_note/join/2014/522330/EXPOJOIN_SP(2014)522330_EN.pdf (last accessed on 16/04/2014), p. 4. It has also led to enormous increase in funding of Frontex operations (EUR 7.9 million for 2013) conducted in the Mediterranean (*Ibid.*, p. 9).

external land and sea borders as well as to air borders and to checks at other border crossing points at the discretion of individual participants.[65]

As in case of other techniques, this tool has also established a linkage between (irregular) immigration, crime control and internal security of the EU. Besides, it has invoked a "humanitarian" discourse, namely "saving lives at sea". This discourse was underlined in a statement by the Council attached to the Eurosur Regulation stating "Eurosur will contribute to improving the protection and the saving of lives of migrants".[66] Furthermore, its operational setting follows the same secutarian logic. For example, "in order to make the system operational, Frontex will cooperate with EU and international partner organizations and institutions such as Europol".[67] The opponents of the system argue that:

> These new measures will only lead to abuse. The ability to spy on African beaches has the potential of criminalizing immigrants before they even leave their border. To critics, EUROSUR is a product of European intolerance, fuelled by groups that advocate returning immigrants to their countries of origin before they ever reach European shores, so they don't become the European Union's responsibility.[68]

Similarly, it is stated that "Eurosur is a preemptive measure designed to solve the problem of illegal immigration before it reaches EU shores, rather than lowering death rates and providing humanitarian assistance".[69] Eurosur has also been on the top of the EP's agenda. Particularly its effectiveness in saving lives at sea has been questioned. For example, Ska Keller, MEP from the Greens stated:

> EUROSUR amounts to 'Fortress 2.0', using new technologies such as drones to close off Europe's borders. This skewed approach to immigration misses the point and it represents cynicism to claim that EUROSUR will actually help the boatloads of migrants that risk their lives to leave persecution or destitution. There is not any provision in the proposal on how to save lives at sea.[70]

On the other hand, Spain has also implemented various technologized border control practices in order to 'fight' irregular immigration from

65 Frontex, "EUROSUR"

66 *Ibid.*

67 *Ibid.*

68 Franceschi-Bicchierai, L., "Europe Wants Drones to Spot Illegal Immigrants at Sea", 2012, available at http://www.wired.com/2012/07/euro-immigrant-drone/ (last accessed on 02/09/2014).

69 Pelissier, J. P., "EU Plans Drone Network to Nab Illegal Immigrants", *Reuters*, 27 July 2012, available at http://rt.com/news/eu-drones-illegal-immigration-202 (last accessed on 04/10/2014).

70 European Council on Refugees and Exiles, *op. cit.*

Africa. For example, Guardia Civil constructed a double fence around Ceuta and Mellila. Initially, a fence with a length of 8.3 km was introduced surrounding Ceuta in 1993. This first fence was doubled in 1995 as it was not seen high enough to secure the city.[71] In case of Melilla, the first fencing system was constructed in 1996. Following this, in January 1998, Juan Cotino (People Party), the chief executive officer of the Spanish National Police from 1996 to 2002, presented a new project, called 'Plan Sur' targeting Spanish southern borders. The key objectives of this project were defined as "strengthening of border controls, a more intensive surveillance of air and seaports, a tightening of deportation procedures, and a closer cooperation with Moroccan and Algerian authorities".[72] It was decided to supplement this project with advanced technical equipment including new vehicles and helicopters from the Spanish army. Another significant technologized strategy came with the introduction of the so-called Integrated System of Exterior Surveillance (Sistemo Integro de Vigilancia del Estrecho – SIVE) in 1999 with a budget of about 150 million euros for the period from 1999 to 2004. The main aim was to enhance the surveillance of Gibraltar; thereby detecting unauthorized entries of *pateras* (small boats) and *cayucos* (different types of rafts). The SIVE run by the Civil Guard became an integrated system of radars, infrared cameras, planes, helicopters and boats allowing early detection and central command.[73] In the following years, this system was further extended and deployed in other coastal areas with the financial help of the EU. Another project is the satellite communication system called Seahorse project, which was introduced by the leading IT Company Indra in cooperation with the Spanish Ministry of Interior. This project commenced in 2006 and financed again by the EU with more than 6 million euros devoted to the period of 2006-2010. Initially, the system included Portugal and South-African states such as Mauritania, Senegal, and Cape Verde. In 2009, it extended to Morocco, the Gambia and Guinea Bissau. The system was designed to facilitate secure information exchange on the movement of irregular migrants, location of suspicious boats and criminal activities such as drug, human trafficking and terrorism along the Atlantic coast of Africa.[74] Further, another aim

71 Alscher, S., "Knocking at the Doors of "Fortress Europe": Migration and Border Control in Southern Spain and Eastern Poland", *CCIS Working Papers*, University of California, San Diego, 2005, p. 10.

72 *Ibid.*, p. 12.

73 Albahari, M., "Death and the Moral State: Making Borders and Sovereignty at the Southern Edges of Europe", *CCIS Working Papers*, University of California, San Diego, 2006, p. 10.

74 See European Migration Network, *op. cit.*; Artega, *op. cit.*

is to enhance the "coordination of rescue operations and interception of illegal boats".[75]

Concluding Remarks

This chapter explores the securitization of migration as a regime of biopolitics with a special focus on the "border" between the EU/Spain and Africa. The analysis demonstrates that biopolitical governance in general and securitization of migration in particular aims to regulate and contain the so-called threats and instabilities relating to (African) immigration. The strategies and practices seek to identify and filter those migrants deemed to be a threat to the "well-being" of the EU/member states. This means that certain group of migrants, including refugees, asylum seekers, those so-called "economic migrants" originating from the poor regions of the world, has become subjected to intense technological and militarized surveillance practices. Most importantly, all these securitarian practices have been justified with a reference to the discourse of "saving the lives at sea" and the politicians and policy makers have not fully discussed the reverse effects of these practices. Hence, the "humanitarian argument" which is invoked in every occasion by the EU/member states, is likely to remain a powerful method of masking political and normative questions relating to human rights violations around the borders. To conclude there is a need for critical reflections on the current practices and discourses dominating the migration regime of the EU and member states. This is fundamental in order to end up with a humanitarian framework especially in the face of ongoing human tragedies in the Mediterranean.

Respect for fundamental rights at the door of fortress Europe

The particular situation of Ceuta and Melilla in the Schengen area

Alejandra Germán DOLDÁN

Abstract: Immigration experts and the humanitarian organizations, which work to defend human rights on both sides of the southern frontiers of Europe, estimate that, over the last twelve years, more than 5,000 immigrants have been deported from Spanish territory, by-passing legal procedure and without following the appropriate administrative processes. Spain approved Organic Law 4/2015 to justify this legislative distortion, establishing a special regime for Ceuta and Melilla that is intended to give an air of legality to these summary expulsions of people who are intercepted in the perimeter area between the frontier fences, but who have already entered Spanish national territory. The objective of this investigation is to analyse these measures. It shows how the victims are left with little or no recourse to the fundamental laws foreseen in the Spanish legal order and the minimum standards set down in Community norms, and regional and international human rights law, and that these practices therefore continue to be illegal even in view of the new regulation.

Introduction

While as a lingering effect of the global economic crisis there has been a decrease in migratory flows into developed countries, the total number of migrants worldwide has not declined in recent years. Every year thousands of people risk their lives in small overloaded boats or by jumping over a triple 6m high fence surrounding the cities of Ceuta or Melilla, in an attempt to reach Southern Europe by land or by sea. These migratory flows that occur between north and south have as a particularity that Spain is the only country of the European Union (EU) that has territorial limits with the African continent, such that it constitutes the frontier of both a country and a continent. Border fences stand between them both, separating the most unequal frontier of the planet between rich and poor: the GDP of Spain, with 47 million inhabitants, is higher than the sum of the GDP of 53 African countries with their 1,300 million inhabitants.[1]

This proximity has not meant a priority foreign policy, but on the contrary, historically, the different national governments have lived with their backs turned to Africa, as various Spanish presidents have themselves acknowledged.[2] This has been turned into a continuous history of meetings and disappointments with its southern neighbour, Morocco, with which Spain maintains a complex relationship up until today. In the case of migratory policy, which is nothing more than one aspect of that relationship, it has been characterized by a constant list of rebukes over mutual incompliance, one of the principal topics of which is the incessant debate over (in)sufficient supervision of the border fences that separate the Spanish-Moroccan frontier and the treatment meted out to those who manage to get around one of those fences.

The border between Spain and Morocco

The first great assault on the fences that separate both frontiers dates back to 2005, when the first crisis of the perimeter fences around Ceuta and Melilla took place and subsequently collective assaults have taken place, with an increase over recent years. The Ministry of Home Affairs reported that 63 people climbed the border fence of Melilla in 2011, 390 in 2012, 830 in 2013[3] and 4,176 in the first six months of 2014 in both cities; figures that the government has cited as "extraordinary migratory pressure".[4] With regard to these people who enter Spanish territory in an irregular manner and through unauthorized border posts, this work will specifically concern itself with those who have managed to pass the first of the three border fences and who therefore find themselves on Spanish soil and who are subsequently deported to Morocco in an illegal manner. These actions

1 Flores, O., "Pasado, presente y futuro de las infraestructuras críticas y servicios esenciales", in S. De Tomás (ed.), *Retos del derecho ante las nuevas amenazas*, Dykinson, Madrid, 2014, p. 84.

2 President Zapatero did not manage to seal concrete agreements with Senegal to slow the massive arrival of illegal immigrants to Spain, Libertad Digital, 05/12/2006, available at http://www.libertaddigital.com/php/ imprimir_pagina.php?cpn=1276294243; Rajoy justified his trip to Malabo with the following words: "Africa is important to us, we want to help them, we want them to help us", Europa Press, 23/06/2014, available at http://www.europapress.es/nacional/noticia-rajoy-justifica-viaje-malabo-africa-nos-importa-queremos-ayudarlos -nos-ayuden-20140623132451.html (last accessed on 15/04/2015).

3 The above figures are taken from the Annual Report "Balance de la lucha contra la inmigración irregular", Ministry of Home Affairs, for the years 2011, 2012, 2013.

4 National report submitted in accordance with paragraph 5 of the annex to Human Rights Council resolution 16/21. Spain. Human Rights Council Working Group on the Universal Periodic Review Twenty-first session 19-30 January 2015. Doc. A/HRC/WG.6/21/ESP/1, par. 44.

have popularly been called: "hot returns" or "hot expulsions". Understood as such an "action carried out by the law enforcement authorities and [that] consists of handing the foreign citizens who have been intercepted by those authorities in the area under Spanish sovereignty over to the Moroccan authorities on a *de facto* basis without carrying out the legally established procedures or meeting the internationally acknowledged guarantees".[5] In the present work, we will avoid the use of this term coined by the media and will instead use "illegal returns" in its place, so as not to lose any of the emphasis and legal weight that the term illegality carries with it, as these practices are not in line with any legally envisaged procedures, nor are they respectful of the rights of immigrants.

In accordance with the reports from NGOs that work in the area, the first documented illegal expulsion of an immigrant in Melilla dates back to 2001, but it was not until 2005 when the NGO Pro Derechos de la Infancia (Pro.De.In) obtained the first audiovisual evidence of this working practice of the Civil Guard and presented it the *Fiscalía General del Estado* [Office of the General State Prosecutor].[6] It showed various civil guards guiding a group of fifteen sub-Saharans between the two fences and, after opening a gate in the barbed wire fence, handed them over to the Auxiliary Moroccan Forces. Three months later, on 22 November 2005, the first secretary of the *Defensor del Pueblo* [Public Ombudsman] presented a devastating report in Congress against the Socialist government in which it reported that three of the seventy-three Sub-Saharans illegally returned by Spain to Morocco, on 7 October of that year, were refugees recognized as such by the United Nations High Commissioner for Refugees (UNHCR). Such a procedure was qualified by the Ombudsman as a "radically incorrect" one, when rightful access to legal counsel and respect for current laws was not forthcoming. Likewise, Amnesty International reported in a similar way, saying that it was "concerned about the irregularities in the procedure used to expel people from Spain and Morocco. Many are expelled from the area between the two border fences, others are expelled from Spain to Morocco and some from Morocco to neighbouring North African countries".[7]

---

5 "Hot returns": When the State acts outside the Law. Legal Report, 27 June 2014, available at http://eprints.ucm.es/27221/1/HOT%20RETURNS.%20WHEN%20DE%20STATE%20ACTS%20OUTSIDE%20THE%20LAW.%20Legal%20report.pdf (last accessed on 10/04/2015).

6 Médicos sin Fronteras, *Violencia e inmigración. Informe sobre la inmigración de origen subsahariano (ISS) en situación irregular en Marruecos*, September 2005, p. 17; Amnesty International, *Spain and Morocco: Failure to protect the Rights of migrants-one year on*, 26 October 2006, p. 22.

7 *Spain and Morocco: Failure ...*, doc. cit., p. 11.

It would be in June 2014, that Pro.De.In. once again showed the shame of the southern frontier; violent blows and more blows. From the Moroccan agents and from the Spanish – as the videos distributed by the NGO show[8] –, and that prompted the opening of a judicial investigation. Not because of the aggressions, but because of the illegal returns that took place on those days and which the Government qualified as "refusal at the border" and considered legal, despite criticism from Brussels, the Spanish Ombudsman, NGOs and a well-knit group of jurists.

The following arguments were highlighted, among those that the Minister of Home Affairs used to justify the legislative distortion[9]: i) interpreting that "the internal fence materializes the border that the State, in a free and sovereign decision, delimits as its national territory for the sole purpose of the immigration regime"; according to which the territory between the different fences for these purposes is not Spanish soil; ii) the second argument to justify the "hot returns" is based on the idea that it can expel, on a *de facto* basis and without the need to use any procedures, any person who is anywhere in Spanish territory, provided that they have entered irregularly, since only those who have entered through authorized border posts are in national territory, a theory that was declared null and void and was fully banned by a judgment[10]; iii) the third argument of the Ministry of the Home Affairs was based on the Agreement between the Kingdom of Spain and the Kingdom of Morocco regarding the circulation of people, the transit and the readmission of foreigners who enter irregularly, signed in Madrid on 13 February 1992. However, that Agreement does not provide sufficient legal grounds for the so-called "hot returns" to the detriment of applying the proceedings established in the immigration legislation. Also, its provisions do not justify handing over foreign citizens to the Moroccan authorities on a *de facto* basis.[11]

With the aim of providing a legal basis to these illegal returns, the Government, through the Popular Parliamentary Group in Congress,

---

8 Asociación Pro.De.In Melilla, *Violencia, ilegalidad e impunidad sin límites en la frontera de Melilla*, 18/6/2014, available at https://vimeo.com/98687161 (last accessed on 15/04/2015).

9 Appearance of the Minister of Home Affairs to report on the events at the border of the Ceuta Autonomous City, 13 February 2014.

10 The Supreme Court Administrative Division issued ruling No. 488/2001 of 20 March 2003, which stated that, in this sort of case, the legally established procedures for enabling, where applicable, foreign citizens to return to their countries of origin or provenance were the administrative sanctioning proceedings for an illegal stay in the country.

11 Each of these points has been rebutted in a Report by a group of prominent Jurists, entitled "Hot returns": When the State acts outside the Law. Legal Report, 27 June 2014.

in the course of processing the Draft Law on the protection of public security, introduced an amendment in Organic Law 4/2000, on the rights and liberties of foreigners in Spain and their social integration (LOEx).[12] In the first, the legal definition of "refusal at the border" was introduced as a special regime for the cities of Ceuta and Melilla, seeking to give these practices an air of legality. It is necessary to include a summary analysis of the controls over entrance and residence, so as to contextualize this legal modification, and to understand the particular situation of the cities that are of interest in this study.

Legal framework for foreigners in Spain

Since the Spanish Constitution (SC) entered into force in 1978, there have been various attempts to prepare a norm that, with a generalist intention, would legislate on the legal situation of foreigners in Spanish territory. In 1985, the first law on foreigners was published[13], which brought with it greater legal certainty, as it merged a large number of Circulars and Instructions from the Government in a single text, which were in many cases unknown as they had not been published in the official bulletins of State.[14] This regulation had the purpose of upholding the "constitutional mandate" foreseen in art. 13.1 Spanish Constitution.[15] It was not however the ideal legal response, as it neither corrected the technical shortcomings, nor managed to incorporate the international commitments to which Spain subscribes.

After a period of fifteen years in force, the Organic Law 4/2000, on the rights and liberties of foreigners in Spain and their social integration was approved, which implied an advance in the recognition of the rights of foreigners, including a set of rights for those who found themselves in an irregular situation. Since then, this Law has undergone a total of seventeen modifications[16] - each of which has implied a reduction in the

---

12 Organic Law 4/2000, of 11 June, on the rights and liberties of foreigners in Spain and their social integration (*Ley Orgánica 4/2000, de 11 de enero, sobre derechos y libertades de los extranjeros en España y su integración social* or LOEx), Official State Bulletin BOE No. 10 of 12/01/2000.

13 Organic Law 7/1985, of 1 July, on the rights and liberties of foreigners in Spain, BOE No. 158 of 03/07/1985.

14 Vidal, C., "La nueva ley de extranjería a la luz del texto constitucional", *Revista Española de Derecho Constitucional* No. 21, No. 62. Mayo-Agosto 2001, p. 180.

15 Art. 13.1 SC: "Aliens in Spain shall enjoy the public freedoms guaranteed by the present Part, under the terms to be laid down by treaties and the law".

16 Organics Laws 8/2000, 11/2003 and 14/2003, 2/2009, 10/2011, 4/2013, 4/2015; Laws 2/2012, 17/2012, 22/2013, 36/2014; Royal Decree 16/2012; Sentences of Constitutional Court (STC) [Tribunal Constitucional] 236/2007, 259/2007, 260/2007, 17/2013 and Sentence of Supreme Court [Tribunal Supremo] 350/2015.

rights of immigrants.[17] The last of which was on 30 March 2015, in a reform of the above law on the rights of foreigners, in the form of Organic Law 4/2015 on the protection of the safety of citizens, which introduced a tenth additional provision that foresaw a specific legal regime for the Communities of Ceuta and Melilla, in which the legal instrument of “refusal at the border” was applied to return whoever was detained in the fenced off space or buffer zone between border fences to Morocco. It was approved in the following terms: “Foreigners detected on the boundary line of the demarcation of Ceuta and Melilla attempting an unauthorized crossing of the border in a clandestine, flagrant or violent way, shall be rejected in order to prevent their illegal entry into Spain”.

In the following paragraphs, we will analyse the context and conditions in which the inclusion of this new precept takes place, for which purpose it is necessary to remember the procedures that were applied in the Law of Foreigners before this amendment.

Frontier controls

Migratory control of the people who regularly enter Spain is carried out at official border crossing points situated on the exterior frontiers of the Schengen zone. In other words, on the frontiers or borders between a signatory State to the Schengen agreement and another country outside the zone. When those who seek to enter Spanish soil do so from a State within the Schengen zone, there will be no controls as within this zone there are no internal frontiers[18], except in exceptional cases.[19] If on the contrary, entry was from a non-member state of the Schengen zone, through external borders[20], the person should comply with a series of requirements set by the authority of the Spanish government. If these are met, entry will be allowed, stamping the passport or travel documents

---

17 Conclusions and Summary. Workshop at the World Social Forum in Madrid 2010, migration, available at http://centrodefensaestudioderechoshumanos.blogspot.com.es/2010/04/conclusiones-y-resumen-taller-sobre.html (last accessed on 17/04/2015).

18 In accordance with art. 2.1 “Internal borders may be crossed at any point without any checks on persons being carried out”. Art.1. For the purposes of the Convention, Internal borders “shall mean the common land borders of the Contracting Parties, their airports for internal flights and their sea ports for regular trans-shipment connections exclusively from or to other ports within the territories of the Contracting Parties not calling at any ports outside those territories”.

19 Regulation (EC) No. 562/2006 of the European Parliament and of the Council of 15 March 2006 establishing a Community Code on the rules governing the movement of persons across borders (Schengen Borders Code): Title III, Chapter II, establishes a series of circumstances for the temporary reintroduction of border controls at internal frontiers.

20 Pursuant to Regulation No. 562/2006 ‘external borders’ means the Member states’ land borders, including river and lake borders, sea borders and their airports, river ports, sea ports and lake ports, provided that they are not internal borders” (art. 2.2).

with the security code, or if this is not possible, the document accrediting entry (art. 12.2 and .3 LOEx).

In cases in which the person intends to enter Spanish territory through border crossings located in Ceuta or in Melilla[21], if the requirements are not met, the legal formula to apply will be "refusal at the border", in which case no physical enforcement measures will be required. It is enough to prevent access to the territory or to force the withdrawal from the border crossing so that the person does not set foot on Spanish soil. From what may be understood from the second section of art. 26 LOEx, the return occurs when in the process of "passing from being outside our borders to finding oneself within national territory"[22], the foreigners "do not comply with the requirements established for entry" in the checks carried out at thc official border crossing. This implies that the foreigner does not manage to enter Spain, because the authorities detain the traveller at the border having verified that the legally established requirements have not been met.

On the contrary, when the request to enter is presented at a port or airport, once the traveller has arrived in Spanish territory, these people are considered subjects under Spanish sovereignty and jurisdiction, regardless of whether they remain in what are called the "international zones".[23] In these cases the result will be "denial of entry" (arts. 60 LOEx and 15 of its Royal Decree 557/2011 (RD)[24]) and recourse to the legal mechanism of the "return" process. At all times, it will be a reasoned decision that will provide information on the appropriate appeals process that may be followed, the timeframe to do so, and the authority with which it has to be registered, and the fundamental right to legal counsel and the right to legal representation in court, which could be appointed de officio, and the right to an interpreter if the person has no understanding or comprehension of the Spanish language or any of the co-official languages. All of these procedures are set in motion from the time at which the border crossing control takes place (art. 26 LOEx and art. 15 RD).

---

21 Pursuant to Regulation No. 562/2006, art. 36 "The provisions of this Regulation shall not affect the special rules applying to the cities of Ceuta and Melilla, as defined in the Declaration by the Kingdom of Spain on the cities of Ceuta and Melilla in the Final Act to the Agreement on the Accession of the Kingdom of Spain to the Convention implementing the Schengen Agreement of 14 June 1985".

22 STC 72/2005 of 4 April, Legal Basis 4.

23 Judgment of the European Court of Human Rights of 25 June 1996 *Amuur v. Francia*, No. 19776/92; Decision of the Constitutional Court ATC 55/1996, of 6 March 1996.

24 Royal Decree 557/2011 of 20 April approved the Regulation of Basic Law 4/2000 on the rights, freedoms and social integration of foreigners in Spain pursuant to the amendments introduced by Organic Law 4/2000, BOE No. 103 of 30/04/2011.

In the case of a person who attempts to cross or to get over the border, but without passing through an official border crossing is detained while doing so, it is a matter of "devolution" (art. 58.3 LOEx). The factual circumstance is a person who attempts to enter in an irregular manner, understanding as such whoever fails to comply with the requirements foreseen in Chapter II of Royal Decree 557/2011 and who can at that time be stopped. And it will be carried out when the Law Enforcement agents of the State, who have the duty of supervising the security of borders and the coastline, stop them trying to enter. In such situations they should as swiftly as possible be taken to the nearest Headquarters of the National Police Force for identification. This administrative requires the fulfilment of the guarantees contained in art. 23.1 RD. In other words, they should have access to legal counsel, to an interpreter in case they do not understand or speak the language, and they should have the possibility of preparing submissions relating to any situation that may involve international protection and humanitarian assistance. The legal nature of this distancing measure differs from those previously discussed, as the devolution is fully incorporated in the scope of administrative sanctioning law, insofar as it implies "the exercise of the *ius puniendi* of the State, in the form of forced repatriation to the country of origin with the imposition (or extension) of a period of prohibition of entry into Spanish territory".[25]

And finally, the sanctioning regulations establish that when the person is already within Spanish territory, but is found in an irregular situation without any authorization for the stay or period of residency, we face a procedure of "expulsion". Art. 57.1 of the LOEx lays down with regard to this infraction, "rather than the sanction of a fine, expulsion from Spanish territory may be applied, on the grounds of the principle of proportionality, following the processing of the relevant administrative fine and in a reasoned decision that assesses the constitutive facts of the offence" In other words, after the processing of the relevant file detailing the sanction, it will be decided whether the administrative offence will lead to the sanction of expulsion from national territory or whether on the contrary an administrative fine will have to be paid.

All the aforementioned legal categories envisaged in the LOEx are tied to the concept of "readmission", which may be understood as the procedure that is set in motion following the issuance of a 'return order', which implies the material act of the transference of the person from Spanish territory to the country of origin or of transit, with the consent of

---

25 Moya, D., Hernández, D., "Los controles en frontera: denegación de entrada, orden de regreso y devolución", in D. Boza, F. Donaire, D. Moya (coord.), *La nueva regulación de la inmigración y la extranjería en España. Régimen jurídico tras la LO 2/2009, el Real Decreto 557/2011 y la Ley 12/2009*, Tirant lo Blanch, Valencia, 2012, p. 221.

that country. Hence, transference to the border and the physical crossing of the border by the expelled person could be understood as somewhat different from the orders involving return, devolution, or expulsion. The ultimate aim of readmission would be the successful completion of that order issued in Spain; it is therefore "a closure point of the system"[26]; readmission is the counterpoint of the different removal measures. This brief analysis of entry and residency controls is essential to understand the particular situation of the two cities which are the focal point of this study.

Ceuta and Melilla: the southern doorways of fortress Europe

The southern border of the EU becomes the main destinations of irregular migrations by sea. It is worth noting that this form of immigration, although it is the most highly profiled in the mass media and at the forefront of the political debate, represents less than 10% of total irregular immigration into Spain.[27] The majority of this influx corresponds to migrants who, having entered in a regular way, in compliance with the requirements, overstay the time permitted by their visas or because they cannot renew their documentation.

From among the five Mediterranean member states of the EU, Spain is the only one that has a land border with the African continent, as two of its Autonomous Cities share a border with Morocco. When Spain joined the European Union in 1986, both Ceuta and Melilla automatically became part of the process of the construction of the EU, becoming the only two territorial fragments of the European Union on the African continent. However, they have not joined the Schengen Area[28], and have, ever since, found find themselves under strong migratory pressure. Melilla and Ceuta are two Spanish autonomous cities located on the north coast of Africa

26 Barrerea, F., "La readmisión en origen. La postrera expresión de la política comunitaria de alejamiento de los extranjeros inmigrantes en situación irregular", *Revista Electrónica de la Facultad de Derecho de Granada*, Estudios Doctrinales, 2010, p. 3. Available at http://www.refdugr.com/estudios_doc.php (last accessed 22/04/2015).

27 *Movimientos Migratorios en España. De la década prodigiosa de la inmigración a la recesión económica*, ACCEM, 2014. Available at http://www.accem.es/ficheros/documentos/pdf_publicaciones/Movimientos MigratoriosEspana.pdf (last accessed on 29/04/2015).

28 Regulation (EC) No. 562/2006 of the European Parliament and the Council of 15 March 2006 establishing a Community Code on the rules governing the movement of persons across borders (Schengen Borders Code), art. 36. The Schengen *acquis* as referred to in Article 1(2) of Council Decision 1999/435/EC of 20 May 1999, OJEC L239, Vol. 43, 22 September 2000.

and sharing a western border with Morocco with an area of 12.3 km^2 and 18.5 km^2, respectively.

Location of ceuta and Melilla in relation to the spanish mainland

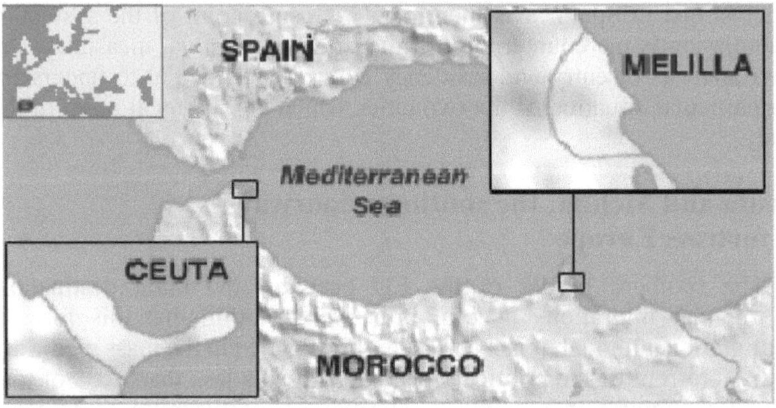

Hence, migration is one of the main issues to have occupied Spanish-Moroccan (and EU) bilateral relations. This was reflected in the first readmission agreement signed by Spain, by virtue of which Morocco engages itself to readmit to its territory "the third-country nationals who have illegally entered the territory of the requesting State from the requested State" (art. 1).[29] The result of this agreement, however, was not as the Ministry of Home Affairs wished; a legal document that could justify the illegal returns, despite the application of the procedures established in the LOEx, as the object of their regulation did not coincide in both cases. Insofar as the Law establishes the means of removal measures that may be used to return the person to his place of origin or transit, the Agreement undertakes to facilitate the readmission of the person, in other words, to regulate the way in which the coactive departure is carried out when the destination is Morocco. Nevertheless, the agreement on readmission will only be activated when the Spanish administrative authorities have taken a decision to return a person.

Neither is the amendment introduced by Organic Law 4/2015 applicable to these cities by setting up a legal regime for both cities, establishing the possibility of "refusal of entry" of whoever is stopped "on the borderline of the territorial periphery of Ceuta and Melilla while they try to surpass border security controls to cross the border in an

---

[29] The *Agreement between the Kingdom of Spain and the Kingdom of Morocco on the movement of people, the transit and the readmission of foreigners who have entered illegally* entered into force on 21 October 2012. It had been provisionally applied since 13 February 1992, date of its signature. BOE No. 100 of 25/04/1992.

irregular way".[30] In accordance with what is envisaged in Organic Law 4/2000, the refusal may only go ahead when the irregular migrant has yet to enter Spanish territory, but the people have already cleared the first of the three fences, and they are therefore on Spanish soil. The applicable legal norm would therefore be devolution, which is applicable to those circumstances in which the person in stopped at or around-about the border while seeking to enter Spain at an irregular border crossing point. A procedure that entails a series of rights and guarantees that disappear with the application of the newly approved legal statute. Leaving aside therefore the interpretation given to this new legal provision that has been incorporated and beyond whatever was the purpose of the legislative reform, it may not be legally sustained that the tenth additional provision provides normative cover to the illegal returns as they have been taking place.[31]

The violation of fundamental rights in cases of illegal returns

The modification of the LOEx, when it affects the removal measures impacts directly on various fundamental rights envisaged for those who cross or attempt to cross at unofficial border crossing points, bringing with it a series of doubts over their compatibility with the requirements to which Spain has subscribed. Both those established in the Constitution itself and those arising from community legislation and regional and international human rights law; notwithstanding the declaration that contains the tenth additional provision of Organic Law 4/2015 under section 2, incorporated in the LOEx: "In any event, the return will take place with full respect for international human rights law and the international protection to which Spain is a party".

This quote should leave us with the certainty that regardless of what is meant by "refusal", it should be done out of full respect for fundamental rights and guaranteeing the possibility of requesting international protection and humanitarian attention. Hence, the form in which these illegal returns are being carried out should be completely banished from the practice of the Civil Guard, in their border control work. Nevertheless, "there are important indications that suggest that summary returns will continue to be carried out in the way that they have been done up until now".[32]

---

30 Organic Law 4/2015 incorporates a 10th additional Regulation "Régimen especial de Ceuta y Melilla" [Special Regime for Ceuta and Melilla] to Organic Law 4/2000.

31 *Rechazos en Frontera: ¿Fronteras sin derechos?*, Legal Report, 13 April 2015.

32 *Ibid.*, p. 4.

Among these rights, the violation of which will continue, we may refer to the right to life and physical and moral integrity of those who try to come onto Spanish soil. That much is regulated in art. 15 SC, to which everybody is entitled regardless of their nationality, in other words both for Spanish nationals and foreigners. And their interpretation, according to the previsions of art. 10 SC, it will be done in accordance with what is recognized in arts. 3 and 4 of the Universal Declaration of Human Rights (UDHR), in arts. 6 and 7 of the International Covenant on Civil and Political Rights and in arts. 2 and 3 of the European Convention on Human Rights. Its violation was made quite patent in February 2014, when a group of immigrants, trying to swim to the Spanish beach of El Tarajal, in Ceuta, from Moroccan soil, were targeted by rubber bullets and tear gas, as a consequence of which 15 people died. There is also the question of degrading and violent treatment that accompanies the expulsions.

The following right that is provided for in section 3 of art. 13 of the Spanish Constitution, which envisages the right to asylum in Spain and its application in the light of art.14 of the UDHR[33] and art.18 of the Charter of Fundamental Rights of the European Union.[34] According to the Amnesty International Report on the border with Morocco, Spain continues to deny acceptable procedural access to people fleeing from violations of human rights in other countries, and refuses to grant them asylum, despite having affirmed that the principle of *non refoulement* "has been and remains the cornerstone of the Spanish system of international protection".

The LOEx states that irregular migrants who are intercepted at the border have the right to legal assistance and access to translation and should be taken to a police station as soon as possible to proceed with their identification and, when appropriate, their return.[35] This fundamental right is envisaged in art. 24 SC, which establishes "everybody" as beneficiaries, and so do articles 8 of the UDHR, art.114 of the ICCPR and art.6 of the ECHR. When the LOEx refers to the judicial protection of foreign citizens under art. 20, it does nothing more that reiterate what

---

33 Article 14.1: Everyone has the right to seek and to enjoy in other countries asylum from persecution.

34 Article 18: The right to asylum shall be guaranteed with due respect for the rules of the Geneva Convention of 28 July 1951 and the Protocol of 31 January 1967 relating to the status of refugees and in accordance with the Treaty establishing the European Community.

35 Art. 58 of Organic Law 4 /2000 and art. 23 b) of Royal Decree 557/2011, Directive 2008/115/EC of the European Parliament and of the Council of 16 December 2008 on common standards and procedures in Member states for returning illegally staying third-country nationals, OJEU L 348/98. Council of Europe 2000 on the rights and freedoms of foreigners in Spain and their social Integration.

may be taken from the individual constitutional text.[36] Also in relation to this right, the regulation of the right to free legal assistance for foreign citizens assumes special interest, in as much as the legislation recognizes this right for everybody who is found in Spain in relation to administrative and judicial procedures that may facilitate refusal to enter, their return or expulsion from Spanish territory, or which may involve procedures in matters of asylum. So far this year, nearly 3,000 people have attempted to enter European territory through the fences and fifteen people have died in the attempt, but only around 20-30% of the migrants who manage to climb over the fence enter the Short-Stay Migrant Centre (Centro de Estancia Temporal de Inmigrantes). This gap can only be explained by the fact that they are intercepted before getting to a police station and returned to Morocco, without respect for the Spanish Law on Foreign Persons, the Readmission Agreement with Morocco, or International Refugee Law. The migratory pressure on Ceuta and Melilla from Morocco is also obvious in the official data collected by various statistical sources and allows us to envisage the other side of the coin, those people who do not appear in the statistics.

Disclosures and reports from social organizations on human rights, which question the respect of Morocco for the human rights of migrant persons, should not stop referring to breaches of the fundamental human rights in their contents of people who are attempting to enter Spanish territory in an irregular manner, especially when they are of Sub-Saharan origin. Therefore, before proceeding to the expulsion of these people, the treatment that they will receive should be classified once they are handed over to the Moroccan authorities, as in accordance with the recommendation from the European Committee for the prevention of torture, "in the light of the risk of ill-treatment by members of Moroccan Auxiliary Forces of irregular migrants returned to Morocco, the CPT recommends that the Spanish authorities ensure that no person is handed over to them".[37]

All the aforementioned rights are enshrined in the constitutional text itself and, therefore, they should be interpreted by taking art. 10.2 of the SC into account, which makes international texts ratified by Spain "valuable instruments with which to configure the meaning and the scope of the rights".[38] After all, the highest normative regulation of the

36 STC 107/1984, 115/1987, 99/1985, 116/1987, 91/2000.

37 *Report to the Spanish Government on the visit to Spain carried out by the European Committee for the Prevention of Torture and Inhuman or Degrading Treatment or Punishment (CPT) from 14 to 18 July 2014*. The Spanish Government has requested the publication of this report and of its response. The Government's response is set out in document CPT/Inf (2015) 20, p. 24.

38 STC 38/1981, of 23 November, Legal Basis 4.

Spanish State orders that all interpretations of the rights and liberties that it enshrines should be in accordance with the Universal Declaration of Human Rights, and with the treaties and international agreements on the same matters ratified by Spain. This provision, Vidal Fueyo affirms, is of great relevance for foreigners, as the international regulation of human rights has, some decades ago, moved beyond the classic distinction between national and foreigner, proclaiming the existence of a set of rights applicable to all human beings, creating what has been called a minimum international standard of rights.[39]

Compliance with this minimum standard is not forthcoming at present with the illegal returns and the new legal precept of hot returns; as it is being carried out by the Government, it is incompatible with respect for the rights that have been described. Its application therefore fails to comply with the provisions of the constitution, the community and international human rights law, as well as with the requirement of the second section of the tenth additional provision of the LOEx, such that it may not be interpreted nor applied in a way that allows the observance of the aforementioned rights.

Final reflexions

The Organic Law on Foreigners 4/2000 has been modified by Organic Law 4/2015, on the protection of public safety, to provide a legal screen for the actions of the Civil Guard – endorsed by the Ministry of Home Affairs –, in the cities of Ceuta and Melilla. These actions consist of handing over people who are intercepted within the frontier perimeter to Moroccan forces, on a *de facto* basis and by passing any administrative procedure.

To do so, the modification of the law includes the legal concept of 'refusal of entry', with which the intention is to return whoever is detained within the perimeter between the fences or who has already crossed these fences to Morocco, regardless of the rights foreseen for these situations in the present Organic Law on foreigners. It takes place having distorted the legal definition of border returns previously foreseen in the law, the requirement for the application of which consists in not having passed into Spanish territory; a situation that does not occur in the cases in question, taking account of the undeniable reality that those fences are entirely located in national territory. The people who are found in the gap between the fences or who have passed over them are on Spanish soil and the legal sanction that should be applied to them is repatriation and not "hot return" or denial of entry at the border.

39 Vidal, C., La nueva ley…, *op. cit.*, p. 195.

These practices carried out over the past ten years are therefore illegal returns, even with the modification of the LOEx that is in force, so they fail to comply with the text of the constitution and community and international regulations. This is so, because they prevent access to a procedure in which the right to a hearing of the interested party, to the assistance of counsel, to an interpreter and to the possibility of requesting international protection are not respected; as well as placing at risk the life and the integrity of whoever attempts to negotiate the infrastructure of border security.

When carrying out the returns through the gates in the fences, the people are not even identified and this lack of individualization prevents any administrative action. It makes the impossibility of controlling the actions of the Spanish State quite evident, as if they are not identified, they do not even have the remotest possibility of appealing against these actions, whether as individuals or as groups.

It is not, as the Minister of Home Affairs Fernández Díaz has recently affirmed, that more or less everybody is allowed through who, "in a continuous massive and illegal manner, and on many occasions in a violent way, seek to enter Ceuta and Melilla, which is to say Spain, and the EU, illegally".[40] Rather, the controls at the border posts should be carried out with respect for fundamental rights, so that the treatment meted out to people on the southern border is therefore proof of the level of democratic quality and the Rule of Law of the Spanish State and of the constitutional values in which it is grounded.

---

[40] F. Díaz questions the reasons for requesting border reinforcements in the EU and not in Ceuta and Melilla, Diario La Vanguardia, 23/01/2015. Available at http://www.lavanguardia.com/politica/20150123/54423925277/f-diaz-cuestiona-que-se-pida-reforzar-fronteras-en-ue-y-no-en-ceuta-y-melilla.html (last accessed on 27/04/2015).

Immigration policy within “Fortress Europe”

The legalisation of “hot returns” in Spain*

Lucía PAYERO LÓPEZ

Abstract: This chapter will analyse both “hot returns”, *de facto* expulsions of immigrants in Ceuta and Melilla, and the recent creation of a legal procedure of exit for illegal immigrants, rejections at the border, that is aimed at legalising “hot returns.” It will try to show how this new policy is a good example of a nationalist discourse which intends to avoid community disintegration in a particularly sensitive time of economic crisis.

It don’t take no nerve to do somepin when there
ain’t nothin’ else you can do
John Steinbeck, *The grapes of wrath*

“Hot returns” and their justification

As a southern European country, Spanish borders are also the limits of the so-called “Fortress Europe”. In Spain this frontier is not only maritime, but also terrestrial: two cities in the north of Africa, Ceuta and Melilla, are under Spanish sovereignty. Two barriers have been built to separate Spain from Morocco or, in other words, Europe from Africa: one surrounding Ceuta (8 kilometres long) and the other around Melilla (12 kilometres long). The barriers actually consist of three wire fences of 6 metres high each, with blades and a special design to avoid people climbing over. The gap between the fences is filled with a tangle of steel wires. Providing the former is not enough, Civil Guard agents patrol the border behind the three fences with the aim of preventing anyone from entering. In addition to these six obstacles, Morocco has built another fence and dug a moat of several metres deep which has been reported to be full of glass at the bottom.[1]

* I would like to thank Dr. Sarah Hackett, from Bath Spa University, and Ian L. Bytheway for reading a previous draft of this article and suggesting very interesting ideas. I am also indebted to the anonymous reviewers whose comments helped me to improve the final version of this work. The opinions expressed, however, are only mine.

1 Vargas, J., “Nada cambia en la frontera sur con la ‘ley mordaza’”, *Público*, 28 March 2015.

Immigrants have tried to enter the Schengen Area through both of these fences – the one in Ceuta and the other in Melilla – for years: this is not new. Neither is the illegal expulsion of sub-Saharan people who breach the frontier novel: experts on migration and NGOs calculate that around 5000 immigrants have been returned on the spot since 2001.[2] These expulsions are called "hot returns", a practice which consists of handing the foreigners who have been intercepted by the Civil Guard or the National Police "in the area under Spanish sovereignty over to the Moroccan authorities on a *de facto* basis, that is, without carrying out the legally established procedures or meeting the guarantees" that are recognised in international treaties.[3] The originality now lies in the public reaction of the Spanish government to those unlawful actions committed by Civil Guard agents. The controversy generated after the death of 15 foreigners who were shot by the Civil Guard with rubber bullets while swimming to the coast of Ceuta[4] led the Spanish Home Secretary, Jorge Fernández Díaz, to justify "hot returns". Two main arguments were used: the coining of the concept of an "operational" border and the absence of an obligation to follow any formal procedure to expel aliens who try to cross the frontier illegally.[5]

The concept of an "operational" border means that aliens are understood to be in Spain only when they have crossed the three fences or, in case they arrive in Spain by sea, after having surpassed the imaginary line formed by the agents who guard the frontier. According to this reasoning, immigrants who are intercepted when they have either climbed onto one of the fences, are in the space between them, or swimming near the beach have not crossed the border yet, so they have thus not entered Spain. This "operational" border is only used for migration purposes: outside this context, the Spanish borders are those which have been established in international treaties.

2 Blasco de Avellaneda, J., "España lleva 12 años expulsando ilegalmente inmigrantes en Melilla", *Eldiario.es*, 19 November 2013.

3 Martínez Escamilla, M. *et al.*, "'Hot Returns': When the State Acts Outside the Law", Legal Report, 27 June 2014, p. 2.

4 These events took place on El Tarajal beach (Ceuta) on 6 February 2014. A very complete research project carried out by independent journalists from 6 February 2014 to 6 February 2015 can be read in Sánchez, J. L., Sánchez, G. (coords.), "Las muertes de Ceuta", *Eldiario.es*.

5 Additionally, it was also said that the Agreement between Spain and Morocco regarding the circulation of people, the transit and the readmission of foreigners who have entered illegally provided a legal backing to "hot returns". However, this line of reasoning falls outside the remit of this chapter. A well-justified criticism of this argument can be read in Martínez Escamilla, M. *et al.*, "'Hot Returns': When the State Acts Outside the Law", *op. cit.*, pp. 10-12.

The Home Office also maintained that summary expulsions were allowed providing the foreigner had not entered through authorised border posts. The reason is that the immigrant was not considered to have reached the territory of Spain and, consequently, Spanish migration laws were not applicable.

Both reasons admit sound counterarguments. First of all, the concept of an "operational" border lacks legal grounds. Frontiers are established by international treaties with binding effects on any state.[6] According to these rules, all Spanish beaches and their coastline, including those of Ceuta and Melilla, are undoubtedly under Spanish sovereignty (territorial water); the same can be said of the external fence: it was erected on Spanish, rather than Moroccan, territory. Secondly, no law legitimises a border concept that can be determined whimsically *ad hoc*. The reason is that such a concept would violate at least two essential principles: legal certainty and the prohibition of arbitrariness (section 9.3 of the Spanish Constitution).[7] Thus the idea that the government is allowed to discretionarily modify the limits of state territory cannot be defended on a legal basis, even if that change is introduced only for migration purposes.[8] Thirdly, even if the concept of an "operational" border is accepted, Spanish police and civil guard officers are always subjected to the Constitution and the rest of the Spanish legal order when they perform their duties.[9] This is not only the case if the actions are carried out in Spain, but also abroad.[10]

6 See the Decision of the First Instance and Instruction Court No. 2 of Melilla (Auto del Juzgado de Primera Instancia e Instrucción No. 2 de Melilla), of 11 September 2014.

7 Section 9.3 of the Constitution establishes: "the Constitution guarantees the principle of legality, the hierarchy of legal provisions, the publicity of legal statutes, the non-retroactivity of punitive provisions that are not favourable to or restrictive of individual rights, the certainty that the rule of law shall prevail, the accountability of public authorities, and the prohibition of arbitrary action of public authorities".

8 The same is also applicable to the delimitation of border posts. Although the establishment of border posts falls within the state jurisdiction, it should be done by general rules rather than by an *ad casu* norm.

9 According to the European Court of Human Rights Judgment of 27 February 2012, case of Hirsi Hamaa and others vs. Italy, "whenever the State through its agents operating outside its territory exercises control and authority over an individual, and thus jurisdiction, the State is under an obligation under Article 1 [of the European Convention on Human Rights] to secure for that individual the rights and freedoms under Section I of the Convention that are relevant to the situation of that individual" (paragraph 74).

10 See Sentence of the Constitutional Court 21/1997, of 10 February (Legal Basis 2).

Secondly, when immigrants are intercepted at the Spanish border, the Immigration Act[11] (hereinafter, LEX) and the Immigration Decree[12] (hereinafter, REX) contemplate three different procedures of exit: expulsion (section 57 LEX), refusal of entry (sections 26.2 LEX and 15 REX) and return (sections 58.3b and 23 REX).

The *expulsion* is one of the sanctions which can be applied to a foreigner who is in Spain and lacks due authorisation to be there. According to section 57.1 of the LEX, "when the offenders are foreigners and carry out the actions classified as very serious or serious in paragraphs a), b), c), d) and f) of article 53.1 of this Act[13], the expulsion from Spanish territory can be applied, instead of a fine, on the basis of the principle of proportionality, after the corresponding administrative file is processed and a reasoned decision is made that assesses the facts that constitute the breach". Therefore, when a foreigner is found on Spanish territory without due authorisation to stay and/or live there, he/she can be either fined or expelled from Spain. In the cases the expulsion is applied, an administrative file must be processed and a reasoned resolution taken. As can be seen, the sanction of expulsion does not contemplate acting on a *de facto* basis.

The *refusal of entry* is not a sanction, but the process applicable when foreigners intend to enter Spain through the authorised border posts and they do not meet the entry requirements. In that case, they will be "refused entry through a reasoned resolution, with the information about the appeals that can be filed against this decision, the deadline for doing so, and the authority where they must formalise it. They will also be informed of their right to legal assistance, which can be provided free of charge through the legal aid system, and to an interpreter, which shall start at the time that the control is made at the border post" (section 26.2 of the LEX). Two remarks may be made. First, immigrants who enter Spain by climbing the fences of Ceuta and Melilla or through the beaches of these two cities do not fall under the scope of section 26 of the LEX because they are not asking for access at an authorised post. Second, the refusal of entry also excludes *de facto* actions.

Finally, section 58.3 b) of the LEX states that "no expulsion file is required for returning the foreigners [...] who plan to illegally enter the country." The REX specifies that "foreigners who are intercepted at

11 Organic Act 4/2000, of 11 January, on the rights and freedoms of foreigners in Spain and their social integration.

12 Royal Decree 557/2011, of 20 April, approving the regulation of the Organic Act 4/2000.

13 Section 53.1 a) of the LEX establishes that it is a serious breach to stay or reside illegally in Spain, that is, lacking the proper administrative authorization.

the border or in its vicinity shall be considered to be included for such purposes" (section 23.1 b). The *return* is not a sanction either, but an administrative activity which naturally excludes factual channels.

According to this, it seems that the return is the procedure which, at least, should be used at the southern border of Spain when aliens who are intercepted at the fence or in its vicinity plan to enter Spain through an area that has not been authorised for that purpose. Therefore, "hot returns" are being used in circumstances in which immigration legislation contemplates a specific procedure: the return. The return is an administrative procedure which includes a number of requisites: foreigners must be taken to a police station; a lawyer must be appointed for them; when they do not speak Spanish, an interpreter must be provided for them; they must be identified; a resolution for their devolution must be issued; and the devolution itself must be carried out by the national police force[14], not by the Civil Guard.

In conclusion, handing immigrants over to the Moroccan authorities on a *de facto* basis when they are trying to enter Spain through the fences of Ceuta and Melilla directly infringes the LEX and the REX.

"Rejections at the border": the legalisation of "hot returns"?

As has been explained, "hot returns" are being used instead of the procedure of return. Moreover, "hot returns" lack a legal backing and the arguments employed by the Spanish Home Office to justify these actions (mainly, the concept of an "operational" border and the possibility of expelling aliens who have entered irregularly on a *de facto* basis) are not sound. Being aware of this circumstance, and after receiving harsh criticisms from the EU[15], the Spanish government introduced a fourth

---

14 Martínez Escamilla, M. *et al.*, "'Hot Returns': When the State Acts Outside the Law", *op. cit.*, pp. 4-5.

15 After the tragedy of El Tarajal beach, Cecilia Malmström, the then-Commissioner for Home Affairs, demanded explanations from Spain as to why the Civil Guard used rubber bullets against sub-Saharan migrants who tried to reach the Spanish coast (Gallego, J. G., "Bruselas pide explicaciones a España por el uso de bolas de goma contra inmigrantes en Ceuta", *El Mundo*, 14 February 2014). On 17 October 2014, Nils Muižnieks, Commissioner of Human Rights of the European Council, after watching a video recorded by Prodein in which an immigrant was being expelled on a *de facto* basis, condemned "hot returns" in Facebook (Ferrer Gallardo, X., "Los consejo(s) de Europa", *Público*, 21 October 2014). On 24 October, Cecilia Malmström addressed a letter to the Spanish Home Secretary expressing concern for the alleged beating of that immigrant. Information on the investigation of these facts was also requested (Abellán, L., "Bruselas acusa a España de violar las reglas europeas de fronteras", *El País*, 31 October 2014).

procedure of exit into immigration legislation: the *rejection at the border*. With the intention of providing a legal foundation to "hot returns", an Additional Provision of the Organic Act 4/2015, of 30th March, on the Protection of Citizens' Security was passed.[16] It read as follows:

> Tenth Additional Provision. Special Regime of Ceuta and Melilla.
>
> 1. Foreigners who are intercepted on the border line of the territorial demarcation of Ceuta or Melilla while they are trying to irregularly cross the border by overtaking the obstacles of containment can be rejected to avoid their unlawful entry in Spain.
>
> 2. In all cases, the rejection shall be done in conformity with the international norms on human rights and international protection of which Spain is part.
>
> 3. Applications for international protection shall be formalised at the authorised border posts and processed according to international protection laws.

The new legal figure aimed to circumvent the procedure of return which would be applicable in general terms. However, two questions must be answered. First of all, it should be determined whether "hot returns" fall within the scope of rejections at the border. Secondly, regardless of the response given to the former issue, the compliance of rejections at the border and "hot returns" with international human rights law, EU fundamental rights and constitutional rights should be analysed.

Does the introduction of rejections at the border entail the legalisation of "hot returns"?

Even if the intention of the government was to legalise "hot returns" by means of the creation of this procedure of exit, a literal reading of the Tenth Additional Provision of the Organic Act 4/2015 leads to the opposite conclusion. The reason is that, according to this provision, rejection at the border is not applicable to most of the cases in which the Spanish authorities have resorted to "hot returns."

---

[16] It is interesting to note that although this Provision was added to the Organic Act on the Protection of Citizens' Security, in fact it amounted to an amendment of the LEX. The normal procedure would have been to initiate a reform of the LEX, but reasons of urgency were alleged during the discussion on the modification of the Organic Act 4/2015 in the Congress of Deputies and this section was introduced as an amendment to that bill. According to the Constitutional Court, the use of the parliamentary amendment to include *ex novo* unrelated matters to the main issue is exorbitant (Sentence of the Constitutional Court 119/2011, of 5 July; 136/2011, of 13 September). Moreover, this subterfuge eluded the required legal opinions on the technical suitability and legal compliance of the bill (Martínez Escamilla, M. *et al.*, "'Rechazos en frontera': ¿Frontera sin derechos?", Legal Report, 13 April 2015, p. 9).

First of all, the explicit reference to "border obstacles of containment", structures which only exist on the terrestrial border, together with the mention of "the border line of the territorial demarcation of Ceuta or Melilla", leave out the events of El Tarajal beach, for example. Any attempt to cross the maritime border of Spain does not allow the application of the new procedure of exit: thus, the rejection at the border is designed to be applied only when immigrants are trying to enter Spain by land.

Secondly, the provision also reads "foreigners who are intercepted on the border line of the territorial demarcation of Ceuta or Melilla *while they are trying* to irregularly cross the border by overtaking the obstacles of containment, can be *rejected to avoid their unlawful entry* in Spain" (emphasis added). The words in italics leave no doubt that those immigrants who are rejected at the border need to have not crossed the border yet. Otherwise, they cannot either try to irregularly cross it or be rejected. Specifically, the rejection at the border will not be applicable when aliens are intercepted either after having surpassed the internal fence, in the middle of two fences, or climbed onto one of the three fences. In all these cases, immigrants are already on Spanish territory, not trying to cross the border, so the procedure of return should be used. As has been pointed out, a clumsy writing of the provision prevents it from being applied to the cases it allegedly intended to regulate.[17]

Therefore, the Home Office may employ the concept of an "operational" border in order to sidestep the literal wording of the rule and its uselessness for the purposes it was initially devised for. As has already been explained, this concept lacks legal grounds and must be rejected.

In conclusion, "hot returns" cannot be subsumed in the recently created figure of rejections at the border. Even if the government aimed to legalise "hot returns", a literal reading of the Tenth Additional Provision of the Organic Act 4/2015 excludes it from being applied to the actions in which summary expulsions are being carried out. Rather, the procedure of return should be used.

Rejections at the border, "hot returns" and the respect of human rights

Even if rejection at the border was determined to be applicable to the actions it was initially designed for, attention should be paid to the second paragraph of the Tenth Additional Provision: "in all cases, the rejection

17 Martínez Escamilla, M. *et al.*, "'Rechazos en frontera': ¿Frontera sin derechos?", *op. cit.*, p. 13.

shall be done in conformity with the international norms on human rights and international protection of which Spain is part."

The first question that comes to mind is: why was this paragraph included? One could argue that it serves no purpose. Whatever the rejection at the border takes, it must comply with the international and domestic regulations on human rights, including asylum, just like any law or act carried out by the Spanish authorities. As the specification was redundant, some authors have suggested that the government intended to legalise "hot returns" by means of the creation of this legal figure and, with the vague mention of human rights, avoid some criticisms that summary expulsions had received before that provision was passed. In this sense, rejection at the border would constitute the legal coverage of an illegal practice: *de facto* returns.[18]

Although the provision does not explain the procedure which must be followed to reject foreigners at the border, some minimum requirements are derived from international, domestic and EU law. According to the LEX, the interested party must be heard (section 20.2) and duly informed of the appeals that may be brought against the resolution, which has to be motivated (section 26.2). Moreover, "foreigners who are in Spain are entitled to legal assistance in all the administrative processes that can lead to the refusal of their entry, return, or expulsion from Spanish territory, as well as in all the processes on international protection. They are equally entitled to an interpreter if they do not understand or speak the official language. Both assistances shall be free when they lack enough economic resources" (section 22.2). The alien must be identified and his/her procedure individualised so that the right to asylum can be exercised. In this sense, section 19.1 of the Charter of Fundamental Rights of the EU prohibits collective expulsions of immigrants.

Rejections at the border must comply with the aforementioned guarantees, even if the provision makes no reference to human rights and international protection. "Hot returns" do not respect any of these, so they breach international, EU and Spanish law. The reform of the LEX that introduced a special procedure of exit to be applied in Ceuta and Melilla has been worded in such a way that summary expulsions as have been carried out at the southern border are excluded of its scope; however, in case the official exegesis of this provision included "hot returns" within it, the conclusion would be that the actions carried out at the border of Ceuta and Melilla violate not only international, EU and domestic law, but also the Tenth Additional Provision.

---

[18] Martínez Escamilla, M. *et al.*, "'Rechazos en frontera': ¿Frontera sin derechos?", *op. cit.*, p. 18.

The meaning of the reform of the LEX

If "hot returns" can be neither legalised nor even included within the scope of rejections at the border, what is the reason that explains the creation of this new legal procedure of exit?

The reform of the LEX, by which the figure of the rejection at the border was introduced, is in line with the orientation of the EU's migration policy and, more specifically, that of Spain. Most of the resources and efforts are devoted to control flows of people, with a particular focus on combating irregular immigration. Although it can be debated whether, and to what extent, the official discourse is false,[19] what is beyond any doubt is that all the legal tools and policies use an instrumental concept of the immigrant. In this sense, immigrants are accepted as long as they are useful for the economy of the arrival country. These are the keys of that utilitarian vision: immigrants do the jobs nationals turn down, the domestic population is rejuvenated, and more contributions are paid to the social security system. Thus, immigration is in the interest of the receiving states.

This chapter suggests a critical interpretation of the hegemonic thinking which highlights the underpinnings of the official discourse on immigration.[20] European governments' first commitment is not to fight irregular immigration, but to ensure that capitalism enjoys good health. Capitalism needs a steady labour surplus – or, in Marx's words, an "industrial reserve army"–[21] both to regulate wages and to supply work for sudden expansions in production. Regarding wages, the industrial reserve army is forced to survive in a precarious situation so that it puts pressure on workers to accept progressively worse labour conditions. When people in employment are overloaded with work, the industrial reserve army grows; at the same time, the increasing competition that surplus population exerts on workers condemns the latter to exploitation.

As for work supply, it is interesting to note that the proportion between the industrial *active* army and the *reserve* one does not depend on the

---

19 Millions of immigrants are estimated to be living illegally in the EU (hundreds of thousands in Spain), and the number of expulsions becomes negligible when compared with the number of entries through unauthorised posts (Romero, E., *Un deseo apasionado de trabajo más barato y servicial. Migraciones, fronteras y capitalismo*, Cambalache, Oviedo, 2010, pp. 98-99). In case the official version is true, the conclusion which can be drawn is that EU migration policy and legislation have failed.

20 See also Payero, L., "El asalto a la fortaleza europea. Inmigración y derechos en la película *Cuando naces ya no puedes esconderte* (Marco Tullio Giordana, 2005)", in B. Rivaya and J. A. Gómez García (eds.), *Filosofía del Derecho y Cine*, Universidade da Coruña, A Coruña, 2012.

21 Marx, K., *Capital*, Dent, London, 1930.

demographic cycle, but on the economic one. That is why a decrease in the number of incoming immigrants bears no relevance to the design of migration policy. In order to face sudden market contractions or expansions, a labour surplus is required so that the very existence of the system is guaranteed. The accumulation of wealth on one side implies the accretion of misery and precariousness on the opposite, a *sine qua non* for the smooth running of capitalism: therefore, rather than being one of the goals of the economic system, full employment is anomalous to it.

The industrial reserve army is not only composed of immigrants: a lot of nationals are part of it, especially in times of economic crisis. This situation creates problems of social cohesion which can cause citizens to rise up against governments. In this context the scope of the legalisation of "hot returns" can be properly understood. The reform performs a symbolic function whose message is aimed at Spaniards rather than at illegal immigrants. Five different aspects should be addressed in order to explain the importance of the symbolism contained in this new immigration norm.

First of all, the government is using the LEX as an instrument to feign and/or show that undocumented immigrants are severely punished in Spain. This strategy seems particularly useful in a context of economic crisis where a scapegoat is needed to soothe popular dissatisfaction. The situation is so paradoxical that those who are to blame for provoking the crisis and worsening the position of the working class when trying to respond to it (cuts on public services, privatisation, corruption) are now deviating public attention from themselves to other victims who are depicted as culprits: not only immigrants, but also civil servants and recipients of social benefits.[22] For the particular case of immigrants, they are said to be responsible for the high unemployment rates in Spain as they accept any kind of job for poverty wages. "Spanish people, first" was not only the slogan of the fascist party National Democracy, but it has become a popular idea that receives general approval.[23] This agreement

22 De Lucas, J., "Políticas migratorias, democracia y derechos en tiempos de crisis", *Working Paper*, 2015, p. 7.

23 The main political parties and unions in Spain argue that flows of immigrants should give an instrumental response to the needs of the labour market, an idea that basically means "nationals, first". A good example of it is the comic book edited by the union Comisiones Obreras: Campuzano, L. F., *Sueños de vida*, COMFIA, Madrid, 2008. However, the most serious thing is not that labour organisations and right-wing parties share the same discourse on immigration; rather, what is really worrying is that their vision on immigration has become hegemonic (Romero, E., *Un deseo apasionado de trabajo más barato y servicial*, *op. cit.*, p. 27). In this sense, the 2008 Report on the evolution of racism and xenophobia in Spain, elaborated by the Spanish Observatory of Racism and Xenophobia (an organization that depends on the Ministry of Employment), found that a high number of Spaniards "rejected immigrants in terms

shows that the creation of an external enemy is a good strategy when attempting to foster social cohesion.

This leads to the second aspect involved in the symbolic function of the amendment of the LEX: the construction of enemies to fill citizens with fear. In the aftermath of 9/11, both the US and the EU embarked on a policy which offered security in exchange for liberty. Afraid of the *others*, Western societies closed themselves off into a more and more limited *we*.[24] The financial crisis served as an excuse to deepen this tendency. Treated as enemies, immigrants are not entitled to the rights of citizens, and instead of the rule of law, a state of exception governs: the presumption of innocence, guarantism, or the principle of legality are not applied to them. In this sense, and making a parallel with Jakobs' Enemy Criminal Law[25], it may be said that EU immigration law, including the Spanish LEX, is a good example of an *Enemy Administrative Law*.[26] The

---

of the *preference for nationals* over foreigners. This is one of the central elements to the traditional xenophobic discourse. Those who deliver this speech assert that, although contrary to the *social desideratum*, priority should be given to the domestic population", particularly in the access to medical attention (41% of those polled) and regarding the possibility to choose a school for their children (54%) (Cea, M. A., Valles, M. S., "Evolución del racismo y la xenofobia en España (informe 2008)", Ministerio de Trabajo e Inmigración, Madrid, 2008, p. 131).

24 De Lucas, J., "El miedo en las sociedades más seguras de la historia", *Anales de la Cátedra Francisco Suárez*, Vol. 43, 2009.

25 Jakobs argues that States can fight crime by using two different tools: Enemy Criminal Law and Citizen Criminal Law. Enemy Criminal Law is aimed at enemies, that is, people who "to a not merely incidental extent in their attitude or their occupational life or by their inclusion in an organisation have at any rate presumably permanently turned away from the law and in this respect do not guarantee the minimum cognitive security of personal behaviour and demonstrates this deficit by their behaviour" (Jakobs, G., "On the Theory of Enemy Criminal Law", in M. D. Dubber (ed.), *Foundational Texts in Modern Criminal Law*, Oxford University Press, Oxford, 2014, p. 420). Quite the opposite, Citizen Criminal Law is aimed at citizens, that is, people who despite the fact of having committed an illegal action display a minimum of law-abiding behaviour. Citizens are punished for past actions and this punishment is a form of communication. However, communicating with enemies is impossible: that is why Enemy Criminal Law tries to prevent future acts by isolating the enemy: "*he*, cognitively speaking is a dubious figure against whom we are securing ourselves" (*op. cit.*, p. 421). Thus, Enemy Criminal Law is a sort of anticipatory criminality for future wrong based on the presumption that the perpetrator somewhat permanently has abandoned the law or parts of it. In the end, the enemy is not considered a person and, after being excluded from society, he is combated in war.

26 The recently-coined term "Enemy Administrative Law" refers to the tendency to limit fundamental rights – more specifically, freedom of speech and association, the right to assembly and demonstration, rights of political participation, freedom of movement – through administrative legislation. Protesters, immigrants and other social groups are considered enemies; however, as they typically do not commit crimes, sanctions applied to them fall within the scope of Administrative Law. Be that as it may, the

immigrant is a non-person whose "absent presence"[27] forces him/her to be invisible in the public space. Moreover, like the *homo sacer* in the archaic Roman law, he/she is subjected to unpunished violence.[28] Deprived of basic rights, immigrants are even more useful for the economy of the arrival country: as they are not human beings, they can be treated as goods; and it should not be forgotten than in this globalised world only goods and capital actually enjoy free movement.[29]

The strategy of fear has an internal dimension too, and this leads to the third aspect of the symbolic function the amendment fulfils: the refusal to confer rights on immigrants has an impact on society itself. First of all, the state of exception is capable of being extended to other groups who will become internal enemies: the enactment of the Organic Act 4/2015, popularly known as the *Ley Mordaza* (Gag Law)[30], is a good example of how freedom of speech is being severely limited. Demonstrators, political activists, extreme left-wing parties and anyone

---

underlying philosophy is the same in both cases: punishment is aimed at preventing future actions whose perpetrators have been excluded from the category of (good) citizens. This legislation is justified on security grounds.

27 Sayad, A., *L'immigration ou les paradoxes de l'altérité*, De Boeck-Wesmael, Brussels, 1991.

28 Agamben, G., *Homo Sacer. Sovereign Power and Bare Life*, Stanford University Press, Stanford, 1998, p. 82.

29 Mezzadra, S., *Diritto di fuga. Migrazioni, cittadinanza e globalizzazione*, Ombre Corte, Verona, 2006 (2nd ed.), pp. 54, 72.

30 The reform of the Organic Act on the Protection of Citizens' Security answered to the government's desire of punishing social protest. As Criminal judgments were not severe enough with demonstrators and political activists, the People's Party (PP) decided to change both the Criminal Code and the Organic Act on the Protection of Citizens' Security. Actions included in the Criminal Code as minor offences were introduced into the Organic Act on the Protection of Citizens' Security as administrative infractions. Two main consequences derived from this amendment. First, fines were increased dramatically. Second, legal guarantees of criminal processes are lacking: the administration imposes the fine – not a judge – and testimony given by police officers is enough to accuse somebody – in the criminal process, both parties are on an equal footing –. There is the possibility to appeal against the sanction to an Administrative Court, but the judge will know the facts as they have been presented by the administration. For all these reasons, the Organic Act 4/2015 has been called "Gag Law" or "Act against the 15M movement". Some of the actions that are considered serious infractions according to the new law (fines between 601 and 30.050,61€) are: threatening citizens' security during demonstrations that take place in front of the Congress of Deputies, the Senate or the Legislative Assemblies of the Autonomous Communities, although the chambers are not met, preventing civil servants or authorities from enforcing administrative or judicial resolutions (typically, eviction orders), or using images and personal or professional data of police officers without due authorisation (section 36).

who does not match the stereotype of the "silent majority"[31], all of whom typically come from the working class, are becoming the new enemies. Secondly, the discourse of the enemy provokes not only fear, but also passiveness on citizen participation[32] and the deterioration of democracy itself.[33] With very few exceptions, foreigners are excluded from the rights of political participation. This seems natural in a world divided into nation-states – or states which are considered to take this form –, but infringes the democratic principle which establishes that there must be a correspondence between those subjected to the law and those entitled to vote.[34] Such a poor conception of democracy, which allows millions of people within the EU to pay taxes but not to participate in elections, is gradually expanding its limits: Spanish emigrants, for instance, face great difficulty with postal voting.[35]

The fourth element of the symbolic function of the reform of the LEX refers to the national community and its unity. According to Habermas, national discourse combines elements of the subjective paradigm – republican conviction – with the objective one – national

---

[31] In September 2012 there was a massive demonstration around the Congress of Deputies in Madrid to protest against the austerity measures imposed by the government. Mariano Rajoy was in New York and when journalists asked him about the protest, he honoured all those people who did not demonstrate or appear on the news. Those people were called the "silent majority" (see González, M., "Rajoy rechaza el 25-S y alaba a la 'mayoría silenciosa que no se manifiesta'", *El País*, 27 September 2012). After that, several ministers used the new expression to equally condemn dissent (see "El gobierno dice que una mayoría silenciosa de catalanes no se ha manifestado", *El Periódico*, 11 September 2013; "Santamaría: 'el gobierno escuchará a todos, también a la mayoría silenciosa'", *El País*, 12 September 2013).

[32] De Lucas, J., "Inmigrantes. Del estado de excepción al Estado de derecho", *Oñati Socio-Legal Series*, Vol. 1, No. 3, 2011, p. 4.

[33] De Lucas, J., "Políticas migratorias, democracia y derechos en tiempos de crisis", *op. cit.*, p. 4.

[34] In this sense, Balibar talks of a "citizenship without community" to refer to the fact that "in some circumstances the *traditions*, the more or less fictive 'memories', [...] must be put in question. This is [...] the condition for *some to become active citizens once again* ('authors' of or 'responsible' for the political institution) while *others become active citizens on both sides of a border* (not only a geographical or geopolitical border but a political and anthropological one). [...] But the converse is also true: some can only *become* active citizens for the first time (collective bearers of personal rights to speech, participation, and decision making in the public sphere) if others become active citizens *again*, or exercise once again their capacities in some way other than in a nominal fashion, by heritage and delegation" (Balibar, É., *We, the People of Europe?*, Princeton University Press, Princeton, 2004, p. 76).

[35] Ibarra, A., "El gobierno cierra el censo sin avisar y deja a miles de emigrantes sin votar en las generales", *Público*, 30 July 2015; Castro, I., "La Marea Granate teme que los plazos electorales impidan votar en las generales a miles de inmigrantes", *Eldiario.es*, 30 July 2015.

self-awareness.[36] An excessive relevance of the subjective element results in the break-up of society; that is why growing doses of objectivism are required, particularly in times of crisis. External threats reinforce the feeling of a common identity shared by the members of the nation. Hence the implementation of racist stereotypes which link immigration to fundamentalism – the former attacks national culture and, specifically, human rights and democracy –, rises in unemployment rates – it attacks *our* economic superiority –, organised crime – it attacks security and order – and the deterioration of public services – it attacks *our* welfare.[37]

Finally, it is worth remarking that even if "hot returns" do not fit the legal category of rejections at the border, the creation of the latter has served to spread the message that the former has been legalised. From now on, the problem will have to be confronted by lawyers and judges. Anyway, only experts on law who support a certain exegesis of it will be able to know that "hot returns" have not been – and cannot be – legalised. Thanks to this reform of the LEX, the government has covered its back in the face of public opinion and the EU, temporarily at least.

---

36 Habermas, J., "Citizenship and Cultural Identity", in *Between Facts and Norms. Contributions to a Discourse Theory of Law and Democracy*, The MIT Press, Cambridge (Mass.), 1996.

37 Payero, L., "El asalto a la fortaleza europea", *op. cit.*, p. 165.

Migration-related detention

A focus on the Italian context*

Francesca Esposito, José Ornelas
and Caterina Arcidiacono

Abstract: Inspired by a community psychology ecological perspective, this chapter addresses migration-related detention as part of that set of practices implemented by the EU and the Schengen Area to ensure internal security by strengthening external borders control. In particular, it focuses on the Italian context. Starting from a historical overview of the Italian legal and policy framework on migration, a critical analysis of the rationale for migrant detention and deportation is developed, highlighting the business interests at stake. In this regard, the concept of immigration industrial complex is utilized, emphasizing its similarities with the military and prison industrial complexes. Finally, the case of an Italian migration-related detention center is illustrated. We argue for the use of ecological multilevel analysis to grasp the complexity of these sites of confinement, and shed light on the forces and interests that revolve around them. Alternatives are advocated based on freedom and justice for all.

Introduction

In 2014, the International Organization for Migration (IOM) documented that, since 2000, at least 40,000 migrants have died trying to cross global borders. At least 4,077 of such deaths occurred in 2014, and up to 3,072 of them took place in the Mediterranean.[1] At the time of writing, a terrible shipwreck claimed between 700 and 900 victims, bringing to over 1,650 the number of people who have died so far in 2015 during the Mediterranean crossing.[2] Although dramatic, these data give

* Acknowledgments: The authors would like to thank Nina Amelung, Olivia Fiorilli and Inês Vieira for their valuable feedback on this chapter and support in language editing. Financing: The first author has received a scholarship by the Portuguese Foundation for Science and Technology-FCT (SFRH/BD/87854/2012).

1 Brian, T., Laczko, F., *Fatal Journeys. Tracking Lives Lost during Migration*, International Organization for Migration, Geneva, 2014.

2 See "Naufragio a sud della Sicilia, almeno 800 morti tra i migranti. Superstiti arrivati a Catania: "Salvi perché aggrappati ai morti", *La Repubblica*, 20 April 2015.

an under-estimated picture of the phenomenon since many deaths are not recorded.[3] This evidence calls for us to reflect on the nature, functions, and impacts of border control in conditions of mass mobility.[4] Furthermore, it urges a critical analysis of how the abolition of internal border control within the Schengen Area, in the name of the right of free movement as a basic human right, has been counterbalanced by an increasing concern for the security of external borders, with serious consequences for the lives of migrants, especially those that are undocumented.

As Vacchiano noted "at the same time that the project for an internal space of 'freedom, security and justice' – according to the Amsterdam Treaty prominent formula – was established, 'the need for a more efficient management of migration flows at all their stages' (Tampere Programme, art. 22, emphasis mine) was acknowledged".[5] Significant in this regard is the establishment, on the 26 October 2004, of the European Agency for the Management of Operational Cooperation at the External Borders of the Member states of the European Union (Frontex), whose main objective is to "facilitate the application of existing and future Community measures relating to the management of external borders [including border surveillance] by ensuring the coordination of Member states' actions in the implementation of those measures".[6] In addition, in order to increase the situational awareness and reaction capability of Member states and the [Frontex] Agency to combat irregular migration and cross-border crime, and to prevent the loss of migrant lives, a European Border Surveillance System (Eurosur) was established.[7]

In such a European scenario characterized by the securitization of migration[8], particularly evident through the multiplication of border control devices[9], migration-related detention (M-RD) – which is the practice of

3 See the blog *Fortress Europe*, "La Fortezza".

4 Bosworth, M. (ed.), *Inside Immigration Detention*, Oxford University Press, Oxford, 2014.

5 Vacchiano, F., "Fencing in South: the Gibraltar area as a Paradigm of the New Border Regime in the Mediterranean", *Journal of Mediterranean Studies*, Vol. 22, No. 2, 2013, p. 339.

6 European Council, "Council Regulation (EC) No. 2007/2004 of 26 October 2004 establishing a European Agency for the Management of Operational Cooperation at the External Borders of the Member states of the European Union", *Official Journal of the European Union*, L 349, 25/11/2004, p. 1.

7 European Parliament and European Council, "Regulation (EU) No. 1052/2013 of the European Parliament and of the Council of 22 October 2013 establishing the European Border Surveillance System (Eurosur)", *Official Journal of the European Union*, L 295, 6/11/2013.

8 Huysmans, J., "The European Union and the Securitization of Migration", *Journal of Common Market Studies*, Vol. 38, No. 5, 2000, pp. 751-777.

9 Vacchiano, F., *op. cit.*

confining migrants because of their irregular status[10] – has been increasingly used to achieve immigration-related aims (e.g., identification and removal).[11] This practice, whose instrumental or deterrent effect has largely been questioned[12], involves a considerable financial burden in a period of global crisis. In addition, many NGOs and human rights organizations have denounced the degrading living conditions and violations of human rights to which migrants are subject inside M-RD centers.[13]

In the medical and psychological fields, several studies have highlighted the effects of detention in terms of mental health.[14] Despite the relevance of these investigations, their individual-level focus and their primary concern with asylum seekers and refugees may represent a limitation.[15] Starting from the criticism towards the individual-level focus of traditional clinical psychology, as well as from the interest of some psychologists "in working toward social change, addressing inequities, and challenging oppression"[16], community psychology has been developed as a branch of psychology concerned with the study of

---

10 Flynn, M., "An Introduction to Data Construction on Immigration-related Detention", *Global Detention Project Working Paper*, July 2011.

11 Bosworth, M., Turnbull, S., "Immigration detention, punishment, and the criminalization of migration", in S. Pickering and J. Hamm. (eds.), *The Routledge Handbook on Crime and International Migration*, Routledge, London, 2014, pp. 91-106.

12 See Cadeddu, D., *CIE e complicità delle organizzazioni umanitarie*. Sensibili alle foglie, Roma, 2013; di Martino, A. *et al.*, *The criminalization of irregular immigration: law and practice in Italy*, University Press, Pisa, 2013; Nethery, A., "Immigration Detention in Australia", Phd thesis, Deakin University, 2010; Schuster, L., Majidi, N., "What happens post-deportation? The experience of deported Afghans", *Migration Studies*, Vol. 1, No. 2, 2013, pp. 221-240.

13 Among others, Amnesty International, *Frontier Europe: Human Rights' Abuses on Greece's Border with Turkey*, Amnesty International, London, 2013; Human Rights Watch, *Two Years With No Moon: Immigration Detention of Children in Thailand*, Human Rights Watch, New York, 2014; Medici per i Diritti Umani, *Arcipelago CIE: Indagine sui Centri di identificazione ed espulsione italiani*, Infinito edizioni, Modena, 2013; Migreurop, *Europe's Murderous Borders*, Migreurop, Paris, 2009.

14 Among others, Coffey, G. J. *et al.*, "The meaning and mental health consequences of long-term immigration detention for people seeking asylum", *Social Science and Medicine*, Vol. 70, 2010, pp. 2070-2079; Robjant, K., Hassan, R., Katona, C., "Mental health implications of detaining asylum seekers: systematic review", *The British Journal of Psychiatry*, Vol. 194, 2009, pp. 306312; Steel, Z. *et al.*, "Impact of immigration detention and temporary protection on the mental health of refugees", *British Journal of Psychiatry*, Vol. 188, 2006, pp. 58-64.

15 Esposito, F., Ornelas, J., Arcidiacono, C., "Migration-related detention: the challenges of an ecological approach with a focus on justice", *BMC International Health and Human Rights*, 15:13, 2015, doi:10.1186/s12914-015-0052-0.

16 Kloos, B., "From the President", *Community Psychologists*, Vol. 47, No. 4, Fall 2014, pp. 1-3.

the links between social systems and individual behaviour.[17] In this light, community psychology scholars have adopted an ecological paradigm for community research and action[18] under the motto of "taking environment into account".[19] This paradigm focuses on the roles played by social, cultural, economic, and political conditions, as well as different types of justice and fairness systems, in determining people's wellness.

Inspired by this perspective, in this chapter we analyse M-RD with a focus on the Italian context. The main question is concerned with what explains the survival and expansion of M-RD centers, in spite of their harmful effects and lack of cost effectiveness. To this end, the historical development of the Italian legal and policy framework is traced in order to allow a contextualized understanding of contemporary practices. Following this, the business of M-RD is discussed, highlighting the role of the various actors involved. Finally, based on the evidence presented in the previous sections, we illustrate the case of an Italian M-RD center.

Historical overview

Until the end of the 1960s, Italy was predominantly a country of emigration: Italians would move to the USA and west-central European countries (approximately twenty-six million people emigrated between 1860 and 1970), or from southern to northern Italy (more than twenty million people).[20] It was from the 1970s that immigration started to become a visible phenomenon.[21] Initially, in the 1980s, Italian authorities addressed immigration as an issue related to the labour market. Indeed, the first legislation, Law No. 943/1986, introduced to enforce the 143/1975 Convention of the International Labour Organization, was aimed at stemming irregular intermediation and employment.[22] Before this, the only provisions addressing immigration were included in the codex of public security law (Royal Decree of 18th June 1931, No. 773),

17 Kloos, B., Ornelas, J., Nelson, G. (eds.), *Community Psychology and Community Mental Health: Towards Transformative Change*, Oxford University Press, New York, 2014.

18 Kelly, J. G., *Becoming Ecological: An expedition into Community Psychology*, Oxford University Press, New York, 2006.

19 Trickett, E., "Toward a distinctive community psychology: An Ecological Metaphor for the conduct of Community Research and the Nature of Training", *American Journal of Community Psychology*, Vol. 12, 1984, p. 265.

20 Sciurba, A., *op. cit.*

21 De Marco, M., Pittau, F., *L'evoluzione storica della normativa sull'immigrazione*, Ufficio Immigrazione Caritas Italiana, Roma, 2013.

22 di Martino, A. *et al.*, *op. cit.*

and required migrants to present themselves to public security authorities within three days after their entry into the country.

The first attempt at setting up a systematic immigration and asylum policy dates back to the 1990s, when the so-called Martelli Law (Law No. 39/1990) was enacted. Apart from establishing provisions for the recognition of asylum seekers, the novelty of this law was that it introduced a system to control and regulate the entry of migrants based, on the one hand, on the possession of specific requirements to get and renew a residence permit, and on the other on annual "flows programming" (subordinating migration to State's economic needs[23]). Moreover, Law No. 39 established the legal procedures for the removal of irregular migrants (coercive in the case of non-compliance with the order to leave). In this regard, it simplified the procedure by assigning to the Prefects the task of signing expulsion orders (before responsibility of the Ministry of Interior).

It was March 1991, when Italy faced the first substantial flow of migrants, i.e., approximately 27 thousand Albanians arriving on its shores. The country, and in particular the city of Brindisi where the ships arrived, were not prepared to receive all of these people. A few months later, in August, more than 20 thousand Albanians landed in the port of Bari. The migrants were transferred from the port to the football stadium from where, after being confined for some days, they were largely deported back.[24] This event marked a decisive step towards the creation of M-RD centers.

In 1995, the Dini Decree was issued (without ever being made into law). Introducing the obligation of residence for migrants subject to removal, it was the first measure to restrict their personal freedom for administrative reasons. Furthermore it highlighted the "primacy of expulsion as a mean to control immigrants' flows"[25]

Finally, in response to the so called "Albanian emergency", the Law No. 563/1995 (so-called Puglia Law) established, for the first time in Italy, centers for the detention of irregular migrants with the purposes of providing first assistance while awaiting identification or expulsion. Three centers, located along the maritime border of the coast of Puglia (in Brindisi, Lecce, and Otranto), were opened. Moreover, the law provided the possibility, in case of "emergency situations", to create such centers in other parts of the country. From this moment, the concept of "emergency" begins to shape the Italian framework concerning immigration control, a process that was also aided by the

23 Sciurba, A., *op. cit.*

24 See "Vent'anni fa lo sbarco dei 27.000 Il primo grande esodo dall'Albania", *La Repubblica*, 6 March 2011.

25 di Martino, A. *et al., op. cit.*, p. 8.

media overexposure of the phenomenon of the landings[26] (this, in truth, only concerned 8% of irregular migrants on the Italian territory[27]). It is also important to highlight that this legislation, as well as subsequent measures, was characterized by an ambiguity between humanitarian and securitarian discourses (assistance vs. maintenance of security/public order). This ambiguity will be a permanent feature of the Italian approach to immigration, and especially of the establishment of a M-RD regime.[28] In this regard, some scholars have spoken about the emergence of humanitarianism as a hegemonic framework.[29]

Addressing, for the first time, immigration as a structural phenomenon[30], in 1998 Law No. 40/1998 was enacted in order to provide a unified framework. Recovering, in part, the provisions enacted in 1995, this law normalized the mechanism of administrative detention for irregular migrants.[31] In this regard, it established the creation of Temporary Stay and Assistance Centres (CPTAs), giving to the *questore*[32] the power to order the custody of irregular migrants whose expulsion by escort to the border, or refoulement, was not immediately executable. The maximum period of detention in CPTAs was set at twenty days, extendable for a further ten days.

The establishment of CPTAs introduced an "exception" to the fundamental principles of the Italian Constitution, which stated that personal freedom is inviolable and limited the enforcement of measures to reduce it to exceptional situations of "necessity" and "urgency", attributing to the judiciary power, rather than to the executive one, the authority to order people's detention (art. 13). The Italian Constitutional Court also highlighted this issue (judgment 105/2001). However, despite these concerns, in 1998 CPTAs opened their doors, showing, right from the outset, the evidence of a management characterized by "arbitrariness and improvisation".[33] For the first time, a criminal justice measure

26 The image of hordes of desperate people who flood in, looking for help was distributed by media.

27 See Sciurba, A., *op. cit.*

28 Cadeddu, D., *op. cit.*; Campesi, G., "Immigrant detention and the double logic of securitization in Italy", in M. Ceccorulli and N. Labanca (eds.), *The EU, Migration and the Politics of Administrative Detention*, Routledge, London, 2014, pp. 145-165.

29 Agier, M., *Managing the Undesirables: Refugee Camps and Humanitarian Government*, Polity Press, Cambridge, 2011.

30 De Marco, M., Pittau, F., *op. cit.*

31 In this act, as in the others, the term "detention" is avoided.

32 High-ranking police official.

33 Sciurba, A., *op. cit.*, p. 149.

was applied in a case of administrative violation, thus highlighting the emergence of "a new expansive form of penal power".[34]

Based on Law No. 40/1998, the Legislative Decree No. 286/1998 brought together other provisions governing immigration in a unitary legislation. This Immigration Law, which is the one currently in force, has been subject to several amendments over the years, resulting in a set of policies often not consistent with each other.[35] Significant in this regard is the Bossi-Fini Law, No. 189/2002, which has further restricted the possibilities to legally enter the Italian territory and to benefit from any kind of regularization once irregular. This Law, designed to counter "the danger of a real invasion of Europe"[36], made removal by forcible deportation to the border the main repatriation procedure, and CPTAs an indispensable tool for implementing it.[37] The maximum time of detention increased from 30 to 60 days, and detention was extended to asylum seekers. Moreover, the transgression of an expulsion order and the irregular stay on the Italian territory became criminal offenses punishable with imprisonment from six months to one year (with Law No. 271/2004, imprisonment was extended from one to four years).

In these years, immigration in Italy increasingly became a subject for media attention and political debate, mainly in relation to the problem of public order and security (media overexposed the crimes committed by migrants). This situation led to an increase of the myths, stereotypes and fears of Italian people, consolidating the representation of the phenomenon as a "dangerous emergency", and legitimizing the criminalization of migrants.[38]

In this context, the so-called Security Package (Law No. 125/2008), introduced the most significant amendments to the Immigration Law, stressing a view of immigration as a security issue.[39] First of all, CPTAs were renamed as Centers for Identification and Expulsion-CIEs. Moreover, a new aggravating circumstance was introduced, making all crimes punishable with a harsher penalty if the offender was irregular.[40] All migrants (even those coming from EU-countries) sentenced to

34 Bosworth, M., "Subjectivity and identity in detention: Punishment and society in a global age", *Theoretical Criminology*, Vol. 16, No. 2, 2012, p. 134.

35 di Martino, A. *et al.*, *op. cit.*

36 Senato della Repubblica, "Disegno di Legge No. 795. Modifica alla normativa in tema di immigrazione e asilo", XIV Legislatura, 2002, p. 4.

37 Campesi, G., *op. cit.*

38 Sciurba, A., *op. cit.*

39 di Martino, A. *et al.*, *op. cit.*

40 The Constitutional Court expressed its concerns toward this amendment in the judgment 249/2010.

imprisonment for a period exceeding two years, became subject to expulsion (Art. 235 criminal code). Providing lodgings to an irregular migrant became a crime (punishable with imprisonment between six months and three years and confiscation of the property), and increased penalties were provided for those who facilitated irregular migrants staying in Italy and gave them employment.[41] Many national and international bodies, including the *Unione Camere Penali Italiane*, the Commissioner for Human Rights of the Council of Europe, and the European Court of Justice, expressed concern about these measures and their compatibility with human rights standards.[42]

The 2009 Security Package (Law No. 94/2009) reinforced the intertwining of security and immigration. Among its most significant amendments, this act introduced the crime of irregular entry and stay (fines of up to €10,000)[43], as well as the duty to have a valid resident permit in order to get married and to show it to obtain authorizations and access to public services (with the exception of sports and recreational activities, access to urgent and essential healthcare treatments, and schools). It also extended the maximum period of detention from 60 to 180 days. Furthermore, in April 2011, Circular 1305 prohibited media, independent organizations (with few exceptions), and civil society from entering CIEs and Reception Centers for Asylum Seekers-CARAs. Using the North African "emergency situation" as a pretext, this provision actually prevented any information on the living conditions of detainees. Thanks to a strong mobilization through the campaign *LasciateCIEntrare*[44], in December 2011, the Minister of Interior withdrew the Circular (after 8 months).

In 2011, another Security Package (later converted into Law No. 129/2011) was enacted in order to complete the implementation of Directive 2004/38/EC and transpose the Directive 2008/115/EC. Although it provided voluntary departure for migrants subject to an expulsion order[45] as well as alternative measures to detention, this act ultimately resulted in a further tightening of the system of immigration control. Indeed, only migrants who fulfilled all the

41 di Martino, A. *et al.*, *op. cit.*

42 See judgment 28 April 2011, case El Dridi, in which the European Court of Justice prohibited the imprisonment for violating an order to leave, claiming its inconsistency with the Directive 2008/115/EC.

43 After years of lobbying action, this crime has finally been removed in April 2014.

44 The campaign *LasciateCIEntrare* was set up in 2011 to counter the Circular 1305. It is a civil and political initiative to affirm the right to have access to, to inform and be informed about the conditions of thousands of migrants - men, women and minors - in the centers. Since the withdrawal of the Circular, *LasciateCIEntrare* has been fighting for the closure of all detention facilities, the abolition of administrative detention, and the review of immigration policies.

45 Implementable also by means of assisted return.

strict requirements requested – proving to be neither dangerous nor at risk of escaping – could benefit from these measures, while detention and forced removal continued to be the norm for the majority of people. Moreover, the maximum time of detention in CIEs was increased to 18 months, and the forced removal for reasons of public order was introduced for EU nationals (if they stay in violation of directive 2004/38/EC).[46]

As a reaction to the extension of the maximum period of detention in CIEs, several protests broke out. In many CIEs, detained migrants underwent hunger strikes and set mattresses on fire to claim their right to freedom. The police crushed these protests, often with the use of violence.[47] For a number of years, the Italian Government refused to back down. It was only in October 2014, with Law No. 161/2014, that the maximum term of detention was finally reduced to 90 days (30 days in the case of migrants previously subject to imprisonment for a period of 90 days or more). This achievement was possible thanks to the struggles undertaken by detainees, as well as by No Border groups, civil society movements (e.g., *LasciateCIEntrare*), and associations (e.g., *Melting Pot*, *Associazione Studi Giurdici sull'Immigrazione*, *Medici per i Diritti Umani*). The number of CIEs was also reduced, falling from thirteen (in 2012) to five that are currently operative (Turin, Rome, Bari, Trapani, and Caltanisetta).[48]

The business of migration-related detention

As Nethery[49] points out, examining the expenditure of M-RD is very important not only because it reveals the high financial costs of this practice, but also because it highlights the economic environment in which these costs occur. In a time of global economic crisis, the high expenditure on the detention and deportation of irregular migrants is jarring.

With regard to Italy´s concerns, a Parliamentary inquiry of 2011 highlighted that the annual cost of immigration policies was 460,000,000 (including policies of border control, identification and expulsion of irregular migrants, and integration), and that the "complete management" of an irregular migrant (from identification to deportation) costs approximately 10,000 euro.[50] It has also been estimated that, from 2005 to 2011, the Italian government has annually spent an average of 143.8

46 di Martino, A. *et al.*, *op. cit.*

47 See *Fortress Europe*, "Cie Bologna: protesta al femminile, 3 donne picchiate", 24 August 2011.

48 Source: Ministry of the Interior, 2014.

49 Nethery, A., *op. cit.*

50 Camera dei Deputati, "Interpellanza Urgente 2/01053", XVI Legislatura, seduta No. 464, 14 April 2011.

million euro to construct, manage, maintain, and renovate centers for migrant people (Centers for First Aid and Reception-CPSAs; Reception Centers for Asylum Seekers-CARAs; Reception Centers-CDAs; Centers for Identification and Expulsion-CIEs). In particular, the M-RD system has cost at least 55 million euro a year.[51] Although in October 2014 the maximum period of detention has been reduced, the costs of these centers remain high due to the high turnover of detainees (which ensure that the detention machine works incessantly).

In spite of these enormous costs, the effectiveness in terms of removals carried out (explicit goal of CIEs) is rather low. Indeed, of the 6,016 migrants detained during 2013 (5,431 men and 585 women), only 2,749 have been deported, with an efficacy rate (deported on detained) of 45.7%.[52] Whereas the number of irregular migrants in Italy is estimated to be around 300,000[53], deportation through CIEs affects only a very small minority of people (around 0.9%), usually "selected at random".[54]

In presenting these data, we do not maintain that the ineffectiveness of detention as a tool to remove irregular migrants is the main argument against CIEs. The crucial question is: Why do M-RD centers continue to exist if their effectiveness is questionable and their costs high? Why do governments fail to invest in alternative policies, e.g. in the effective integration of migrants? What is at stake?

We would like to answer by quoting the words of a young North African man, Aziz (pseudonym), who experienced detention in Italian CIEs:

> A car to go forward needs a lot of fuel, us, the immigrants, we are that gasoline. The pieces of the car are all those who work on our skin, all that is around us, such as those who, for example, prepare food for CIEs, who clean the clothes, the embassy, who manage them, doctors, police officers, the militaries who work inside. [...] the simple transfers of immigrants from a CIE to another are used to maintain active the business discourse: indeed, if in a CIE there are no immigrants, the machine does not earn.[55]

---

51 Commissione straordinaria per la tutela e la promozione dei diritti umani, "Rapporto sui centri di identificazione e espulsione in Italia (luglio 2014)", Senato della Repubblica, XVII Legislatura, 2014; Lunaria, "Costi disumani. La spesa pubblica per il contrasto dell'immigrazione irregolare", 2013.

52 Medici per i Diritti Umani, "Chiudere l'arcipelago CIE. I dati completi sui centri di identificazione ed espulsione per centro e nazionalità", 8 October 2014.

53 Fondazione Ismu, *Ventesimo rapporto sulle Migrazioni: 1994-2014*, FrancoAngeli, Milano, 2014.

54 di Martino, A. *et al.*, *op. cit.*, p. 119.

55 Cadeddu, *op. cit.*, p. 19.

Some intellectuals have defined what Aziz described as the "immigration industrial complex".[56] This concept, associated to those of military and prison industrial complexes, refers to the confluence of "public and private sector interests in the criminalization of undocumented migration, immigration law enforcement, and the promotion of 'anti-illegal' rhetoric".[57] In particular, Golash-Boza identified three major features common to the three complexes: "(a) a rhetoric of fear; (b) the confluence of powerful interests; and (c) a discourse of other-ization.[58] In all cases, a culture of fear directed towards undesirable others has been created to justify massive government expenditures, which served, in truth, the interests of powerful groups.

As Angela Davis clearly highlighted speaking about the prison industrial complex, "prison construction and the attendant drive to fill these new structures with human bodies have been driven by ideologies of racism and the pursuit of profit".[59] This is also the case of M-RD centers. Both these sites (M-RD centers and prisons) serve to concentrate "human surplus"[60], transforming imprisoned bodies into sources of profit.[61] From this perspective, they can be considered as self-perpetuating machines.[62] Detainees, as well as prisoners, consume commodities provided by the corporations implicated in the complexes, and can also be used as a cheap labour force (see the case of British removal centers).

Based on these considerations, and returning to our initial question, it appears that the true reason "for maintaining immigration policies that mandate detention for migrants" is "the fixing of capital in detention centers [which] creates political and economic incentives".[63] These incentives not only concern governments and immigration enforcement agencies, but also private companies contracted to run the centers.[64]

---

56 Fernandes, D., *Targeted: National Security and the Business of Immigration*, Seven Stories Press, Saint Paul, 2007; Golash-Boza, T., "The Immigration Industrial Complex: Why We Enforce Immigration Policies Destined to Fail", *Sociology Compass*, 3/2, 2009, pp. 295-309.

57 Golash-Boza, *op. cit.*, p. 296.

58 Golash-Boza, *op. cit.*, p. 306.

59 Davis, A., *Are prisons obsolete?*, Seven Stories Press, New York, 2003, p. 84.

60 Bauman, Z., *Vite di scarto*, Laterza, Bari, 2007.

61 *Ibid.*

62 Golash-Boza, *op. cit.*

63 Mountz, A., Coddington, K., Catania, R. T. & Lyod, J. M., "Conceptualizing detention: Mobility, containment, bordering, and exclusion", *Progress in Human Geography*, Vol. 37, No. 4, 2013, p. 529.

64 Bacon, C., "The Evolution of Immigration Detention in the UK: The Involvement of Private Prison Companies", *Working paper 27*, Refugee Studies Center, Oxford, 2005.

In the case of Italy, CIEs are managed by cultural associations and social cooperatives, which use a humanitarian rhetoric, centered on the idea of "humanizing" these sites of segregation, to hide their profit interests.[65] In fact, while receiving a fee for each migrant detained, these private entities generate a profit by having their facilities filled and keeping detainees for longer periods. The construction of a humanitarian discourse around detained migrants, and the emergence of a humanitarian model of confinement have played a key role in legitimizing and normalizing detention in the public opinion.[66] This military-humanitarian management has served to allay people's anxieties and alleviate their misgivings, gratifying the desire for moral rectitude.[67]

However, it is not only managing bodies that make money from M-RD. Subcontractors that provide services within detention facilities have made these places of confinement their primary markets. Mass media have used immigration and detention as a means to attract viewers. NGOs have received funds to provide detainees (often specific groups, e.g. asylum seekers) with legal aid and psychosocial support. Finally, as scholars committed to this cause, we cannot exempt ourselves from questioning whether we also play a role in this complex. The answer might be uncomfortable.[68]

An Italian case study[69]

Rome's Center for Identification and Expulsion (Ponte Galeria) is the main Italian M-RD center. Operative since 2000, the center can hold up to 354 migrants subject to removal (176 men and 178 women). However, for safety reasons, the number of detainees is usually lower. For example in 2013, the total number of detainees was 1,287, of which 899 men and 388 women.[70] During our fieldwork (March 2014 – to date), the number of detainees never exceeded 130 people (on average 80 men and 30 women). The majority of them came from non-EU countries, e.g., Morocco, Tunisia, Algeria (especially men), Nigeria, China, Ukraine, but there were also Romanians and Bulgarians. We also met many Roma

65 On this topic see Cadeddu, D., *op. cit.*

66 Cadeddu, D., *op. cit.*; Campesi, G., *op. cit.*

67 Bauman, Z., *op. cit.*

68 A reflection on this issue and on how, as researchers, we can deal with this ambiguous moral burden is a relevant topic to address in future contributions.

69 The information provided in this section was gathered in the context of an ongoing ecological study of life in M-RD centers in Italy and Portugal. Participant observation, interviews, and questionnaires are being used to collect data.

70 Medici per i Diritti Umani, *op. cit.*

people, often detained for several months although not being deportable.[71] In such cases, detention had just a punitive purpose.

The facility, which is located near the Fiumicino airport, looks like a prison, since its perimeter is surrounded by high walls and fences, and CCTV cameras monitor all environments, both internal and external. To date, the center is managed by the cultural association Acuarinto in partnership with GEPSA (*Gestion etablissements penitenciers services auxiliares*), a French company that provides services to prisons and that is a branch of Cofely-Italy, member of Gdf-Suez (now Engie), a multinational energy corporation. They assumed the management in December 2014, by means of a public tender on the basis of the most economically advantageous bid.[72] As a consequence of their reduced budget, a lot of services have been cut[73] and many people have lost their job.

Most staff members are migrants themselves. Behind the banner of multiculturalism, waved by the management as an added value, migrant workers actually represent a cheap and more exploitable labour force. Many accept to be "jailers" of other migrants, often their compatriots, clinging to the false illusion of helping them. There are also Italian staff members, some absorbed by the old management, often dedicated workers but without specific skills (they usually do not have an adequate background and no ad hoc training is provided by the management body). Many need that work to survive. Quoting a staff member "There is no work, we are already in danger of losing it! Many of us remained at home!".

The mission perceived by the staff, in general, is to "try to make detainees stay better in the center".[74] This mission, defined by Cadeddu as "humanizing correction"[75], is impossible to pursue as inherently paradoxical. However, the illusion of its viability helps staff members to face the conflict between their subjective and ascribed identities (i.e., as helpers and jailers).[76] The ambiguity between humanitarianism and

---

71 Usually they were not registered, at birth, at the register office, or the civil registers of their cities were destroyed during the war in former Yugoslavia.

72 They asked 28.8 euro per day per detainee, while before the cost was of 40.9 euro.

73 Before the socio-psychological service was available every day (8-20), and the team consisted of six people; nowadays there are only two psychologists covering a few hours a week.

74 Quote of a psychologist.

75 Cadeddu, D., *op. cit.,*. p. 75.

76 Esposito, F., "Practicing Ethnography in Migration-Related Detention Centers: A Reflexive Account", *Journal of Prevention and Intervention in the Community*, forthcoming.

securitarism also influences detainees' experiences. Police officers who stop and take migrants to CIEs often tell them that they are going to a "shelter" where they will stay a few days to regularize their documents. Therefore, when migrants see the CIE, with its bar fences and CCTV cameras, they get very confused, not knowing exactly where they are. Only once inside, thanks to other detainees, they discover the harsh reality. However, ambiguity still persists. "There are people that it is better that they stay here instead of on the street without food or possibility to take a shower" noted a female detainee during our fieldwork. This chilling comment is paradigmatic of the pervasiveness of the humanitarian rhetoric in terms of detainees' emotional symbolization of life in detention.[77]

Almost 80% of the men detained in CIEs have a criminal background.[78] This evidence highlights the interdependence between immigration and prison industrial complexes.[79] Although politicians, police, and managers are very careful to avoid terms like "detention", "cells", and "escape", it is evident that M-RD centers are the expression of "a new expansive form of penal power … that is not bound by the familiar goals of punishment but exists purely as a means to an end: deportation".[80] The comparison with the prison system is constantly present in the imagination both of staff and detainees. Furthermore, many staff members and immigration officers conceive M-RD as a penal measure to further punish migrants who committed crimes, making them serve a double sentence. Exemplificative, in this regard, are the words of a staff member: "I'm sorry for them, poor people. Yes, some of them I will let them be free. But others I will not. Who raped must stay here!". This dimension is also evident in the hearings with justices of the peace. Until Law No. 161/2014, the presence of a criminal background was a crucial element for a judges' decision to validate or extend detention.[81]

Many detainees claim that prisons are better than CIEs, because they are entitled to lower guarantees and opportunities. "The prison is much better! At least you know why you're there and you have activities to do to pass the time" was an observation usually offered by the migrants we met. This is understandable given that, unlike prisons, CIEs are intended to

---

[77] Carli, R., Paniccia, R. M., *Analisi della domanda: Teoria e tecnica dell'intervento in psicologia clinica*, Il Mulino, Bologna, 2003.

[78] Medici per i Diritti Umani, *op. cit.*

[79] Daves, *op. cit.*; Golash-Boza, *op. cit.*

[80] Bosworth, *op. cit.*, p. 134.

[81] According to Law No. 161/2014, if a migrant was imprisoned for at least 90 days, detention cannot exceed 30 days.

neither change nor prepare detainees for their eventual return to society.[82] "Rather, detention merely confirms their identity as non-citizens that are executable and deportable".[83]

Conclusions

It has been highlighted how, over the years, a strict connection between immigration, security, and emergency has increasingly characterized the Italian political and public debate, which has become the framework for all decisions concerning immigration. This framework has legitimized the application of repressive measures to manage the "immigration problem", using "migrant" as a label to criminalize and dehumanize people. As a consequence, driven by a racist ideology, an immigration industrial complex has been established. This complex, of which M-RD centers are a part, has much in common with the military and prison industrial complexes. However, the emergence of new forms of penal power[84] and of a humanitarian governance of undesirables[85] should be taken into account in its analysis. The relevance of these dimensions in shaping life in detention has been highlighted by the case study of Rome's CIE.

We wish to conclude the chapter by urging scholars engaged in this field to adopt multilevel ecological analyses to grasp the complexity of these sites of confinement, and shed light on the forces and interests that revolve around them.[86] These analyses, especially if based on a critical and reflexive engagement[87], can help to address the roots of the phenomenon of the loss of so many migrants' lives that is occurring in the XXI century, and identify alternatives based on freedom and justice for all.

82 For a critical analysis on the prison system, see Davis, A., *op. cit.*

83 Bosworth, M., *op. cit.*, pp. 134-135.

84 *Ibid.*, p. 134.

85 Agier, M., *op. cit.*

86 See Esposito, F., Ornelas, J., Arcidiacono, C., *op. cit.*

87 Esposito, F., *op. cit.*

Contributors

Adrian-Gabriel Corpădean is a Lecturer at the Faculty of European Studies, Babeş-Bolyai University, Cluj-Napoca. He holds a PhD in History from Babeş-Bolyai University and another from Université de Cergy-Pontoise. His research priorities include the History of European Integration, Communication within the European Union and the Management of European Projects.

Alejandra Germán Doldán is a Lecturer in Constitutional Law at Burgos University, Spain. She participates in various research groups: Immigration Law, Education for Peace, Human Development and Sustainability, and Higher Education Quality with a Gender Perspective. She has published articles in international journals and made presentations at international conferences on the legal status of Foreigners, Constitutional Law and Women's Studies.

Alice Cunha is PhD in Contemporary History (NOVA University, 2013) and research fellow at Instituto de História Contemporânea. She is the author of several publications all related to Portugal and European integration. Her field of research focuses on enlargement studies, Europeanization and the history of European integration.

Ana Isabel Xavier Assistant Professor in NOVA University of Lisbon and researcher at IPRI – Portuguese Institute of International Relations, she holds a PhD in International Relations (European Studies), University of Coimbra. Her main research interests and publications include the European Union, Security and Defence, Human Security, Human Rights and Globalization.

Burcu Toğral Koca is Assistant Professor in the Department of Political Science and Public Administration at Eskişehir Osmangazi University. She received her PhD in Political Science from the University of Hamburg. Her fields of research interests are securitization of migration with a particular focus on the EU and Turkey, biopolitics of security, and racism.

Carlos Coelho is Member to the European Parliament (PSD, EPP), having been chair of the Temporary committee on the Echelon interception system and Temporary Committee on the alleged use of European countries by the CIA for the transport and illegal detention of prisoners. He was also rapporteur of several reports; such has on SIS II, the new Schengen evaluation mechanism or the enlargement of Schengen to Bulgaria and Romania. He was Member of the Portuguese Parliament and of the Portuguese Government. Author and co-author of many publications, he is currently President of Instituto Francisco Sá Carneiro, the think tank of PSD.

Caterina Arcidiacono Full Professor in Community Psychology and Coordinator of the Doctoral program in Gender Studies at the University Federico II of Naples. She was President of the European Community Psychology Association (2011-2013). Her current research concerns migration and a critical approach to community psychology with reference to qualitative research.

Cristina Blanco Sío-López is an Experienced Researcher in European and Global Studies, Project Manager and Principal Investigator. She is also EUI Ambassador and Associate Researcher at the IHC and holds a PhD and a MRes. in History and Civilization from the EUI. She previously worked at the Luxembourg Ministry of Research, the European Commission, the EP, the US Congress and the RSCAS.

Francesca Esposito Phd candidate in Community Psychology at the ISPA-IU in Lisbon. Her project is an ecological study of life within migration-related detention centers in Italy and Portugal. Her current research interests also include gender violence, racism and discrimination, self-help, and feminist approaches to community psychology.

José Ornelas Associate Professor with Aggregation at the ISPA-IU, in Lisbon. He is Director of the Community Development course and the Community Psychology Masters and Doctoral programs. Over the last 25 years he has developed research and practice in the field of Community Psychology, particularly in the domains of community mental health.

Leila Giannetto is a PhD student at the University of Trento (Italy). She has worked at the Jean Monnet European Centre (Trento), researching democratic theories applied to the EU. She holds an MA in European Studies. Her research interests include migration policies, accountability, and civil society participation in the EU.

Lucía Payero López obtained her PhD in Law at the University of Oviedo (2014). Her research interests lie in the fields of Legal and Political Philosophy and Constitutional Theory. She has published articles and presented papers at international conferences on issues relating to nationalism, self-determination of peoples, federal theory, constitutionalism, immigration and citizenship.

Marta Silva is PhD candidate at NOVA University. Her research areas include broadly Social and Oral History and she works mainly on illegal networks of smuggling, recruitment and passage of clandestine emigrants in the framework of the Portuguese dictatorship of the Estado Novo. She has a special interest on the social organization of the rural world and on the intermediary powers in migrations.

Nicolae Păun is the Dean of the Faculty of European Studies, Babeş-Bolyai University, Cluj-Napoca and a member of the European Union Liaison Committee of Historians. He is the author of numerous books and internationally-published articles pertaining to topics from the area of European integration and its history.

Octávio Sacramento PhD in Anthropology, assistant professor at the University of Trás-os-Montes and Alto Douro (UTAD) and researcher at the Centre for Transdisciplinary Development Studies (CETRAD-UTAD) [octavsac@utad.pt].

Rui Frederico is BA and MA in Political Science and International Affairs. He earned his PhD in Sociology from ISCTE-IUL. Integrated researcher at IHC-UNL since 2013.

Simone Paoli PhD in History of International Relations at the University of Florence, is Research Fellow at the Department of Political Science, Law and International Studies of the University of Padua and member of the Research Project "History of the Commission Consortium, Vol. 3 (HISTCOM3)" at the Université catholique de Louvain.

EUROCLIO – Published Books

N° 92 – *Que dire à l'Espagne ? De l'isolement franquiste à la démocratie européiste, la France au défi, 1957-1979,* Pablo MARTIN-PAÑEDA, 2015

N° 91 – *Francis Delaisi, du dreyfusisme à « l'Europe nouvelle »,* Éric BUSSIÈRE, Olivier DARD, Geneviève DUCHENNE (dir.), 2015.

N° 90 – *European Parties and the European Integration Process, 1945-1992,* Lucia BONFRESCHI, Giovanni ORSINA, Antonio VARSORI (eds.), 2015

N° 89 – *Européanisation et démocratisation des États baltes dans la période de préadhésion à l'UE. Le rôle de la conditionnalité politique des organisations européennes,* Anne-Sylvie PIGEONNIER, 2015.

N° 88 – *Le Continent basket. L'Europe et le basket-ball au XX*e *siècle,* Fabien ARCHAMBAULT, Loïc ARTIAGA, Gérard BOSC (dir.), 2015.

N° 87 – *The Convention on the Future of Europe. How States Behave in a New Institutional Context of Negotiation.* Francesco MARCHI, 2015.

N° 86 – *Christian Democrat Internationalism. Its Action in Europe and Worldwide from post World War II until the 1990s. Volume III. The European People's Party Continental and Social Cooperation.* Jean-Dominique DURAND (ed.), 2014.

N° 85 – *Pela Paz! For Peace! Pour la paix ! (1849-1939).* Maria Manuela Tavares RIBEIRO, Maria Fernanda ROLLO, Isabel Maria FREITAS VALENTE, Alice CUNHA (eds.), 2014.

N° 84 – *Economic Crisis and New Nationalisms. German Political Economy as Perceived by European Partners.* Antonio VARSORI, Monika POETTINGER (eds.), 2014.

N° 83 – *European Constitutionalism. Historical and Contemporary Perspectives.* Alexandre DUPEYRIX, Gérard RAULET (eds.), 2014.

N° 82 – *Cross-Border Cooperation Structures in Europe. Learning from the Past, Looking to the Future.* Luis DOMÍNGUEZ, Iva PIRES (eds.), 2014.

N° 81 – *The European Community and the World. A Historical Perspective.* Giuliana LASCHI (ed.), 2014.

N° 80 – *Christian Democrat Internationalism. Its Action in Europe and Worldwide from Post World War II until the 1990s. Volume II: The Development (1945-1979). The Role of Parties, Movements, People.* Jean-Dominique DURAND (ed.), 2013.

N° 79 – *Christian Democrat Internationalism. Its Action in Europe and Worldwide from Post World War II until the 1990s. Volume I: The Origins.* Jean-Dominique DURAND (ed.), 2013.

N° 78 – *Investment Banking History. National and Comparative Issues (19th-21st centuries).* Hubert BONIN & Carlo BRAMBILLA (eds.), 2013.

N° 77 – *Citizenship and Solidarity in the European Union. From the Charter of Fundamental Rights to the Crisis, the State of the Art*. Mariana CANOTILHO, Pedro MADEIRA FROUFE & Alessandra SILVEIRA (eds.), 2013.

N° 76– *The OSCE: Soft Security for a Hard World. Competing Theories for Understanding the OSCE*. Roberto DOMINGUEZ (ed.), 2013.

N° 75 – *Euroscepticism, Europhobia and Eurocriticism. The Radical Parties of the Right and Left* vis-à-vis *the European Union*. Cesáreo RODRÍGUEZ-AGUILERA DE PRAT, 2013.

N° 74 – *Fermer les mines en construisant l'Europe. Une histoire sociale de l'intégration européenne*. Nicolas VERSCHUEREN, 2012

N° 73 – *Reflets de la construction européenne. Réflexions, références et refus du débat sur l'Europe*. Bertrand VAYSSIÈRE (dir.), 2012.

N° 72 – *The International Relations of Local Authorities. From Institutional Twinning to the Committee of the Regions: Fifty Years of European Integration History*. Fabio ZUCCA, 2012.

N° 71 – *Histoire du Conseil de l'Europe (1949-2009)*. Birte WASSENBERG, 2012.

N° 70 – *The EU, Security and Transatlantic Relations*. Finn LAURSEN (ed.), 2012.

N° 69 – *Européanisation au XXe siècle. Un regard historique / Europeanisation in the 20th Century. The Historical Lens*. Matthieu OSMONT, Émilia ROBIN-HIVERT, Katja SEIDEL, Mark SPOERER & Christian WENKEL (dir./eds.), 2012.

N° 68 – *Consensus and European Integration. An Historical Perspective / Consensus et intégration européenne. Une perspective historique*. Daniela PREDA & Daniele PASQUINUCCI (eds./dir.), 2012.

N° 67 – *Générations de fédéralistes européens depuis le XIXe siècle. Individus, groupes, espaces et réseaux*. Geneviève DUCHENNE et Michel DUMOULIN (dir.), 2012.

N° 66 – *Raymond Aron, penseur de l'Europe et de la nation*. Giulio DE LIGIO (dir.), 2012.

N° 65 – *Europe Twenty Years after the End of the Cold War. The New Europe, New Europes? / L'Europe vingt ans après la fin de la guerre froide. Nouvelle Europe, nouvelles Europes?* Bruno ARCIDIACONO, Katrin MILZOW, Axel MARION & Pierre-Étienne BOURNEUF (eds./dir.), 2012.

N° 64 – *Aux origines de la diplomatie européenne. Les Neuf et la Coopération politique européenne de 1973 à 1980*. Maria Gainar, 2012.

N° 63 – *Europe and the Middle East. The hour of the East?* Birte WASSENBERG & Giovanni FALEG (eds.), 2012.

N° 62 – *Quelle architecture pour un code européen de droit international privé ?* Marc FALLON, Paul LAGARDE, Sylvaine POILLOT-PERUZZETTO (dir.), 2011.

Euroclio European Network

together with the SEGEI Network

Coordination : Chaire Jean Monnet d'histoire de l'Europe contemporaine (Cehec)
Collège Erasme, 1, place Blaise-Pascal, B-1348 Louvain-la-Neuve

Germany
Jürgen Elvert
Wilfried Loth

Belgium
Julie Cailleau
Jocelyne Collonval
Yves Conrad
Gaëlle Courtois
Pascal Deloge
Geneviève Duchenne
Vincent Dujardin
Michel Dumoulin
Roch Hannecart
Pierre-Yves Plasman
Béatrice Roeh
Corine Schröder
Caroline Suzor
Pierre Tilly
Arthe Van Laer
Jérôme Wilson
Natacha Wittorski

Spain
Enrique Moradiellos
Mercedes Samaniego Boneu

France
Françoise Berger
Marie-Thérèse Bitsch
Gérard Bossuat
Éric Bussière
Jean-François Eck
Catherine Horel
Philippe Mioche
Marine Moguen-Toursel
Sylvain Schirmann
Matthieu Trouvé
Laurent Warlouzet
Emilie Willaert

Hungary
Gergely Fejérdy

Italy
David Burigana
Elena Calandri
Eleonora Guasconi
Luciano Segreto
Antonio Varsori

Luxemburg
Charles Barthel
Etienne Deschamps
Jean-Marie Kreins
René Leboutte
Robert Philippart
Corine Schröder
Gilbert Trausch

The Netherlands
Anjo Harryvan
Jan W. Brouwer
Jan van der Herst

Poland
Józef Laptos
Zdzisiaw Mach

Switzerland
Antoine Fleury
Lubor Jilek